Brands, Trademarks and Good Will

by

Arthur F. Marquette

Foreword by
James Webb Young

Mid-nineteenth-century breakfasts in the United States were formidable exercises in gluttony that often kept the diner at the table for an hour and a half. Oats were considered horse fodder.

But hard-headed German immigrant Ferdinand Schumacher introduced stone-ground oatmeal into the North American diet, beginning a revolution in breakfast food—and a business that soon made him Akron's Oatmeal King.

By the time The Quaker Oats Company was founded at the turn of the twentieth century, following the first major proxy fight in U.S. industrial history, oatmeal was big business and competition was fierce.

"The rise of The Quaker Oats Company exemplifies the peculiar genius of privately owned American industry for devising impossible plans, then forcing them to fruition," suggests author Marquette. Quaker was *the* pioneer in mass-media advertising and effective promotion campaigns. The Company's advances in packaging and marketing techniques paced the field, and its combination of fearlessness and imagination—and an almost unwavering instinct for what was good business—made it a giant.

Brands, Trademarks and Good Will is also the chronicle of three strong and dissimilar personalities—Schumacher, Henry Parsons Crowell, and Robert Stuart—of their contests for power in the cereal industry, and what resulted from the struggle.

The book includes the full story of "The Food Shot from Guns" and the saga of Aunt Jemima. Here also are accounts of the increasing diversification of The Quaker Oats Company—into livestock and pet foods, into ready-mixed baking preparations, and into the fields of chemicals and plastics.

Quaker has imported oatmeal into Scotland, and even pasta into Italy; the book includes an entertaining coverage of Quaker's rapid and seldom-stodgy international expansion.

Twenty-four pages of photographs.

ARTHUR F. MARQUETTE wrote this book out of thirty years of personal association with the people and traditions of The Quaker Oats Company. As a member of the staff of Lord & Thomas and later as president of Sherman & Marquette Advertising Agency, he served Quaker Oats as advertising counsel during three management regimes. He is also a former Assistant Professor of Advertising and Marketing in the University of Chicago School of Business.

Brands, Trademarks
and Good Will

BRANDS, TRADEMARKS
AND
GOOD WILL

The Story of
The Quaker Oats Company

Arthur F. Marquette

New York   Toronto   London

McGRAW-HILL BOOK COMPANY

Brands, Trademarks and Good Will
The Story of The Quaker Oats Company

Copyright © 1967 by McGraw-Hill, Inc. All Rights Reserved.
Printed in the United States of America.
This book, or parts thereof, may not be reproduced in any form
without permission of the publishers.

Library of Congress Catalog Card Number: 66–28510

First Edition

40465

Contents

Brands, Trademarks
and Good Will

On a Sense of History
by James Webb Young

AN EMINENT French scholar once told me that he believed the history of France was better documented than that of any other country, solely because so many Frenchmen had been given to the writing of memoirs. It may be that Julius Caesar set the fashion when he chronicled the subdivision of all Gaul. Be that as it may, certainly the Frenchman's deep sense of history is the wellspring of his newly emerging national strength.

Indeed, among western Europeans this sense of history seems to be more widely nurtured than it is among us in America. Not uncommonly in England, for instance, a schoolboy can recite in order the names of all the English kings and queens. Or a university student may concentrate his entire course of study on one historical period. There also one finds a high annual production of raw material for historical studies, in such books as *Life in a Noble Household: 1641–1700*—a record of every pound, shilling, and penny of income and outgo of such a family. One result of all this is a Winston Churchill, who was notably enriched by his sense of history.

In our much shorter life as a nation, with a continent to subdue and to develop, we have been too busy making history to record all of it that we might now profit from.

This is notably so in the area of business history, even though we are more often than not thought of as a nation of businessmen.

The history of The Quaker Oats Company is an abundant record of the contributions of an industrial corporation to the national economic and social life. In a sense a national culture developed because of national advertising which persuaded the populace, wherever located over a vast landscape, to accept products and ideas in common. Quaker, one of the great pioneers in the theory and practice of national advertising, illustrates this point very well. In a real sense, national advertising and The Quaker Oats Company developed together. And national advertising and national marketing provided the economic sustenance for our present mass communications media.

When I entered publishing and advertising at the turn of the century, and for some three decades thereafter, all the businesses I dealt with—even the largest—were family-owned and -controlled. In the case of Quaker, two families were principally involved, but the principle was the same. The managers were the original entrepreneurs and/or their offspring. These managers had either lived their business history, improvising and creating, or had received it directly from their fathers and expected to transmit it to their sons. On balance, their sense of history seems to me to have given these managers a useful perspective from which to approach business decisions. Today's professionally trained managers are somewhat differently motivated and oriented. Their strength is the mastery of techniques. Their schooling emphasized the technologies of their accomplishment.

Through books such as this history of Quaker, the sense of historical continuity of American business is

enhanced. The first mass production followed the realization that national distribution might be achieved
through national advertising. In turn this advertising
revenue—along with editorial vitality—became the lifeblood of the publishing business, and the total volume of
advertising became each publisher's blood bank. Gradually both businessmen and publishers conceded that
the advertising specialist was an essential adjunct to
their own goals, and the creative agency developed. Out
of this concept grew the whole of modern agency service. Quaker had pioneered that concept of advertising
long before it was generally embraced by the agencies.

The agency with which I was associated made its
most significant contribution to the new trend by in-
novating the hiring of the Ph.D. and educators of high
stature to introduce educational techniques into advertising. This concept of advertising as education plus
persuasion, a form of applied social science, led to many
of the first Simon-pure advertising successes, thus helping to establish advertising as the indispensable means
of communication to the national market. Thanks to it
women were taught for the first time by advertising we
prepared for Quaker, among others, many practical
means to a better living.

This book makes an important contribution to modern
business management by its examination of an important result of advertising—the organic growth of a business. It begins with a basic economic unit, the processing and distribution of farm products for consumption,
and progresses from modest beginnings to world operations. The key roles of the individual entrepreneurs, risk-
takers, innovators, and canny enterprisers and advertisers in the development of the American economy are
revealed clearly. Here is exactly the kind of material

from which we can acquire a sharpened sense of business history. The experiences lived by these eminent industrial creators will interest and help the managers of today, and be useful in our schools of business administration for training the managers of tomorrow.

Chapter 1 * Quaker—
an American Phenomenon

THE RISE of The Quaker Oats Company exemplifies the peculiar genius of privately owned American industry for devising impossible plans, then forcing them to fruition. Nineteenth-century industrial leaders were a tough-minded breed of visionary, motivated not by utopian fantasies but by more substantial daydreams in which they saw a rewarding future of almost limitless expansion. Such visions demanded insight unblurred by conventional business thinking. Converting the dreams to substance required new and intricate business mechanisms for which no patterns existed. So, having dreamed the dreams, these practical prophets built new forms of enterprise beyond the conception of their tradition-bound predecessors. Imaginatively they brushed aside the limitations of geography, looking beyond local markets to stimulate broad demand and forge a pattern of national distribution for their consumer goods. They were inspired rather than deterred by the vastness of the American land, which challenged them to shake off the provincialism of centuries of European tradition and to pioneer as boldly in merchandising as others had in settlement. New sales concepts, techniques, organizational structures, and procedures exploded across a continental span of 3000 miles with such speed that in the mid-twentieth century the millions of customers who benefited from this creativity were only two generations removed from the innovators.

The Quaker Oats Company is directly in the mainstream of American industrial expansion. Its history is in fact the story of modern merchandising. Many of the imaginative innovations on which today's sales programs are based began with the founders of The Quaker Oats Company. These concepts caused immense social change, although some historians tend to ignore or deprecate the influences of American industry upon the establishment and development of the American culture. The Quaker Oats story documents the monumental social impact of American industrial creativity.

The corporation called The Quaker Oats Company is not a straight-line evolution from the first phase of American commerce. The enterprise did not rise, as did many industrial creations, from the genius of a single founder who created or filled a consumer need and established a baronial empire for himself and his sons. Rather, Quaker emerged from the second phase—the company was the confluence of several separate streams into a combination of forces financed in the modern manner by public stock offerings and managed by a team of specialists. In this respect, Quaker was one of the first of the truly modern American corporations— and it paid the penalty of public ownership by encountering one of the first proxy fights in American business history.

Quaker escaped the handicap of many personally founded companies. It was not held back by a strong-willed founder who continued to rule after his contributions had become obsolete. Nor was it stifled by absentee ownership vested in an affluent, indifferent second generation. It was not swallowed up, as many other enterprises have been, by a third-generation merger, the result of inadequate hereditary management talent.

Quaker was modern from its birth, free to pioneer and to innovate, to thrive on the sum of several personalities with special skills, and to pass on the burden of leadership to the fit. Quaker was a joint effort even before it became The Quaker Oats Company. Most important to the team in the initial phases were an aggressive pioneer miller, Ferdinand Schumacher; a management and financial organizer, Robert Stuart; and one of the most creative merchandising minds in American history, Henry Parsons Crowell. What they and their associates did changed the breakfast habits of the nation, revolutionized food marketing, created national brand food advertising and, in passing, demonstrated to industry that diversification of management talent and product lines is the life of trade.

Ferdinand Schumacher lived and worked in the handicraft age of North America, and founded his business on the model of the Middle Ages. Except for the use of steam power, his early milling techniques were essentially those of the fifteenth century. His career extended into the period of America's eruption as an industrial nation, a condition to which he, in effect a medieval businessman, could not adjust. Stuart and Crowell then literally pioneered America's modern concepts of national consumer selling.

Henry Crowell was one of the strongest forces in the creation of modern advertising. He induced predictable responses by building his campaigns on a soundly conceived estimate of human reactions. He was one of the first industrialists anywhere to develop an enterprise philosophically rather than simply by craftsmanship and sweat. He studied his problems, and solved them by innovation based on logic, rather than blundering through trial and error to procedures based on experience. As a result, he was twenty years ahead of the trend toward national distribution of a continuously advertised brand. National advertising of breakfast cereals began not with any creative advertising agency—none then existed—but with Crowell, in 1882. His associate Robert Stuart permitted him to do so, a fact remarkable in itself, considering Stuart's financial conservatism. Many bankers of that day, suspecting all advertisers of being charlatan patent-medicine men, refused to lend money to companies that advertised. Thus reputable manufacturers tended to be as conservative in the exploitation of their wares as the medical profession is today, a condition difficult for our advertising-oriented generation to believe. And Stuart had, among other attributes, those of a banker. For Quaker he was the architect of a prototype of national and international organization so successful that Quaker became one of the first truly world-wide corporations.

Quaker was the first American company to develop a theory and practice of modern consumer advertising that spanned the effort from supplier of raw materials to ultimate consumer. Quaker was first to approach packaging of merchandise as a sales lure rather than as a mere convenience of distribution and handling. Quaker was first to make a national food label significant, first to market a breakfast cereal nationally, first to promote a food by national advertising, first to register a cereal trademark. Founder Schumacher was a pioneer in providing ready-mixed feeds for farm animals; as a result Quaker, in its early days, could boast that it was "the largest manufacturer of feeds for horses, cows, calves, hogs and poultry in the world." As the company expanded, Quaker pioneered in irradiation of foods for vitamin enrichment. Through the Aunt Jemima line it extended the concept of ready-mixed food preparations so helpful to the modern housewife. And, through Ken-L Ration, it led in developing a shaky novelty into today's burgeoning pet-foods business.

In its unending quest to find commercial use for its milling byproducts, Quaker developed the first commercial production of furfural and thus entered the chemical industry. Furfural is a prime organic chemical with scores of uses in the plastics, synthetic fabrics, and oil-refining industries, and its derivatives give it position as one of the world's most versatile chemicals.

By 1966, Quaker Oats was the largest-selling breakfast food in the world, and the company was one of the foremost manufacturers of cereals in existence. The *Quaker Oats* and *Mother's Oats* labels (the products are identical) together supply more than half the total hot-cereal market in the United States, and one-tenth of all cereal sales, hot or ready-to-eat. Only The Quaker Oats Company has national distribution of such maize products as corn meal, grits, self-rising corn flour, and corn-meal mixes. The Quaker dog- and cat-food lines—*Ken-L Ration* and *Puss 'n Boots*—lead their fields in total sales. The company remains one of the largest manufacturers of livestock and poultry feeds, and has expanded impressively in chemicals and such baked goods as crackers and cookies under the *Burry* label. Quaker did a world-wide business in 1966 nearing $500 million a year.

How all this—and much else—was accomplished, the social implications attendant upon Quaker history, and Quaker's ongoing contributions to America and to the world in our time, this book will show.

Chapter 2 * *An Industry Is Born*

THE bells of Saint Bernard's church had just chimed the hour of two in the morning when the cry of *Fire!* woke slumbering Akron, Ohio. The night was crisp and cold, no hint in it of the spring thaw of 1886 that soon would mire every road into the city. Against this annual mud, which bogged delivery of agricultural products across gumbo roads for months, prudent miller Ferdinand Schumacher had just brimmed his bins with 100,000 bushels of oats, plus a supply of other grains sufficient to carry him until the summer harvest. In Akron, Schumacher was saluted as The Oatmeal King, and so he was. He accepted the accolade as his due. He had reared the mightiest oat-milling complex in the world; his *Jumbo* mill, only three years old, was five stories high and a mechanical wonder. Schumacher had introduced to America the use of oatmeal as a human food. He had created both an industry and a staple substitute for meat. His *Rolled Avena* was known to wholesalers throughout New England and the East, as far west as Denver, and even exported to that sanctum of porridge, Scotland. Schumacher was the largest employer, the heaviest buyer, the biggest industrialist in Akron. The economy of the area had grown up around him. So the disaster of fire at the mill affected, directly or indirectly, almost everyone in town.

There was some delay in reporting the flames to the Sixth Ward firehouse. By the time a pumper had built steam and raced behind four horses to the blaze, a crowd of sightseers almost blocked its way. Hose lines were flung, but the equipment generated no pressure. For some unknown reason, the machine failed to function. A new alarm went out. The fire's glow in the sky radiated to the nearby town of Kent, and also to Cleveland, thirty-three miles off. The Kent firemen responded, but their hose couplings had the wrong-gauge thread to fit Akron hydrants. A pumper from Cleveland, dispatched by special train, was derailed when the engine struck a handcar on the railroad tracks. Every piece of Akron's firefighting equipment had responded by 3 A.M., but the Schumacher mills were spread over so much acreage that the hose supply was inadequate.

"The elevator," said a special edition of the Akron *Daily Beacon* that day, "became food for the insatiable thrust of the fire fiend. The flames quickly licked up everything of a consumable nature, and within a half hour it was an utter ruin. Then the roof [of the great *Jumbo*] fell in, and the walls fell with a deep rumbling crash." When Saint Bernard's chimed six, there were five streams of water sizzling the ruins, but the conflagration, with nothing left to feed on, was sated.

The immigrant miller, "of iron nerve and inexhaustible will power," as the newspaper described him, watched his life work go. He was scarcely insured for the value of his elaborate $100,000 office, the pride of Akron, coveted by tycoons as far away as millionaire-studded Cleveland. The mills, the grains newly laid in storage, were a total loss. "Why weren't you insured?" a reporter asked at the climax of the blaze. "They want a fearful price for the premiums; I wouldn't pay," Schumacher replied in heavy German-accented English.

Only once did he become provoked with the inade-quacies of the primitive fire-fighters. The *Empire* mill, his best building until the *Jumbo* had been built, escaped the flames for a long time. Schumacher suggested that hoses played from inside that building to the flames round about would preserve it. "Save the *Empire* and you save me," he pleaded. But the firemen had no more hose. Soon the timbers began to smoke. Suddenly, like flaming mice, tiny flecks of yellow scudded up and down the building, and in another moment, with a spontaneous roar, the *Empire* was fully ablaze. Schumacher watched the calamity, strange calm masking his despair.

The disaster tempered Ferdinand Schumacher. Until then he had been an arrogant Dutchman who cooper-ated with nobody and crushed all opposition ruthlessly. Now he was severely crippled financially, and, of equal significance, he had nothing to sell. Into this double vacuum surged two competitors who, in different ways, reflected the new approach to industry hesitantly abroad in the land. An era had begun of combine, monopoly, national marketing, and technological advance that pro-duced America's first financial and manufacturing giants: Morgan, Rockefeller, Vanderbilt, Carnegie, and the rest.

Like a phoenix rising with greater vigor from its own ashes, from the Schumacher fire emerged the embryo of what today is one of America's great merchant suc-cesses: The Quaker Oats Company.

Ferdinand Schumacher, for all his shortsightedness, created the conditions that made the work of his younger associates possible. Short—less than five and a half feet tall—rotund and little schooled, but as canny and practical in mechanics as he was impractical in business judgments: his failure to insure his plant against fire was typical of him. As his fortune from milling grew, he made other investments that invariably failed. Said a colleague of him, "His private records contained innumerable accounts representing investments in which only two entries appear: a debit for the initial speculation, and a credit to 'bad debt.' . . ." His success as a miller and oatmeal merchandiser was the result of unimaginative persistence in an idea and hard physical labor, elements on which many an untutored but stubborn man has built a career.

Photographs of Schumacher taken about the time he ran for the governorship of Ohio on the Prohibition Party ticket reveal a personality then identified with the Amish: high forehead in a lean, almost gaunt face framed by overlarge ears; short, unruly hair; a prominent square-cut beard without mustache: a conservative, set in conviction, uncompromising, skilled as a craftsman rather than schooled as an intellectual. He poured several million dollars into a communal living colony at Harriman, Tennessee, open only to persons who (like Schumacher) swore no drop of alcoholic beverage had ever crossed their lips. In the old country, he would have remained a country miller all his days. In a new land of opportunity he made several millions, and, equally characteristic of a bounteous land, mismanaged and lost them. His basic idea was sound—that oatmeal was a superbly nourishing human food. Except for a few German, Scottish, and Irish immigrants, Schumacher was alone in his opinion when, in 1854, he set up a hand mill for grinding oats in the back room of his little grocery store.

The mid-nineteenth-century American breakfast was a formidable exercise in gluttony that often kept the diner at table for an hour and a half. Visiting European chroniclers all commented, appalled by the tradition. Even the humblest frontier kitchen followed the pattern to some degree, and no innkeeper who set less than a breakfast banquet survived long. Many accounts describe the New England–Allegheny Mountain breakfast of the period as including salt fish, beefsteak, sausages, boiled fowl, ham and bacon, together with corn bread sopped in gravy, jam or honey as a sweet aside, big dishes of potatoes and other vegetables, climaxed with fruit pie. On the frontier there were also corn-meal or buckwheat cakes and fried venison or chicken. In the South, hominy grits, eggs, hot breads saturated in butter or jelly, dumplings, fresh fish or prawns were added. The immigrants in the crowded cities—as immigrant Schumacher well knew—could neither afford the "hearty feeding" of the time nor see a need for it.

The Schumacher oatmeal was a cheap protein, not merely for breakfast use but as a meat substitute at any meal. German migrants heard about the Akron *Avena* from their Cleveland compatriots, and soon Schumacher was shipping his product in glass jars to New York and Philadelphia, Cincinnati, St. Louis, and other concentration areas of Teutonic stock.

"The general opinion prevailed," Schumacher wrote later, "that our domestic oats were not suitable for the manufacture of oatmeal. After satisfying myself that this was a mistake, I laid the foundation on a small scale of my present extensive milling establishments, and became the pioneer oatmeal manufacturer."

He soon outgrew both the grocery and the hand mill, and in 1856 organized the German Mills American Oatmeal Factory; where, using a water wheel for power, he ground between stones daily enough oatmeal to fill twenty 180-pound barrels. At first, little of it was sold in bulk; it was shipped in two-pound quantities or in wooden crates containing two or three dozen glass jars.

Schumacher had neither education nor training for his role as the first American merchant prince in the cereal line. Born at Celle, Hanover, in 1822, he was a grocer's clerk by the time he was fifteen. One of his duties was to grind oatmeal on the spot for customers, much as he ground coffee in another hand-cranked machine. That was all he ever learned of the trade, for he left soon for employment in a sugar refinery. In 1850 he followed a wave of his countrymen to America, settling with his brother as a farm hand on land now part of Cleveland, Ohio. Marrying a German girl, he moved to Akron to find support for a growing family that ultimately numbered seven children. He took up the grocery trade because it was the only work he knew. From the acquisition of his first mill, he pioneered the techniques.

The milling procedure of his time was not difficult to learn or expensive to finance, and the grain was available in Ohio as a horse feed and chicken scratch. Oats, a newcomer among sophisticated grains but known in wild form by the Romans and earlier, was cultivated in Central Europe during the Bronze Age as a crop that flourished in a cool climate with a short growing season. This was its attraction also for the Scots and Irish, for whom a porridge or gruel of oats was a major dietary staple. By A.D. 1700 it was growing in New England and Virginia, and by the time Ferdinand Schumacher began to buy it, American farmers produced 150 million bushels a year, the best quality and most abundant crops concentrated in Ohio, Illinois, and Iowa. A few other flour and corn millers may have ground a bit of oats for local sale, but Schumacher was the first to establish a brand for human use, first to develop a sale beyond his own doorstep. The marketing was simple. He sold at his own gates, or directly to consumers on mail order for cash, and finally, as business and capacity both expanded, to grocery wholesalers on tight credit terms of thirty to ninety days. He liked to have a full year of orders booked by September, so he would know how much of the new oat crop to buy and in what months to accept deliveries. So he took advance orders, where possible, for shipment after October 1, when he began to grind the new crop. Thus could he deliver oatmeal freshly ground, free of the risk later in the year of a dirty and mildewed product. Most of Schumacher's raw-material purchases were from local farmers who came by wagon to his elevator at seasons when dry roads were firm or icy tracks unmired.

A new influx of German and Irish immigrants in unprecedented numbers in the 1870s and 1880s greatly expanded the demand for Schumacher's wares. By 1880 the 180-pound barrel of bulk oatmeal bearing Schumacher's label was found in city general stores east of the Rocky Mountains except where local competition undersold it. But no consumer had ever thought of buying it by brand name.

The absurdity of an oat cereal for human food attracted jocose attention from the press, editorial writers, and cartoonists. Oat-eaters were accused of robbing horses, of developing a whinny, and of acquiring spavins. Heretofore oatmeal, imported from Scotland or Germany, had been dispensed only by apothecaries in half-pound packages to make an easily digestible pap for invalids and convalescents. Now even *The New York Times* turned caustic humor on the novelty of a human appetite for oatmeal:

A Scotchman [said an editorial], finding that oatmeal will sustain life and that it is the cheapest of all articles of food, naturally lives on oatmeal. Of course he does not like it any more than he likes his hereditary Calvinism, but he is entirely willing to eat it as long as it is cheap. . . . If the oatmeal craze continues, the next generation of Americans will be as dyspeptic and Calvinistic as the majority of Scotchmen.

This joke was so widely reprinted that *The Times* a few weeks later added to the fun. "It appears," a new editorial said, "that it is all a mistake to assume that oatmeal is the cause of the national Scotch dyspepsia . . . a real Scotchman . . . explains . . . the true cause of Scotch dyspepsia is the result of listening to the bagpipes."

Such public comments nevertheless propagandized widely for the virtues of oatmeal and increased its use—to the benefit of Schumacher, who refused to advertise in newspapers, relying on word-of-mouth recommendation to spread his product. The comments on economy attracted the indigent and frugal, especially the immigrants. Schumacher fueled the controversy by replying to *The Times*. Employing a prominent nutrition expert, Dr. Henry A. Mott, he published a panegyric on oats as a human food, proclaiming that the cereal contained every nutrient needed to keep man and child healthy—at a pittance compared to the cost of meat—and was gentler on the digestive system. Then, cudgeling directly *The Times*' charge that the Scot ate oatmeal only because it was cheap, Mott's booklet said, "On this theory, if water and champagne were on the table, the Scotchman according to this brilliant writer should ask for the water." But Schumacher the prohibitionist could not refrain here from a comment of his own, killing his own argument with the interpolation "He would certainly show good sense in doing so. *F.S.*"

Gradually the native American also began to find virtue in oats as human food, particularly after Schumacher's *Jumbo* mill introduced a tastier, easier-to-cook rolled oats in 1883. The saving in kitchen drudgery of the new recipe was enormous, an important attraction to the housewife that did not escape Quaker marketers a few years later. The first standard American cookbook to contain a recipe for oatmeal except as a sickroom gruel appeared in 1873, with a formula for oatmeal mush. A year later Schumacher's recipe for oatmeal as a complete breakfast food was included—an enormous victory for Schumacher and one that marked his first acceptance by native-born Americans. The stubborn German's missionary work had paid off. In thirty years he had made the nation breakfast-oatmeal conscious and had destroyed a prejudice against such a pedestrian substitute for the traditional gluttony. At Schumacher's zenith, just before the fire, he was selling 360,000 pounds of oatmeal a day, chiefly in 180-pound barrels to the retail-grocery trade on direct shipments, bypassing wholesalers and middlemen. His two-pound export tin was known in Scotland, a supreme accolade to his milling skill. His factories also produced wheat and barley flour and corn meal.

As both heavy immigration and native acceptance increased the American demand for oatmeal, competitors appeared in many localities. A mill capable of grinding a few thousand pounds a day was cheap to build. It needed a set of stones, water power or a windmill, and a few wagonloads of oats. Ten bushels (320 pounds) of cleaned oats made one 180-pound barrel of rolled oats. The technology, with rare exceptions, was centuries old.

The first significant modernization in milling was Schumacher's 1875 innovation of a machine to convert hulled kernels into coarse meal, with a resultant product Schumacher called *Steel Cut Oats*. The process, developed by Schumacher and an assistant, was improved in a patent issued to another employee, William Heston, an action that led directly to the founding of the Quaker brand in competition with Schumacher. At Rockford, Illinois, a miller named George Cormack (also to become part of the Quaker organization) invented labor-saving systems for moving grains in and out of the mill. In 1878 Schumacher imported porcelain rollers from England to manufacture rolled oats, a cereal soon in such demand that in 1881 he converted his entire oatmeal production to the succulent, easily cooked variety. Housewives now could prepare a breakfast by use of a double boiler in one hour, as against a minimum two hours plus enormous preparation for the traditional banquet breakfast, and at an infinitesimal fraction of the cost.

Cutting manufacturing costs became important. Never in his life, however, did Schumacher improve a product primarily to cultivate greater consumer acceptance; that theory of selling emerged, under the Quaker label, with the next generation of management. Schumacher developed rolled oats because the rolling process flaked grains instead of crushing them, eliminating the unsalable powdery oat flour that had wasted one-fourth of the oats in earlier grindings.

A collateral advantage was an enormous competitive edge over the strident imitators who had copied his steel-cut method despite legal efforts to protect his patent. "A recent decision by Judge Gresham of the U.S. Circuit Court of Illinois," Schumacher wrote at the time, "confirms my right to the patents for cutting oatmeal. The use of this device in one form or another has been unlawfully appropriated by almost all oatmeal millers . . . I shall soon take steps . . . to prosecute all such to the fullest extent of the law." Twenty competitors began to produce oatmeal east of the Rocky Mountains, chiefly in Illinois and Iowa, in answer to the Schumacher-created demand. By 1885 the American oat-milling industry had a combined capacity of 3940 barrels (709,200 pounds) a day, twice as much as the retail needs of the nation could absorb. Fierce price wars resulted.

The food industry was just beginning to consolidate specialty retailers into general stores which answered the needs of the expanding urban culture. Until the Civil War, America had been an agricultural nation. As late as 1840 there were only 131 towns in the nation of 2500 or more. Each family—certainly each community—was virtually self-sufficient. Every town had its miller of grains; each family grew its vegetables and meats and kept poultry. Housewives baked the bread, churned the butter, made the candles and often the clothing. On the frontier, trading posts bartered for furs with kitchen wares, farm implements, drugs, coffee, tea, and spices. Gradually the trading posts succumbed to itinerant peddlers who in turn settled down at a crossroads and opened a general store.

As cities expanded—there were 1737 American cities by 1900—the town food industry specialized. The housewife stopped a few moments with the grocer, then the butcher, then the vegetable-fruit merchant, the baker, the dairy operator, the spice retailer, and possibly even a specialized cheesemonger and fisherman: eight stores to collect the raw materials for a single meal. Portents of the future were just beginning to appear. In 1859 the Great Atlantic & Pacific Tea Company expanded into a chain of specialty shops. In 1865, John Wanamaker in Philadelphia put firm prices on his merchandise, ending haggling. In 1866, to sell by mail, a tobacconist developed the first retail consumer package, the Bull Durham tobacco bag. The open-shelf help-yourself dime store was created by F. W. Woolworth in 1875. But these innovations were primitive in Ferdinand Schumacher's day. He made his living from the 90,000 grocery and 100,000 general stores, each individually owned and operated.

These merchants bought their wares and ran their establishments in individualistic fashion. Their only consideration was price. No customer bought by label, except an occasional buyer who wanted Bon Ami, Gold Dust, Babbitt, Fairy or Ivory soap, perhaps Bull Durham. Scant attention was paid to cleanliness, and there was no government inspection for purity, standard, or honest weight.

From such local manufacturers as millers, bakers, and dairymen the retailer purchased what he could to save commissions and freight. Fresh fruits and vegetables in the main came from the countryside, as did eggs and poultry when the farmer's wife came to town on Saturday afternoon. Winter-keepers, such as russet apples, rutabagas, and turnips, prolonged the fresh season into December in northern latitudes.

For "foreign" supplies, the grocer relied on commission men from wholesale houses. These traveling salesmen ranged the countryside from store to store booking orders, advancing credit as much as a year until the next harvest in the community brought the merchant his annual settlement from his customers and promising future deliveries, often months off. Rolled oats, for example, were best bought shortly after October 1, when the freshly milled grains were new; later purchases were apt to be weevily following months of storage in a dank warehouse. For other than local distribution, the wholesaler was the key to the trade. What he stocked the retailer sold; what he ignored the grocer did without.

The general store, and in smaller measure the grocery, was actually a warehouse strewn with crates and boxes of many sizes, shapes, and weights, jute and cotton sacks, and—behind the counter—high-stacked shelves. Up front, near the door, a pyramid-shaped stack of perforated-metal trays supported the perishable vegetables, kept fresh by a spray of water showered from above. On the counter, usually close to a huge roll of wrapping paper and a ball of twine suspended from the ceiling, rested an 80-pound Swiss cheese under glass, with a cheese knife the size of a cleaver nearby. Meats were tinned, smoked, or salted, there being no refrigeration, and salted fish in bales lay at random, victimized by dogs and houseflies. Most of the "foreign" imports were sacked by the grocer in small quantities from bulk purchases and weighed up haphazardly on an untested scale. A standing jest was that the grocer (or meat man) weighed in his thumb each time. Coffee purchases were weighed out from a gunny sack and ground in a hand-cranked Hobart mill kept in the rear of the store near the vinegar barrel.

There was no standardization. The confusion of containers included oatmeal, corn meal, crackers, flour, barley, rice, salt fish, and kerosene in barrels of one sort or another that held from 50 to 250 pounds; dried figs, apricots, and prunes in boxes; pickles in brine; sugar in sacks the same size as those that held onions and lentils. A battery of glass-topped boxes revealed chocolate marshmallow and coconut-topped cookies, ginger snaps,

and other "city goodies," and hard by in an oaken rack
an assortment of spooled threads and kits of needles,
and perhaps behind them on a shelf a few bolts of cotton
goods. Under glass were penny candies—licorice twists,
lemon drops, molasses kisses with peanut-butter centers,
creamed filberts, jawbreakers, peppermint chews, hoar-
hound drops, peanuts, stick candy, gumdrops, jelly-
beans, and gum. The same case held smoking and chew-
ing tobacco and 2¢ cigars. Hanging from the walls were
turkey-feather dusters, mops and brooms, pails and
washtubs, washboards and baskets, and often a bunch
of bananas. There were tinned meats and fruits on the
shelves, along with Mason jars, wax and paraffin, tooth-
picks, phosphorus matches, English lavender, flypaper,
mousetraps, insect powders, candles and cocoa, lard and
bottled grape juice, baking and rising sodas, lemon and
vanilla extracts, paste and glue, macaroni and noodles,
bay rum, Vaseline and Epsom salt, animal crackers in
circus-wagon boxes, ginger in stone jars, and sets of
dishes and silverware. In season, a rack of vegetable and
flower seeds was mandatory. Under the counter was a
cash till; beside it usually was the box that held the
green trading stamps.

In all this confusion there was little room for loafers
or browsers, but they were there, out of the rain or snow
or summer heat and unevictable, because usually the
store was also the post office and the grocer the post-
master. No one helped himself, except to pilfer an occasional cookie or cracker or pickle. The grocer personally
waited on every buyer. He also had a big book from
which he could answer such questions as What is the
difference between condensed and evaporated milk?
What is the difference between white and gray lobster?

What are sardines in salad oil? What are pimentos? What is succotash?

The open food receptacles were havens for mice, rats, flies, roaches, and sometimes served as a bed for the store's cat. When a woman asked for a nickel's worth of oatmeal, the grocer obliged her by scooping out and weighing into a paper sack the measure she requested, ignoring any collateral ingredients that might have infested it. For her nickel, the weight in oatmeal would be a pound and a quarter.

The miller delivered his 180-pound barrels of oatmeal to wholesalers as far east as Boston or west to Denver in 1885 for about $4.50, his price to his local customers being perhaps 75 cents less. The wholesaler's markup to the grocer was about a half-cent a pound, the retailer's another penny. Until aggressive competition hit him, Ferdinand Schumacher made several million dollars at such prices. But by 1886, when the mill burned, Schumacher was selling nothing in Iowa or within fifty miles of Rockford, Illinois, and wholesalers were offering him as little as $3.75 a barrel in St. Louis and Philadelphia. There was little profit left in the trade for anyone.

Perhaps with this in mind, Schumacher, when asked amid the embers of the fire if he would rebuild, answered curtly, "I do not propose to borrow money to rebuild." He still had a small output in other locations—the Cascade Mills, the Starch Mills—totaling perhaps 600 barrels a day. "I'll live on it the best I can," he said.

But events outran him. The vogue for mergers and stock companies had begun. Schumacher was precipitated into the new day despite himself. He could no longer flourish as a lone figure of power in the emerging era of investor stockholders whose only interest in the business was a generous profit. Schumacher the craftsman was incapable of understanding such a system; to him success was strength, not money. He had no comprehension of the tools of the twentieth century, but the nineteenth had taught him enough about infighting to sustain him in transient adversity. He was burned out, temporarily eclipsed. But he had not abdicated his oatmeal throne. In his own mind, and in the eyes of Akron's admiring citizens, he was still the king.

Chapter 3 ✳ *Three*
Millers Get Together

THE FIRE that engulfed Ferdinand Schumacher was scarcely cold when the grocery trade received this letter in the mail:

Gentlemen:
Please note advance in values which is this day established. The change has been made necessary owing to the supply formerly furnished by Mr. Schumacher of Akron having been cut off. His mills were burned on Saturday morning of last week.

The opportunist who capitalized first on Schumacher's disaster was not his largest rival, but his nearest and most energetic competitor, Henry Parsons Crowell. From a small mill at Ravenna, Ohio, sixteen miles from Akron, Crowell had seriously undermined Schumacher's sales by aggressive marketing of steel-cut oats under the brand name *Quaker*. His product was good and his methods unusual: he put up two-pound measures of his oatmeal in filthproof paper boxes, with explicit cooking directions on the carton. He advertised his wares in the newspapers of cities which contained large concentrations of German, Scottish, and Irish immigrants. To Schumacher all this was nonsense.

Further, the Quaker package displayed a picture of a

lean, austere member of the Quaker religion of Colonial times, holding in his hand a scroll that displayed the word *Pure*. The equation was effective; the Quaker group was admired for its frugality, thrift, neatness, orderliness, and—above all—its integrity. The Quaker label capitalized on these assets through advertising. By the time of the Schumacher fire, Crowell had a nice little business.

With the collapse of Schumacher, Crowell saw an opportunity for personal leadership. Perhaps the time had arrived to organize the millers into a trust similar to the highly profitable, though publicly condemned, combines that had been created in oil, coal, steel, and sugar. Such an amalgamation would end the suicidal price war then in progress, and might enrich the partners. Crowell burned to earn big money—he had promised God that he would. In the preceding year Crowell and a much more important miller, Robert Stuart of Cedar Rapids, Iowa, and Chicago, had organized a voluntary association of grain processors; it had collapsed because Schumacher alone refused to support it. With Schumacher's ability to dominate the industry now removed, a merging of milling interests, discussed by Crowell and Stuart privately, might be accomplished. Crowell's quick price increase was the first move in a much greater scheme.

Schumacher had said contemptuously that Crowell knew nothing about the business. This was precisely Crowell's advantage. He had no tradition, no prejudices, no check rein on his soaring imagination, no experienced sage to warn him that his innovative ideas were impractical or imprudent. Before entering the milling trade in 1882, Crowell had read diligently the history of the craft and of business methods generally. From this study certain truths had seemed to him self-evident, the chief one being that the milling industry was a century behind the times.

Henry Parsons Crowell was the descendant of an aristocratic New England family in which the genes transmitted a congenital vulnerability to tuberculosis. Crowell's grandfather, father, and two brothers all died of a pulmonary ailment—which young Henry also contracted and which should have killed him. But, as he said later, he made a compact with God that if he were spared, he would dedicate his talents to amassing money with which to finance Christian evangelism.

Metaphysical motivations goaded Henry P. Crowell for the remainder of his life. For half a century, during which his income was impressive, he dedicated 65 per cent of his earnings to Christian causes (chiefly Presbyterianism and the eclectic Protestant fundamentalism of the wide-ranging evangelist Dwight L. Moody). Because Crowell believed that God was his partner and had indeed endowed him with many of his ideas, Crowell seized boldly on all the new merchandising trends of the turbulent generation that finished turning the United States from an agricultural into an industrial nation. As the developer of national markets for giant corporations, Crowell was as creative as any industrialist of his time.

Crowell's father had reached Cleveland in 1853 from West Hartford, Connecticut. The citizenry was impressed with this arrival in the Western Reserve—less because of his dignity, elegance, and obvious wealth or even his bride, a stylish, handsome member of the Hartford family of Parsons, which bent a social knee to nobody, even in Boston, than because the method of his coming was perhaps unique in the Territory. He and his bride were borne by a regal private stagecoach drawn by four horses. No such personal equipage had ever been seen in the region before. With the former Miss Parsons was a collection of Hepplewhite furniture, Paul Storr and Bateman, silver, elegant imported brocades. Her home, with its harp in the drawing room, immediately set a new *ton* for the frontier town. Crowell established himself as a wholesaler in fine shoes and boots, an out-station of the family business in New England. By the time he died at forty-three of the congenital lung weakness, he was handsomely established; the oldest of his three sons, a sickly boy of nine, was being tutored privately for the family tradition of eastern preparatory school and Yale University education.

At Greylock, a now defunct Berkshire Mountain academy not far from Hartford, young Henry Parsons Crowell gained all the academic education he would ever receive. In his fifth year there, the school buildings burned. Seventeen-year-old Henry was too weak from a progressive physical wasting from lung trouble to be admitted to another school. He returned home to die. En route, he consulted a specialist in Philadelphia who recommended seven years of outdoor life in the dry climate and rarefied air of the western mountain states.

Young Henry recognized in this prescription the Biblical "seven lean years" during which he would be tested and made whole as a prelude to living out his days off the fat of the land. He pledged that if God forged him a healthy manhood, he would henceforth help to finance Christ's work on earth. In August 1874 he set out alone for the West in absolute confidence that he would be cured. He was. The lean years ended; he returned to Cleveland in 1881 for the promised fat ones, rich from western land speculation, horse breeding, and a $27,000 inheritance. He was now a dapper young man of the eastern prep-school breed: something of a dandy, meticulously tailored in the eastern fashion of tight-fitting clothes, with elegant mustaches sweeping back into his cheeks and carefully oiled black hair. But his blue eyes were calm with the serenity of unusual inner peace. His recent illness was suggested only by a pale complexion, a lean, almost gaunt face, an ascetic countenance punctuated by thin lips. His associates soon began to call him the "Godly autocrat." He was pious; he was benign, never raising his voice in anger or reproach—but he always had his own way. The decision-making role was his natural attitude; men deferred to him both because of this and because he seemed instinctively accurate. This trait, combined with his assurance that God motivated him and therefore he was infallible, was difficult to contravene. Few men of that generation quarreled with the Almighty. Schumacher was perhaps the only man in all his life who ever met Crowell head-on in a test of power.

Crowell had been home only a month when a family connection suggested that he buy the Ravenna oatmeal mill, then almost bankrupt from inept management. The company had only two assets. The first was a franchise to use without payment of royalty a patent for the manufacture of steel-cut oats otherwise assigned exclusively to Schumacher. The process had been developed in 1877 by Asmus J. Ehrrichsen, a Schumacher employee, the first real advance in oat-milling technique since the Middle Ages. When Schumacher built his original mill in Akron, he hulled the raw oats by grinding them between two circular stones rotating in opposite directions. The composite of oat grain, hulls, and useless residue was cleaned in sifters and blowers and reduced to hulled oat grain, called groats. The groats were crushed through another set of millstones. The result was a meal which in three or four hours of cooking was edible, but it was pasty as a result of the floury residue from the grinding, and often became lumpy and glutenous. Ehrrichsen's improvement discarded the millstones. By steam or water power the hulled oats were cut into meal by fine knife blades, thus eliminating the flour. The result was a meal of uniform pleasant taste and flaky composition.

(Another employee of Schumacher's, William Heston, observing Ehrrichsen's machine, produced and patented an improvement in the cutting process, in effect securing the Ehrrichsen–Schumacher invention for himself. He placated his angry employer by licensing his device to Schumacher with the reservation that he might also use it himself. This he did in the water-powered mill at Ravenna, financed by several partners.)

The Ravenna establishment's second asset was the Quaker name. Heston was of Quaker descént, which may have motivated the trademark, but this is doubtful. More probably one of the partners, Henry Seymour, searching an encyclopedia for a virtuous identity that would instill buyer confidence, saw in the article on the Quaker sect exactly the connotation he desired for his steel-cut oats. Possibly his eye was on the large Quaker population in nearby Ohio towns and villages. At any rate, the Quaker symbol was given commercial form in 1877 when the Quaker Mill Company registered as a trademark the "figure of a man in Quaker garb," to which in 1895 the name *Quaker* was added in another registry. The 1877 filing was America's first registered trademark for a breakfast cereal.

None of the partners in the Quaker Mill Company was an experienced businessman, and the venture languished. For a time it passed to a distiller, Warren Corning, who extended the Quaker symbol to a whiskey he bottled in Peoria, Illinois. By 1881, Corning had found profit in spirits but none in oats; he sold the Ravenna establishment to Crowell, but continued the Quaker name on his liquor product, a brand that has survived but has no connection with The Quaker Oats Company.

Crowell believed that, as with all his major decisions, his attention had been turned to the Ravenna company by Providence, showing him the way to make money. He sat down and wrote a remarkably clear-headed memorandum on his goals. He purposed to establish at Ravenna the first element in a world-wide organization that would sell the best-quality oatmeal improving technology was capable of turning out. The scheme was grandiose and, to his competitors, ridiculous. The possessor of a unique patent for a sewing machine might establish a world market, perhaps—but a food product that must compete with local supply everywhere was unsuited to such distribution. Crowell saw the venture developed beyond even his dreams in his lifetime, for Quaker became before 1910 a true world organization, the first American food processor to reach this pinnacle.

No annal records what Crowell's 10 per cent partner, James H. Andrews, thought of all this. Andrews was a perfectionist. He knew milling, in which specialty Crowell left him alone, even though Andrews, in his zeal for efficiency, was such a driver that laborers worked for him only if no other employment were available. *Do it now* was the motto that motivated him, an admirable lash with which to drive Crowell's imaginative schemes to full production. So utterly was his motto followed by his employees that one Saturday afternoon, when he mentioned to a foreman that a company-owned vacant lot in downtown Akron should be fenced in, the employee at once hired 150 carpenters, twenty teamsters with wagons to haul lumber, and completed the job before dark that day.

In the mills the regimen was similar. By 1882, under the Andrews whiplash, the Ravenna mill was the first in the world to maintain under one roof operations to grade, clean, hull, cut, package, and ship oatmeal to interstate markets in a continuous process that in some aspects anticipated the modern assembly line. This efficiency gave Quaker Oats, which by 1883 rolled as well as steel-cut to compete against Schumacher's new *Jumbo* rolled oats, a cost advantage. Crowell needed this margin to cover the extra cost of packaging, which added half a cent a pound to expenses. In the year of the Schumacher fire, Quaker put up its brand-established product for the trade in a case of three dozen five-pound packets, or a smaller case of three dozen two-pound cartons; these were cut oats. Quaker Rolled White Oats were offered in twenty-four-ounce cardboard boxes. In addition, the Quaker Mill Company sold its steel-cut oats in 180-pound barrels, its rolled oats in 90-pound kegs. The product lines included fine-quality wheat meal, hominy grits, graham flour, cracked wheat, rolled wheat, farina, and corn meal. Schumacher answered this competition by offering his *Rolled Avena* domestically in his two-pound export tin, conspicuously marked "The Original Packaged Oats."

With Crowell to plan and Andrews to execute, the Quaker label became established and well-distributed in the larger cities east of the Rocky Mountains. By the time of Schumacher's misfortune, Crowell's position was impressive. An advance in price of the only oatmeal buyers requested by name—and were apt to buy despite the price rise—demonstrated his influence in the industry. And this was its intent.

The Crowell message was no cryptogram to flourishing miller Robert Stuart in Chicago. He interpreted it correctly, and moved at once to procure in the shift of power a dominant position for himself.

Canadian-born, Stuart was Scottish as porridge. A thin-faced, unobtrusive merchant, his scholarly bent intensified by eyeglasses, in speech and conversation frugal, in manner reserved, Stuart asked of his colleagues only that he be allowed to do his work, shunning the limelight of company presidencies or other impressive trappings of business success. He complemented the flamboyant Crowell as a mortise does a tenon; together later they interlocked perfectly, each supplying only his own part of a mutual function, each supremely respecting the undoubted and indispensable talents of the other. Stuart's jaw was clean-shaven, his mustache conservatively Victorian, his clothing impeccable but unobtrusive. He called no undue attention to himself.

Stuart's father had been much the same. The elder Stuart, John, had migrated in 1850 from a bleak glen in northern Scotland to Canada and had settled at tiny Embro, scarcely on the map of Oxford County, Ontario, and an unlikely location for a man who aspired to make a living as an exporter to Europe of Canadian fruits, grains, and cheese. He worked as a field hand for a time on the farm of a Joseph Meadows. Growing restive after the birth of Robert, he traded his key-winder watch for a gray colt and rig. As a Scot he had an affinity for oatmeal, and Oxford County, generously supplied with water power, was full of it. Several Scottish millers had settled there, including George Cormack—who later at Rockford, Illinois, became the industry's first scientific engineer. From the farmers John Stuart bought oats, after riffling it through his fingers with a fine touch for plumpness and other manifestations of superior quality. He had no trouble persuading miller James H. Monroe to trade these oats for one-third their weight in oatmeal. Then, traveling by wagon, Stuart bartered his meal from farm to farm until he reached Goderich on Lake Huron, where he traded his accumulated provender for dried fish. On the return trip, the fish were converted into oats for restocking at the establishment of James Monroe. By 1860, when Robert Stuart was eight, he was his father's chief helper. The trade waxed slowly, and enveloped a sawmill in Ingersoll, Ontario, which was converted into an oatmeal factory. This he advertised in the Oxford County Directory of 1862 as follows:

JOHN STUART

FLOUR AND FEED STORE

MANUFACTURER OF OATMEAL, AND PROPRIETOR OF

NORTH STAR MILLS

INGERSOLL, D.W.

The highest price paid for oats.

But he was too far from any large market to prosper, and as Robert Stuart grew older he, like many pioneer country youths, spread his dreams to far horizons. To make a living at all, John Stuart supplemented oat milling with a small export trade in Ontario fruits, grains, and cheese through the lake port of Goderich. In bulk, his oatmeal went to Scotland, and possibly to Germany. But this business was not even large enough to absorb the capacity of the North Star which, at twenty-five barrels of production a day, was the smallest in the county. Seeking an exit from this dead-end commercial venture, Robert made several exploratory trips to the United States. Finally he saw what he wanted: the most magnificent-quality oats in the world in abundant supply. They were grown in the eight-foot deep topsoil of eastern Iowa, where the weather was cool enough in spring to nurture the crop but hot enough in summer to mature and dry the seasoned grains. Nobody had ever seen such oats. And at Cedar Rapids, on the swift-flowing Cedar River, there was a likely and available site for a mill. He and his father had nothing to lose by leaving Embro, the boy argued. John Stuart agreed. His confidence in a twenty-year-old son was remarkable, for he uprooted his life, turned the North Star over to his brother, and migrated to Cedar Rapids in 1873. He was impressed. The oats were right. Four railroads and the waterways of the nearby Mississippi River connected a thriving little city with the great world; water and coal were cheap and abundant. Why, the seven thousand residents of Cedar Rapids were a market in themselves! And there was a Presbyterian Church, built by Scots immigrants.

Cedar Rapids already had been marked by a different sort of authority, Abraham Lincoln's onetime secretary of state, William H. Seward. "Of the towns which have sprung up on the plains," he had written, "we notice Cedar Rapids—not for its superiority to others, but as a specimen of an inchoate Western city. During a ten-minute stay there, we saw the suburban cottages, with pointed roofs, of the Bohemian settlers, surrounded by dark green meadows covered with flocks of geese and eider ducks. We heard airs from *Trovatore* on a Chickering piano from a dwelling house not yet painted and plastered. We saw the mansard mansion of a speculator in city lots. . . . There seemed to be all sorts of churches for all sects of Christians." Seward neglected to mention that Coe College had been founded there in 1851, or that a less desirable element of horse thieves and other riffraff had once made the town's pioneer inn headquarters.

John Stuart remained considerably longer than ten minutes in Cedar Rapids, and reached his judgment concerning it in fewer words than did Seward. But the enthusiastic conclusion was identical. Noted the Cedar Rapids *Daily Republican:* "Mr. John Stuart of Canada has recently purchased the large stone warehouse near the depot, and will immediately convert it into a manufactory for the making of oatmeal. . . . His son Robert will be here next week and will superintend the establishment." Robert was already there, but typically avoided any publicity. His eye had caught what the news reporter's had not, the fact that the acquired warehouse fronted on one of the choicest footages of the Red Cedar River in Linn County, admirably suited for a water-powered mill, large enough for future expansions. The cost was $5500. During the mill construction, John Stuart fell and fractured a leg. He returned to Embro, leaving Robert to complete and operate the business, which had an original capacity of 300 barrels of oatmeal a day. This was small, but it was more than ten times the capacity of the old North Star, and a daily peak production would supply 5400 pounds of oatmeal for sale: a goodly beginning.

Another Scot, George Douglas, obliquely assessed young Robert Stuart's success, and liked what he saw. More directly, he surveyed the young man at the Presbyterian Church, and had little cause to fault the newcomer. Being an able businessman himself, Douglas employed a hedging operation: he introduced young Stuart to his attractive niece, then gave the couple ample exposure by inviting Stuart often to Sunday dinner. He figured that loneliness and proximity might be a powerful compote, and so they were. Soon Stuart and Maggie had an "understanding." The maneuver was typical of Douglas, who had prospered mightily by keeping his eyes open and taking advantage of what he saw. He had been a strong-backed stonemason on his arrival in the United States in 1845, but he discovered soon enough that the western railroads had need of his talent to build bridge abutments. He contracted the work and grew rich, investing the profits in choice Iowa farmlands he crossed in his railroad-construction work. The land made him a millionaire. He bought a plug hat, a frock coat, and a gold-headed cane, and settled in Cedar Rapids as its leading citizen. But his appearance was deceptive. Two thugs, seeing him in his dude clothing, made the mistake of attempting to take from him a payroll sack he carried for one of his Cedar Rapids enterprises. He knocked both thieves senseless.

Such a direct actionist as Douglas was not one to let a likely nephew-in-law escape. As Stuart prospered, he married and settled into the social group of the Presbyterian parish, Douglas now having moved across the Mississippi River to Dixon, Illinois. But young Stuart was restive. Cedar Rapids was too far from the *big* markets. What he wanted was a more metropolitan outlet for his other aptitude, a demonstrated instinct for profitable speculation on the grain exchange. Drawing-room conversations on the subject of wider oatmeal markets in Chicago beguiled Douglas when Maggie and Robert visited him. In 1879 a partnership, Douglas and Stuart, was formed to finance and operate a new mill in Chicago.

Ferdinand Schumacher with his steel oat hulling machine which enabled him to build world-wide oatmeal business

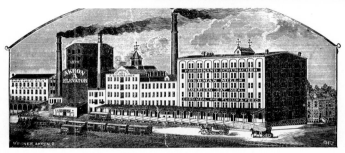

By 1886 these mills produced 360,000 pounds of oatmeal a day, as Schumacher made the nation oatmeal conscious

This fire destroyed Schumacher's great empire in 1886, motivating the combine which became Quaker Oats Company

Robert Stuart, a co-founder
of American Cereal Company

Earliest Stuart oat mill,
Embro, Ontario, about 1850

Portland-bound special, here loading at Cedar Rapids,
gave Quaker its first nation-wide distribution in 1891

Henry P. Crowell expanded Quaker into a world symbol

Quaker trademark was born at this Ohio mill in 1877

Typical Crowell promotions: above, Quaker pavilion at 1893 Chicago fair; below, float in parade for W. J. Bryan, 1896

*This great product symbol, "the man in Quaker garb,"
was America's first registered trademark for a cereal,
familiar nationally by 1893, in world trade by 1910*

Trademark for Pettyjohn's
Cereal, the first
diversification in 1893

Ingenious puffed rice gun
created a new cereal in 1902

Secret lab hidden here
in grain bin from 1902

Early advertisement for
product acquired in 1911

By 1912 sales exceeded $15,000,000 a year. At Cedar Rapids (top right); 500 girls loaded cartons (left); other signs of expansion: the Empire Mill at Akron (center) and first Canadian plant at Peterboro, Ont.

Home of Aunt Jemima, the world's first ready mix
food (upper left) from 1890; Nancy Green (right)
personified the trademark for thirty years; Quaker
acquired label in 1926, streamlined production
(below) at St. Joseph

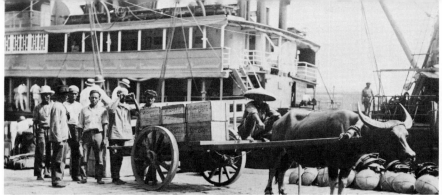

Quaker's trademark was the world's best known, product most widely distributed, even before World War I. Some conveyances in use: above, Singapore docks; left, Tokyo; below, Karachi; bottom, Cedar Rapids

Soon the Imperial Mill, for years a Chicago landmark, was in operation at the corner of Dearborn and Sixteenth streets. Stuart joined the Chicago Board of Trade, where he became one of its most canny traders, not only for his company but for his own account. With his father, he continued to produce milling products in Cedar Rapids. The production of the two factories was marketed under common labels and also packaged for Baltimore and Philadelphia wholesalers under private labels. The line of flours and milled grains, including oatmeal, was marketed throughout the Midwest, but principally in Chicago, Milwaukee, and Detroit, a market large enough to absorb most of the oatmeal production without making serious inroads on the operations of either Schumacher or Crowell.

Douglas and Stuart also exported three grades of oatmeal to Scotland through a broker in Glasgow. A very coarse grind was popular in porridge. A medium grind cooked in shorter time but was less flavorsome to the Scottish palate. A fine oat flour was shipped as the basis for a soft drink, taken in hot weather as a restorative and stimulant. Workers in the Stuart mills also were offered this drink. In summer, barrels of ice water were laced with fine oat flour into a milky liquid which employees were encouraged to consume to produce greater energy.

The ambitions of Stuart in Illinois–Iowa and Crowell in Ohio, mutually stifled by Oatmeal King Schumacher, inevitably drove the younger men toward each other. Schumacher, by controlling half the total oatmeal-production facilities, could fight price wars without the least dismay. He could offset a cut in one market with a compensating advance in another. On volume alone he could show a profit where other millers operated at a loss. When, early in 1885, the rush of competition in oatmeal milling made a shambles of the market, Stuart and Crowell met, probably in Chicago, though there is no record of this encounter.

The result, months later, was the formation of a trade group, The Oatmeal Millers Association. Everyone of consequence in the industry was represented: Cormack in Rockford, Stuart in Chicago, Crowell in Ravenna, and fifteen others. The only important nonparticipant: Schumacher.

Haughtily he refused to attend the organizational meeting as a waste of time. He was correct, in fact. The Association set a minimum price below which members pledged not to sell oatmeal: $6.50 a barrel for steel-cut, $3.57½ for a half-barrel of rolled oats. At this price all prospered, non-member Schumacher most of all. Penalties were devised against members of the group who undercut the price structure by rebates, discounts, unusual credit terms, or free merchandise. For a few months the experiment succeeded. Then a miller in Fort Dodge, Iowa, broke the agreement. Within a week everyone had met his reduced prices, and the association succumbed. Crowell and Stuart were convinced that had Schumacher contributed his name and business volume to the Association, the group might have exerted sufficient sanctions on the industry to maintain the Association's objectives.

With Schumacher's mills destroyed by fire, the situation was agreeably changed for all except Schumacher. Not only was the visible supply of oatmeal reduced drastically, thus strengthening the market, but the old Association members were in position to force Schumacher's compliance. Members of the defunct Association began a vigorous exchange of correspondence, nurtured by Stuart. In a few months a convocation of the nation's chief millers was scheduled at Davenport, Iowa, a convenient rendezvous about midway in the oat belt between Crowell and Schumacher in Ohio, Stuart and Cormack in Illinois, and lesser processors scattered across Iowa to Omaha, Nebraska.

Meanwhile, Schumacher had reorganized and was again a strong force in the trade. He had absorbed his local competitor, the Akron Milling Company, an archaic organization one unit of which was a stone mill built in 1832; it had, however, a new oat-rolling mill that spewed out greater production than the owners could sell. They therefore proposed a merger with Schumacher, who had markets but little production. So dominant were Schumacher's personality and reputation that the new enterprise became the F. Schumacher Milling Company, and the master miller put his entire family on the payroll, with himself as unquestioned leader. So Schumacher set out for Davenport confident that despite his misfortunes, he remained the Oatmeal King, and as such would dictate the decisions of the meeting.

On the first Tuesday in November 1886, half a year after the Schumacher fire, the King boarded the Rock Island noon train at Chicago, accompanied by both Stuart and Crowell, who provided him careful escort to his elegant suite in Davenport's Kimball House. The older man appreciated sumptuous luxury, the visual trapping of his kingship.

But the next morning Schumacher discovered that he had been dethroned. Represented at the table were 4110 barrels daily of oatmeal production, not counting his own; he therefore produced less than one-fourth of the oatmeal represented at the meeting. In addition, 1600 barrels daily were under control of local small millers who, had not joined the old Association. Schumacher now was merely a peer among equals. The participants realized at once that something more was required than a voluntary and unenforceable agreement.

What evolved from the discussion was the Consolidated Oatmeal Company. It was not a unanimous venture—only twelve members of the old Association subscribed to it. It was a pool, of a type illegal today but licit and popular then. It attempted to control production and pricing by allotting each of its partners a sales quota based on its percentage of the industry's oatmeal capacity, a specific geographic area in which to sell, and a fixed price. The management was authorized to curtail production in periods of oversupply. Financing was provided to buy out competitors or to lease their plants and keep them idle. Stuart and Crowell were delegated to act as commissioners who would monitor the performance of Consolidated's members, with authority to levy fines for noncompliance. Henry P. Crowell, who liked the limelight, was elected president; Robert Stuart, who sidestepped publicity, was the managing vice-president, and Ferdinand Schumacher, who liked to run everything in which he was involved, was relegated to the role of treasurer. He never forgave Crowell and Stuart this insult, and harassed them in many petty ways during the remainder of his career.

The Consolidated, chartered May 4, 1887, as an Illinois corporation, had a significant weakness: it controlled only half the trade. Too much of the total oatmeal production remained outside for the pool to dominate the market. Lesser millers delighted in undercutting the monster wherever possible. As a result, maintenance of a price structure and division of markets was impractical. Nor was Consolidated able, as it had planned, to obliterate this competition. The cost of financing a new oatmeal mill was so small that opportunists rushed to open mills merely for the purpose of

selling or leasing them to Consolidated. Before Consolidated was two years old, twenty-one nuisance mills had been built. In 1888 Consolidated paid $112,500 to acquire facilities it immediately closed down, drawing off half its net earnings. Non-pool millers, to protect themselves, had raised enormous cry in the press and in state legislatures against the "giant" that had been created to destroy them. In other industries, too, pooling had become a common device and lawmakers were swamped with protests from manufacturers disadvantaged by these arrangements. As a result, such pools were outlawed by the legislatures of most Midwestern states. Consolidated collapsed.

Near the close of 1888, the seven largest cereal mills in the nation, having abandoned the pool, united under a holding company chartered in West Virginia as the American Cereal Company. Together they represented 2240 barrels (more than 400,000 pounds) of daily oatmeal-producing capacity. But now there were 29 other mills with 3470 barrels (620,500 pounds) in competition, or about 60 per cent of the total. Six of the participants exchanged all the assets of their individual businesses for stock in the new company—but not Schumacher. He asked too high a price, one which would have given him immediate control of the enterprise. Therefore he was accepted on lesser terms. He was not absorbed, but merely transferred to the combine his oatmeal patents and trademarks, and agreed to pay the holding company a fair share of the profits from the oatmeal portion of his business.

This, of course, was an impractical arrangement. Members soon complained that Schumacher charged most of his milling overhead to the oatmeal operation, thus eliminating any profit payable to American Cereal. Several powerful operators threatened to withdraw unless Schumacher joined as a full partner. After much persuasion by Stuart and Crowell, during which Schumacher now was in position once again to dictate terms, the American Cereal Company was reorganized as an operating company under Ohio law. It issued $3,400,000 in capital stock and $1,600,000 in first-mortgage bonds. These were distributed to the seven component members in exchange for their physical resources. At last an effective merger of seven big millers had been accomplished physically.

At the creation of American Cereal in 1888, the Chicago *Times,* noting that the new giant's headquarters were in Robert Stuart's Empire Mill in Chicago, commented that Ferdinand Schumacher's vacated crown had settled upon the head of the young Scot on Dearborn Street.

The announcement was premature. For his mills in Chicago and Cedar Rapids, Stuart received in the American Cereal reorganization of 1891 about 12 per cent of the stock and bonds, valued at around a half-million dollars. Crowell, for his Quaker brand and Ravenna plant, accepted an equal amount. George Cormack of Rockford received less than half as much as did Stuart and Crowell, and three others fared no better.

The King's share—more than 50 per cent and therefore voting control—went to the presumably dethroned old miller Ferdinand Schumacher, a holding valued at $2,500,000.

Schumacher exercised his authority immediately by dislodging Crowell as president and installing himself in the chair. Crowell became vice-president and general manager. Stuart was the secretary-treasurer.

Schumacher was back on top.

Chapter 4 * Pioneer
in Advertising

FOR FIVE YEARS a combination of unusual talents
pushed the American Cereal Company to impressive
earnings; in two years it doubled its surplus, despite a
severe financial panic in 1893. Oatmeal proved itself a
depression-proof commodity; its sales expanded in times
of economic hardship. Competition forced a 20 per cent
price cut in 1894, but American Cereal's gross revenues
advanced by more than a million dollars.

Schumacher drove the organization hard and untact-
fully. There was immediate friction between him and
Crowell over the sales organization. Quaker had an ag-
gressive group of "drummers" who called on the retail
trade in large cities and knew the urban market. But
Schumacher insisted on retaining for American Cereal
the commission men who had represented him for years.
As a result, Crowell's agent in New York City, K. B.
Newell, was superseded by Schumacher distributors
Charles and R. W. Muns. Reluctant to lose Newell,
Crowell appointed him "advertising manager," one of
the first in industry outside the patent-medicine field.
The advertising headquarters in New York were to Schu-
macher a luxury American Cereal could not afford.
Muns transferred to his staff dynamic New York–New
Jersey Quaker salesman L. C. Ruch. In important cities

everywhere, Schumacher demonstrated his will and his power in the new milling company by uprooting or subordinating the Crowell and Stuart personnel. Soon his rule over the sales force was absolute.

But the influence of his associates thrust the company forward, often over his loud objections. He could understand the contributions of George Cormack, whose Rockford Milling Company had entered the combine. For American Cereal, Cormack continued to invent labor-saving and quality-improving machines. He devised the first mechanical sorter to separate oat grains by size rather than by weight, ventilation systems that reduced grain spoilage in storage elevators, escalators and endless belt carriers for speeding grains and products through the mills from one process to another and ultimately to hoppers in the packaging rooms. This ingenuity cut costs, and Schumacher applauded.

Schumacher also acknowledged the genius of Crowell's original partner, James H. Andrews, and gave to his charge the management of all the Akron mills when the plant at Ravenna was abandoned. Andrews supplied the mechanical skills for exploiting Cormack's inventions. Crowell designed a bright new multicolored box for each of a dozen Quaker and F. S. Brand products, in the flashy red-blue-yellow that were to identify Quaker labels for two generations. Andrews then supplied the semiautomatic filling machines that loaded these cartons at the sensational rate of twenty packages a minute while adding gift premiums—metal spoons at first, then fragile chinaware. And Andrews designed and constructed economical machinery to box the tiny half-ounce samples of Quaker Oats soon to be scattered by thousands from door to door and from coast to coast.

Under Stuart's alert eye, all these improvements were

added to ever-increasing production at Cedar Rapids, which soon became American Cereal's most important milling unit. Stuart argued the necessity of two mill complexes, either of which could produce the company's vaulting volume of sales, so that a disastrous fire at one plant would not interrupt the flow of products to expanding markets at home, in Canada, and in Europe. Schumacher did not understand the necessity for a $600,000 capital expenditure as a protective measure, even though Stuart pointed out that growth of the company soon would absorb this reserve capacity. Further, Schumacher desired his own monument, the Akron mills, to be improved, rather than a plant far removed from his personal control. Stuart antagonized several other stockholders whose obsolete mills, part of the original combine, were dismantled or sold. Under Stuart's efficiency program, the minor mills were jettisoned one by one. For some years after 1893, when the Rockford factory burned and was not rebuilt, the company's entire output emanated from Cedar Rapids and Akron. This concentration of facilities, with its lower unit costs and greater economy of management, contributed greatly to American Cereal's ability to prosper during the economic depression of 1893–1894. But the stockholders who, with their sons, had lost their jobs as salaried managers and thus had lost both income and prestige, blamed Stuart for their predicament, causing a schism in the Board of Directors.

From his Chicago office, Stuart also preempted, in collaboration with Crowell, other management decisions, which disturbed the company president and whittled at his authority. As treasurer, Stuart regulated the company's cash flow, thus keeping the fluid resources from the hands of Schumacher and his ambitious son Hugo.

Stuart bought the grains for all the mills, and controlled the extension of credit to customers. He gave the company its first diversification, spending $7500 to acquire the American Health Food Company, and $12,340 (plus $50,000 of plant improvements) to absorb Pettijohn's California Breakfast Food. The Pettijohn purchase was significant: it removed Quaker's most annoying competitor in hot cereals. Stuart picked up the company at a bargain during the panic of 1893 and tucked it into the milling operations at Cedar Rapids. Schumacher regarded this as foolish, if not spendthrift.

In its first year, American Cereal offered an ambitious price list of milled products for the grocery counters, plus sidelines in baby cereals and animal feeds. Its sales book for the New York market in 1891 priced Quaker Oats, in cartons containing three dozen two-pound packages, at $3.35 per case wholesale. At retail, each package sold for 13 cents. Schumacher's *Avena* was also offered under the company president's initials, the F. S. Brand, its price identical to that of Quaker. In barrels, rolled oats cost $5.65, but an unbranded 200-pound barrel fetched $4.95. The line included a rolled wheat cereal, cracked wheat, farina, hominy, white and yellow corn meal, all in distinctive packages; also, wheat and corn meal, buckwheat groats, white, wholewheat, graham, rye, and oat flours in 180-pound or 200-pound barrels and 90-pound kegs, and a variety of animal feeds made from mill tailings at from $18.50 to $25.50 a ton. Pearled barley sold in hundred-pound kegs. An experiment in diversification was an exorbitantly priced baby cereal called Schumacher's Infant Food. Made of grape and cane sugars, albuminoids, soluble carbohydrates, dextrine, starch, and fat, it retailed for nine dollars a pound. Company salesmen peddled the products at list price to retailers on ten days' credit, to wholesalers at a discount of 10 per cent, plus an additional 10 per cent rebate four times yearly if quarterly quotas were met. Small discounts were offered to grocers on five-case lots of the packaged goods. The varied weights of bulk products were caused by lack of standardization among the seven millers involved in the merger. Two years later, the price list had remedied this confusion, but it still offered competitive brands in F. S. and Quaker.

Innovation and expansion of product lines soon followed, under the impetus of Stuart in Chicago, who held the theory that a company was twice as strong with products in two different sales lines and far less susceptible to volume declines, since a slump in sales of one product might not affect the other. Survival thus dictated variety, to say nothing of the greater growth opportunities. In 1892 a poultry feed was offered in hundred-pound sacks and proclaimed a stimulant to egg production by the testimonials of happy users.

More significant was a new household product, a self-rising cake flour. In 1893, Quaker's Dietetic Pastry Flour, an improvement over the self-riser, won a "highest" award at the Chicago World's Fair. Toward the end of 1893, American Cereal salesmen began to peddle the newly acquired Pettijohn's wheat cereal and more aggressively to push Cornucopia, an old Schumacher corn-meal mush that cooked in four minutes. Already Crowell had become sensitive to the housewife, and sought to give her foolproof mixtures to release her from some of the kitchen drudgery. In Board meetings, Schumacher rumbled against Crowell's foolishness.

More raucous and angry were Schumacher's protests against the "huge" sums spent by Crowell on advertising and on a three-ring circus of promotions designed to keep the Quaker name before the public constantly. The Quaker Oats trademark blazed from the sides of buildings, illuminated billboards at eye-vantage points carefully chosen in crowded districts, caught the gaze of streetcar riders from car cards, and flashed unexpectedly from the news columns of daily papers from coast to coast. Metal signs were hung on rural fences facing roads; gold letters spelling QUAKER ROLLED WHITE OATS were glued to grocery-store windows and doors. Calendars, blotters, dodgers, and cookbooks deluged the mails, and missionary exhortations on the merits of Quaker were printed on the reverse side of the Sunday bulletins in scores of city churches. Extensive use was made of small six-inch-deep newspaper advertisements featuring the "man in Quaker garb," with a brief message; some advertisements were placed in select groups of magazines. Week-long cooking schools were held in important grocery stores after little boys had been hired to placard every house in the neighborhood with advance heralds of the event. Entire cities were canvassed and a small free sample of Quaker Oats left at every doorstep. Important county, state, and national fairs and expositions found Quaker represented with a booth that dispensed free samples, the public being apprised of the Quaker location by brilliantly colored postcards of pretty children, nostalgic scenes, and other souvenir-value pictures. Soon the Quaker label was ubiquitous.

The exact credit for all this creativity is unallocated in company archives. Possibly some programs, particularly the cooking schools and booths at fairs, were the work of the advertising manager, K. B. Newell. But Crowell unquestionably was responsible for the theory of constant exposure—a completely new concept in marketing—and for many of the original ideas as well as much of the advertising copy.

Every device of the advertiser's art was used by American Cereal Company between 1890 and 1896. Techniques later men claim to have innovated were tested by Crowell as early as 1893. In his ads he appealed to love, pride, cosmetic satisfactions, sex, marriage, good health, cleanliness, safety, labor-saving, and status-seeking. His boldness, at the height of prudish Victorianism, reached its peak in 1898 in an advertisement in *Birds* magazine and several other periodicals of the day. The illustration was a voluptuous, bare-breasted girl, her torso draped in Roman style, sitting on a Quaker Oats box. The caption under this display—respectable by reason of its classic tone—

> *Ceres, fair goddess of the harvest fields*
> *Now to the world her choicest treasure yields.*

Crowell also pioneered scientific endorsements, customer testimonials, cash-prize contests, sampling, market testing, giveaways, and boxtop premiums—all generally considered creatures of latter-day advertising agencies. He appealed directly to the children's market long before this device was "discovered" by network radio. He created the thesis of educating the ultimate consumer to ask for a specific brand name for a cereal product, thus forcing the retailer to stock it. (This technique had been developed by the patent-medicine promoters.)

The sum of Quaker exploitation was keyed to the distinctive package, easily distributed but difficult and expensive to imitate. Here Crowell was distinctly an innovator because his box was essentially a sales message and recipe rather than merely something to hold the merchandise. Tin-can packing of foods had been known for a century, developed by the French during the Napoleonic wars to supply soldiers on campaigns far from home. The glass bottle, forerunner of the Mason jar, appeared in America in 1820 from Europe, and was used by Schumacher for his first domestic oatmeal shipments, though he exported in tin. The first American patent for a paper bag was granted in 1859. The folding carton, used by Crowell for Quaker Oats, was scarcely perfected at the time, a patent having been in effect less than ten years.

The distinction of the Crowell carton was the prominent display of a printed trademark in impressive colors and the printing of sales and recipe information. This was possible because the unfolded carton lay flat and could be passed through the impression rollers of a printing press. Crowell proclaimed the "man in Quaker garb" and offered attractive premiums to consumers who would cut out the Quaker figure and mail it to him, thus further impressing the trademark upon them. This approach, never tried before, doomed merchandising in bulk. Crowell was the first food processor to package distinctively a nationally advertised food product in a four-color printed carton, and also the first to reproduce a miniature of his carton for house-to-house sampling. His success in packaging was noted and imitated, and in the food industry the paper carton became the major receptacle for merchandising of grocery products not sold in tins.

For the first time, the housewife in 1886 picked up a food package and read on it a sales message:

We would call your special attention to the purity, rapidity of preparation, and the fact that they did not sacrifice sweetness and flavor for the sake of rapid cooking.

And now the recipe:

For breakfast porridge: Stir slowly one part Rolled Oats into 2½ parts fresh boiling water, salting water to taste before putting Rolled Oats in. Boil 20 minutes and serve with sugar or cream, or syrup if desired. If a double boiler is used, do not stir [these three words are in boldface] the Rolled Oats while cooking.

For fried pudding: Take the cold breakfast porridge and fry it on a griddle like Indian pudding or hominy, and serve with butter or syrup.

Delicious pancakes, or gems: Can be made by the ordinary recipe, putting in a suitable quantity of Rolled Oats, and wheat flour.

Quaker bread: For each loaf, soak overnight a sponge of yeast dissolved in a pint of warm water and a cup of sifted flour. In the morning take a cup of Rolled Oats, pour over it a cup of boiling water and set it to stand until nearly cold. Add two teaspoons of melted butter, two tablespoons of sugar, and a pinch of soda. Add all to the sponge and stir in white wheat flour until it is as stiff as can be stirred with a spoon. Let it rise until night, and bake one hour.*

To make an infant feed: Boil 1½ ounces in a quart of water for our hour, strain through a sieve, and sweeten.

Pancakes: One quart milk, thicken with oatmeal to a batter as for griddle cakes, add two eggs well-beaten, salt. Cook on a well-greased griddle.

Recipes also were printed on other products. To a cracked-wheat box of 1886 Crowell appended this message:

This product is made from the choicest white wheat, thoroughly cleaned, pearled and denuded of its outer silex coat, so irritating to most digestions. With most of the products on the market, this silex coat is left on or imperfectly removed. By our own superior process its removal is completely effected, thereby rendering our Pearl Cracked Wheat, when thoroughly cooked, easy of digestion to the most delicate stomach. . . . Stir a half pint of the wheat into a quart of boiling water, stirring constantly to prevent burn-

---

* In the 1950s Quaker offered an oatmeal bread the housewife could prepare merely by breaking open the package, adding one egg, and popping into the oven in its self-contained aluminum pan. It did not survive.

ing. Boil for an hour, then if a dry mush is desired place it on the back of the range to evaporate the water. Serve with butter, sugar, cream, and if desired with fruit preserves, stewed apples, etc. Also can make a pudding by pouring into forms with raisins and currants added. Next day prepare a custard of six eggs, 3 tablespoons of sugar, 1 quart milk, boil until set. Put cracked wheat preparation in a deep dish, pour custard on top, put in oven to brown top slightly. Serve cold.

The recipes illustrate, if nothing else, the kitchen drudgery of the era, and make understandable the modern "convenience" packaging of foods which has emancipated the housewife from four hours a day in food preparation over a coal or wood range.

Advertising agencies as known today did not exist when Crowell began constructing Quaker Oats' international reputation. Booking agencies or advertising agents were simply clearing houses: they took the advertiser's message and placed it in the desired media. Most of them styled themselves "advertising bureaus," although a few offered unique services. J. Walter Thompson advanced a theory that across-the-board advertising in his standard list of thirty magazines would guarantee national exposure. Most of his customers were patent-medicine makers or the manufacturers of such hard goods as sewing machines, coffee grinders, and carpet sweepers, though the meat and fruit canners made limited use of his list. In Philadelphia, N. W. Ayer & Son provided space in 700 newspapers. Charles Moyen and Company booked space in all the German-, French-, and Polish-language newspapers in America. One company arranged, for a fee, to mail company advertising to any desired category of the population, from a list which included 101,500 general stores, 91,000 grocers, 2278 wholesale grocers, 19,500 newspapers, and other lists broken down by profession or trade. Several brokers specialized in tramway car cards, a few in outdoor billboards. Charles H. Fuller in Chicago placed exclusively in agricultural and religious journals. Some agencies had a monopoly on the space in a particular magazine. Nowhere was there an agency, however, that wrote advertising copy, offered any theories about inducing sales response, or, for that matter, had even evolved any philosophy of advertising. So Crowell devised a philosophy and a mechanic to do the job.

Until Crowell's pioneering broke the prejudice, reputable manufacturers shunned the use of advertising space as a vehicle for an effective selling message as something identified with patent-medicine charlatanry. The dignified way was to offer an announcement card of their line of business without any sales story whatever. It fell to Crowell to explore the persuasive magic of words in advertising. Crowell made people want what he had to sell. He created a market. He inspired a demand, then satisfied it. His advertisements were—some subtly, some bluntly—arguments to convince the consumer he or she could not do without Quaker Oats, a concept on which the entire modern advertising technique is based. Crowell pioneered it. He used print to sell his merchandise, not merely announce it. He leveled his message at the consumer, not the storekeeper:

One pound of Quaker Oats makes as much bone and muscle as three pounds of beef. Is it worth trying?

This was Crowell's earliest effort. It provided a reason *why*. One early argument said "Clear head, firm hand and steady nerves for the adult; strong bones, sound teeth and rosy cheeks for the children." Again, reasons *why*. Another: "A delicacy for the epicure, a nutritious dainty for the invalid, a delight to the children." Crowell spoke directly to his potential buyers. To mothers: "It makes children strong, rosy and healthy, and gives them good teeth." To the thrifty: "Perhaps we are mistaken in making the quality of Quaker Oats the highest, instead of the price; but if so, it is our loss, your gain." Over each of these brief salvos appeared the "man in Quaker garb." Such eye-to-eye communication in advertising was a daring departure indeed from the conventional business card of the day.

Crowell used "blind" ads in newspapers profusely, paying for space devoted to stories disguised as innocent news. In an old Company scrapbook the collection of these first subliminal advertisements is noted "Convincing talks—very effective." Examples:

A SUMMER STORY

A queer thing happened at the county jail a few days since that has just come to light. It seems that a man was arrested for vagrancy who was so thin that he could crawl out between the bars and it was found necessary to place a watch over him to prevent his escape. The watchman placed in charge was a lazy fellow who set his wits to work to devise some means to keep his prisoner safe without the necessity of watching him all the time. There were no shackles small enough to hold him, and the only way to accomplish the desired end was to fatten up the vagrant and that pretty quick. The watchman consulted physicians as to the best food for this man, and was universally advised to give him Quaker Rolled White Oats. Inside of three days the prisoner could not squeeze out, and before he had finished the sentence he was under correspondence with all the prominent dime museums in the country with a view to being placed on exhibition as the fattest man in the country.

(Untitled)

It seems as though (enter name of city) is about to be treated with a most sensational divorce case. The parties interested all occupy high social positions, and if the case is really brought to trial there will be some pretty racy reading matter on the court records of the next term. The charge of cruel and wilful neglect will be made by the wife, who is a young and beautiful woman, raised in the lap of luxury and wealth. On four successive occasions she has asked her husband to bring home a package of Quaker Rolled Oats, and each time he has failed to do so. We await developments with interest.

Here is one with a "get your man" theme:

GOT ENGAGED AT THE EXPOSITION

Everybody likes to see living examples of "love's young dream." A few days ago the people on Washington Street were treated to a sight they will not forget very soon. A young man from the country had brought his best girl in to see the fair. They did not attract any particular attention until they were coming up the street about five o'clock. The young man had his strong right arm around the waist of his girl; she was trying to balance her head on his shoulder . . . A kind-hearted policeman tapped the fellow on his unoccupied shoulder and called his attention to the guying he was receiving. "Oh, that's all right, Mr. Policeman," said the happy fellow, "me and Julie come in to see the balloon, and dog-gone if we haint got engaged. I got up early this morning and went over to Julie's for breakfast, so as we could get an early start; Julie had cooked some Quaker Oats. I kin taste 'em yet, and I've been thinking about it ever since. Gosh! I don't know if the balloon went up or not, for about that time I says to Julie, says I, 'Julie, can't we-uns get married and have them Quaker Oats for breakfast every morning?' And Julie, she says, 'Yes,' and say, Mr. Policeman, where kin I get a license, for I want to make sure of them Quaker Oats for tomorrow morning?" The big copper gave him the desired information.

A variety of the "convincing talk," which was not labeled an advertisement and thus caught many an unwary reader, was the sales poem. In the 1890s, poetry was popular with the entire public and was thus an effective advertising medium. Crowell used bits of doggerel in his newspaper promotions, each intended to awaken some desire in the reader. Examples:

THE BELLE

As she tripped along the street,
　With her cheeks all aglow,
She was the prettiest maid you'd meet,
　No matter where you go.

Her face is always a-smiling,
　Each movement shows a wealth
Of beauty most beguiling,
　Indicative of perfect health.

Her friends she numbered by the score,
　She has wondrous golden hair;
In wealth she has a million more
　Than wealthy John L. Blair.

Now this maiden known both near and far
　Whom no woe can ever reach,
Can thank her very "lucky star"
　For the lesson she can teach.

For all her fortunes, wondrous good
　To account for there's but one reason;
Quaker Oats is always her food
　In every kind of season.

THE MODERN GIRL

Josephine Ester in your graceful tennis suit,
From your pretty sailor hat to your dainty canvas boot,
You are like a new Diana, with a racket for a bow,
You have strung upon its stringlets one or two good hearts,
　I know.

As you skim above the greensward, swinging high your
　weapon light,
There's no limit to the poetry I feel I ought to write;

But there is one good old saying over which I always gloat,
If you wish to keep your beauty, you must eat Quaker Oats.

JOY

The Orient's wealth
The diamond's gleam,
The clink of gold—
Are but a dream.

The lust for power,
The greed for gain,
Ambition's thirst—
All, all in vain.

Who holds but these
Can never feel
The joyful thrills,
That o'er me steal.

When breakfast's called
In cheery notes,
I eat my dish
Of Quaker Oats.

Crowell and Stuart early committed themselves to the policy of advertising world-wide only one brand of oatmeal—that with the magic name of Quaker Oats. The trademark was easy for consumers to remember, and carried implications of exceptional worth. Crowell strove to keep people talking about Quaker advertising. "What will those Quaker people think of next?" was a question Henry Parsons Crowell sought from the man on the street with one wily scheme after another.

Schumacher, however, thwarted complete success of Crowell's strategy by insisting that his own F.S. brand be sold in competition with Quaker in every market. Consequently, Crowell was unable to cash the full impact of his advertising, which extolled F.S. brands as well as Quaker. This was a house divided. To circumvent

old Ferdinand, Crowell smothered the Schumacher
brand under a blanket of anemic announcements, all
identical, in 1892, hoping to kill off the paradoxical rival.
This message said:

> The trademark F.S. stands for Ferdinand Schumacher, who
> is probably better known than any other man in the country
> as a manufacturer of Pure Food Products. The brand F.S.
> on a package of flour or cereal is a guarantee to the pur-
> chaser that the quality is the *best* that can be had in the
> market.

Obviously this nonselling, old-fashioned statement
(which Schumacher himself might have written a generation earlier) convinced no consumers of the F.S.
brand superiority over Quaker. Sales of F.S. products declined as Quaker volume rose. But this did not persuade
Schumacher of the validity of Crowell's work. Rather he
was infuriated; his pride was hurt. In his stubbornness
he sought to prove that his old methods could stimulate
sales without costly advertising. He let F.S. undersell
Quaker by discounts and rebates, until the wholesalers
and grocers were confused. He insisted on carrying high,
unsalable inventories of F.S. products. Also, he loaded
the executive payroll with relatives and unemployed directors, thus reducing profits and helping to lay the
groundwork for his spurious complaints that Crowell
was throwing away profits in exchange for extravagant,
useless publicity.

The inevitable result was a collision between the
handicraft generation of the aging Schumacher, who
until the day of his death answered all his mail in ink in
his own hand, and the modern industrial world of Crowell and Stuart, who were dedicated to national advertising and world marketing of the Quaker brand.

The fight was the more bitter because of the Schumacher pride, bedded deep in emotionalism, which rasped directly against the "Godly autocrat" infallibility of Crowell's self-esteem. Between these two egos there could be no compromise because neither knew how to yield. Robert Stuart, in the middle, was the victim of the collision. The clash that ensued precipitated a historical curiosity: a proxy fight for the control of a publicly owned corporation. This also was new to the world of business; in essence it was a controversy between the nineteenth and the twentieth centuries. And it took place in the last year of the old century: 1899.

Chapter 5 * A Proxy
Fight Stabilizes the Future

HENRY PARSONS CROWELL displayed his genius for product promotion in the first year of the American Cereal Company and maintained the pressure for seven years, until 1898. Throughout the period he was deliberately proving out his theory that constant exposure of a trademark was necessary because the consumer is fickle, easily lured by any competing Lochinvar whose wooing is more glib.

In the summer of 1891 Crowell ran a fifteen-car special freight train from Cedar Rapids, Iowa, to Portland, Oregon, to introduce Quaker Oats to the Pacific Northwest. He did this after what today would be called market saturation: he left a sample half-ounce box of Quaker Oats in every mailbox in Portland. The result was a demand on grocers for a specific brand of oatmeal they could not supply. Crowell then rushed 252,000 pounds of Quaker Rolled White Oats, in 126,000 packages, halfway across the nation to "meet the clamor" for Quaker superiority from insistent consumers.

In the old days, salesmen had "loaded" the market with whatever they sold, forcing more goods on the retailer than he required. As a result, stock often accumulated dust on the shelves as resentment against the salesman accumulated in the heart of the gullible merchant. The "best salesman" was the man who sold in carload lots, regardless of the consumer need of the neighborhood.

Crowell reversed this high-pressure method. He embarrassed the retailer by keeping from him a product for which his customers inquired. When the Quaker salesman finally arrived, days after a house-to-house sampling had created a demand, the grocer could not deny shelf room to a product so obviously salable. The grocer's resistance to branded merchandise was broken down; the new ways were forced on him by his customers. At first he resented this. He made more profit, he thought, from the open barrel than from the natty box. But he soon learned that saving in time, reduction of waste from spoilage and rodents, and the reduced ability of his patrons to haggle over price or weight were all to his advantage. And he rid his floor of the ugly, difficult-to-handle barrel, giving his shop a tidier appearance more appealing to his female customers. Crowell, with his Quaker brand, was in the forefront of the educational campaign that changed the grocery from a bulk warehouse into an attractive shop handling packaged foods.

Crowell accomplished more with his special train to Portland than the establishment of the Quaker label. Also aboard the train were a carload of samples, miniature replicas of the standard package. An advance man (recruited from a circus) went from town to town along the railroad line ahead of the "special" to generate a proper excitement by ballyhoo. Carefully he briefed the newspaper editor and his staff—showering them with free samples of his wares—on the expected arrival of the train and the show to be displayed during a brief stop in that city. He whetted the editorial curiosity tangibly by buying at space rates several columns of news space for "convincing talks." Free news stories followed, luring thousands of persons to the various stations to watch the train pass. An organized demonstration, with a brief entertainment, surmounted by a six-foot "man in Quaker garb" atop the engine, was a feature of each stop, while hired youngsters distributed from canvas newsboy bags a free Quaker sample to each eyewitness. This flashy, medicine-show-type promotion was unheard of among "respectable" products. It drew comment as news from papers in Chicago, Philadelphia, St. Louis, and New York as well as from western publications— and greatly enhanced the stature of the Quaker mark. The publicity also gave respectability to Crowell's unorthodox methods. The special train idea undoubtedly originated with Crowell. In his youth he had similarly shipped three hundred Percheron brood mares to South Dakota to advertise a horse farm which he owned and hoped to sell at a fat profit.

American Cereal was not alone in its field. Its former associates in the pool, excluded from the new corporation, undersold the Quaker and F.S. goods in local markets across the land. A miller in Muscatine, Iowa, introduced an oatmeal called Friends, but American Cereal succeeded in enjoining the company against the use of a trademark so similar to Quaker. The boldest competitor was Mother's Oats, which by 1893 had begun to copy Crowell's advertising techniques and thus to establish a name-brand demand. From another source came a damaging competitor who attacked oatmeal directly and cast doubt on its usefulness as a human food: Pettijohn, the wheat-flake-cereal maker.

Pettijohn 1892 advertisements, placed to follow Quaker displays in newspapers and thus to smother incipient Quaker demand, cut into Quaker sales. These broadsides showed a beautiful equestrienne holding a box of Pettijohn's. She stood beside a horse, its nose in a bag of oats. Caption: "My *horse* eats oats." An essay by "M. H. Tipton, A.M., President of Northwestern Christian College," then followed.* It read in part:

> Oats give horses their nerve and strength, and oatmeal in olden times was a good food for Scotch highlanders and English yeomanry who spent their lives in the open air and the active pursuits of agriculture, war and the chase. Most of us have not, however, the strong digestions of either horses or highlanders, and for us—especially the brain workers and business men—oatmeal is too hearty a food and too difficult of digestion. With very many people it overheats the blood, and upsets the nervous system, causing flatulency, biliousness, eruptions and all the other attendants of a disorderly digestion. It is far too heating and produces rash, colic and other troubles. . . . The oatmeal craze, as such, is over.

To this Quaker replied vigorously. "People noted for strength and endurance," said Crowell's rebuttal, "are usually spoken of as being 'strong as a horse.' Any man who handles horses will proclaim that for strength and nerve he feeds his animals on oats. The more muscle and nerve required, the more oats the horse gets. It is the same with men, women and children. The more strength they require, the more food they must have, and the best food is oats. Oats are better than beef, as they contain more nutriment."

Pettijohn's also had a distinctive emblem, a big brown bear on the flank of which was printed, *Bear in Mind Our Trade Mark*. This visible symbol was retained by Crowell in his advertising after American Cereal's purchase of Pettijohn. To it Crowell added his own touch:

* Unrelated to Northwest Christian College at Eugene, Oregon.

"If you are hungry as a bear, Pettijohn's California Breakfast Food will satisfy you."

By 1893, the Quaker symbol had undergone subtle metamorphosis. Printing of the trademark in color on boxes inspired a redesign. The gaunt and austere Quaker gave way to a genial, fat-bellied one, more ostentatious than any Friend would permit—with a red vest under his blue tailored coat, golden buckles on his patent leather shoes. In this role he was a familiar resident of the American scene for many years. So too was the Quaker package, an acknowledged improvement over the unsanitary barrel now disappearing from city stores, replaced by neat rows of two-pound packets on a shelf. As stores became more attractive, housewives frequented them oftener, made them social centers, and the merchant's sales increased. Heretofore, "quality" women had sent servants or children to the grocery with a list to be filled, and delivered by the grocer's boy on a bicycle. Greater confidence in the grocer resulted, the sanitary packaging dovetailing neatly with the medical profession's new warning that tiny organisms called microbes, harbored in filth, possibly caused disease.

The first objective of Robert Stuart and Henry Crowell, envisioned in the formation of the Oatmeal Millers Association in 1886, had at last been realized. This far-seeing pair had demonstrated their thesis as practical. Success in oatmeal marketing lay in a distinctive trademark, the product packaged for purity and ease of handling, and nationally sold on a consumer franchise gained by advertising.

They had experienced the impotence of the trade association to correct the problems of oversupply. They had subsequently theorized that marketing must lure the ultimate user, since neither wholesaler nor grocer could be persuaded to hold any brand loyalty; both were interested only in price. To Crowell and Stuart, oversupply was merely the chronic sickness of underconsumption, cured by creation of demand rather than by reduction of supply. No customer, they reasoned, would begrudge the manufacturer a fair profit on a product that satisfied one or more basic needs.

Crowell acknowledged the evolution of this philosophy, and much broader concepts, by himself and Stuart in testimony years later in an antitrust suit. Their motive, he asserted, in organizing the American Cereal Company was that the enterprise "would make a better oatmeal and cereal of all kinds than had ever been manufactured. That no matter what the cost, it would abandon systems and methods and scrap machinery whenever changes could be made for an improvement of the quality or a lessening of the cost; that it . . . must have its business so broadly distributed that panics or commercial disturbances or depressed times would not seriously cripple or prevent it paying regular dividends. . . . It was to scatter and diversify its business in all parts of the world and do educational and constructive work so as to awaken an interest in and create a demand for cereals where none existed. . . . Its policy in regard to the development of the advertised brands of rolled oats was to develop rapidly in all parts of the world, wherever oatmeal could be sold, an advertised brand. The Quaker brand was retained and made the world brand for the company."

But Ferdinand Schumacher had no use for philosophy. He mistrusted Stuart and Crowell because they dressed like gentlemen and talked without an accent. As a prohibitionist, he was instinctively anxious about a

Stuart who kept whiskey for a nightcap on his sideboard, a Crowell who enjoyed wine with his dinner. Because Stuart and Crowell were the age of his own sons, Schumacher regarded them as immature. Further, abstract notions of any kind were incompatible with his character. He was an artisan, not a thinker. He considered Stuart and Crowell his enemies rather than his colleagues, and he fought their logic with the only sure weapon he had: refusal to agree.

Schumacher resisted the package because of its cost. "But anything," Crowell was heard by colleagues to rejoin, "can get into an open barrel. The right way to sell oatmeal is with packages and advertising." Crowell's biographer records that Schumacher, hostile, suspicious, and explosive, would reply angrily with heavy gutturals: "Crowell, you are crazy. Advertising is silly business. We'll save our money. Let our competitors advertise."

By now Crowell was spending $500,000 a year on advertising and promotion, an enormous sum for the time. But Crowell had watched American Cereal Company's gross sales climb in 1895 to an astounding $7,930,-650, of which $2,617,506 was in oatmeal, and he attributed the success to advertising. Schumacher reasoned that the growth was normal and natural, and that if the money spent on advertising had been added to the year's operating profit of $399,565, the result would have been impressive indeed.

Despite the large gains in sales, the resentment against Stuart for eliminating unneeded executive jobs, and against Crowell for his autocratic self-assurance, gradually caused a division among the directors. A crisis in the first half of 1896 gave Schumacher and friends an excuse to move against the Stuart–Crowell leadership. Large investments in grain and products, construction expenditures of $132,900 at Cedar Rapids, the half-million-dollar advertising budget, and heavy sales expenses in a dozen European countries caused the company to run short of cash. Simultaneously, an unexpected slump in sales occurred. For the first time in its history, American Cereal had an operating loss, an impressive $166,000 for the six months. Only $61,500 cash remained in the treasury with which to meet a payment of interest on the $1,200,000 in bonds and finance daily operations. The dividend for the third quarter was passed.

At the next annual meeting of stockholders, in February 1897, Schumacher requested Stuart's resignation. The action was a formality, since the Schumacher family owned more than half of the voting stock. At the meeting Schumacher ignored the fact that a business upturn in the last half of 1896 had wiped out the deficit, leaving an operating profit for the year of $308,000. In fact, belying any crisis, the directors, after discharging Stuart, declared a double dividend, thus making up the August nonpayment. The vote against Stuart revealed Schumacher's strength: 23,305 votes against 10,957 shares for Stuart, the latter representing the holdings of both Stuart and Crowell.

When Stuart retired to his Chicago interests as a grain dealer and bank director, his departure fatally undermined Crowell's position. As nominal general manager he could now be blamed for every ill of Schumacher's regime. He continued his advertising programs in defiance of the company president, but his promotional budget was cut by the directors to $435,000 for 1897.

Schumacher avoided a decisive conflict with Crowell, since by now the general manager was one of the most important men in Ohio. The rise of the Rockefeller family of Cleveland in the oil business had convinced

Crowell that oil was the cooking and heating energy source of the future. He therefore had bought control of an iron-mongering firm that had patented an oil-burning stove. As the Cleveland Foundry Company, later to become the Perfection Stove Company, this business expanded rapidly into an enterprise at least as impressive as American Cereal. Crowell was as imaginative with stoves as he had been with oats, and used the same advertising techniques. He showed housewives how they could save sixty cents a week by using his stove; with forty cents of the saving they could buy the stove on installments, leaving them twenty cents in spending money—demonstrating himself a master of feminine buying psychology. Sales rocketed. Now he made a deal whereby the 3000 Rockefeller salesmen would push his stove line, thus encouraging the use of their oil. In a few years, Perfection would become the largest stove manufacturer in the world. Crowell's methods, in promoting oats or stoves, had made him a much-discussed and much-admired operator among the important Cleveland bankers and industrialists whose friendship Schumacher cultivated.

Crowell had no economic need for a salaried job with American Cereal. He was now a millionaire, despite generous gifts to Christ's causes. But his substantial pride was bruised: an unmannered immigrant had bested Stuart and himself. Further, he had not yet completely tested his intellectual theories concerning the marketing of branded food products. Therefore he remained, despite Schumacher's antagonism, at his management post. This cavalier disdain for the company president angered the older man further.

Robert Stuart, meanwhile, had moved from American Cereal's general offices in Chicago's Monadnock Build-

ing to an officer's desk at the American National Bank.
Characteristically, he displayed no emotion—even to
himself—over his discharge from the cereal company.
His diary recorded only this laconic observation:

In Akron—attended the annual stockholders' meeting at
10 A.M. and 2 P.M. Left for home about 6:40 via Erie R.R.

A more interesting entry occurred one day in September,
when he noted the visit of Henry Parsons Crowell, accompanied by a corporation lawyer, a Mr. Swift.

This meeting was for the purpose of composing a letter to stockholders of American Cereal, soliciting their
proxies at the next annual meeting to prevent the dismissal of Crowell. Between them, Stuart and Crowell
owned about 24 per cent of American Cereal's stock.
Schumacher replied quickly to advise investors that his
control was unassailable and that his patience with
Crowell's newfangled notions was ended. Joining with
fifteen other stockholders, Schumacher wrote: "There
can never be peace among the stockholders of any company as long as one man claims the right to be absolutely
a dictator." Then, cautiously deferring to Crowell's social
and business eminence, the letter added, "We have nothing to say against Mr. Crowell personally."

As New Year, 1898, presaged an annual meeting only
six weeks away, Crowell addressed a new communication to the cereal company's directors. He accused Schumacher of inventing false charges against Stuart merely
to rid himself of his rival. He listed the disgruntled former mill owners Stuart had refused to employ in fat
sinecures, and stated that their alliance with Schumacher was selfishly motivated. He denied Schumacher's claim that the dividend had been passed at
Stuart's contrivance, a scheme to drive down the price of

American Cereal stock so that Stuart and his relatives in the Douglas family might buy control at a bargain price. The letter pointed out that Stuart had not been present when the dividend was passed: he had been in New York arranging new lines of credit for the company. Crowell charged that the chief reason for Stuart's dismissal was the fact that Schumacher's son Hugo coveted the treasurer's post and residence in Chicago, and that sales of Crowell's advertised brands, resisted by Schumacher, alone had kept the company solvent while losses accrued in unsalable inventories of the F.S. brand. Crowell asked the stockholders to unseat Schumacher and elect a slate of Crowell-nominated directors.

Schumacher answered with contempt: "We now have on hand, ready to vote, much more than a majority. . . . We absolutely and unqualifiedly refuse to serve with Mr. Crowell on the Board of Directors."

The year's earnings also were on Schumacher's side. By eliminating capital spending entirely, he brought in an operating profit of $666,500 for the year—more than twice the 1896 figure, on a sales gain to $9,587,000 gross revenues.

The directors therefore dismissed Crowell, scoffing at Crowell's "philosophy" that the sales of a consumer product such as oatmeal were in direct ratio to the advertising effort. But one director heard the argument and believed it. He, oddly enough, was an "outside" man who, added to the board to replace Stuart, presumably bolstered Schumacher's reputation with the Cleveland bankers. His name was Will Christy.

At Crowell's retirement, James H. Andrews, Crowell's friend and former partner, resigned both as director and as manager of the Akron mills. Now Schumacher was left to operate the company without any advertising genius, without a financial and management wizard, and without one of the most efficient millers who ever lived. Pinching the pennies and riding on the sales momentum built up by Crowell's advertising expenditures, Schumacher managed to produce a good picture. Company earnings for the next two years were new records: in 1898, operating profit of $727,000 on $12,189,000 of sales; in 1899, an $851,000 operating profit on $12,130,-000 of sales.

With Crowell, Stuart, and Andrews all eliminated from American Cereal, competitors mobilized at once. Here was an opportunity to whittle down or destroy a company that had pinched every miller in America. Thirteen of the largest independent millers banded together as the Cereal Bureau, an innocuous-appearing association behind which an important combine developed. In 1901 the group would reveal itself as the Great Western Cereal Company, with production equal to at least half that of Quaker, and an important brand in Mother's Oats.

Crowell established his headquarters at the stove company. From his office there he and Stuart in Chicago were in telephone communication frequently. Their major problem, in any plan to drive Schumacher from American Cereal, was the Schumacher family's controlling stock interest.

Quietly Stuart and Crowell set about the purchase of stock and the acquisition of proxies for the last annual meeting of the century, that of February 1899. This time no fanfare alerted Schumacher. By early summer, the two friends had marshaled a holding about equal to that of the Schumacher family's 17,000 shares. For a majority, they required 17,132 shares, since there were 34,262 shares outstanding. Cautious feelers in Boston turned up 3400 shares owned by New Englanders available at the stiff price of $40 a share. A Mr. Greenshield of Iowa City, Iowa, sold Stuart 46 shares. James Andrews, still resident in Akron, kept the former directors informed of American Cereal's condition. He also uncovered 600 shares available "from an Akron source" who obviously was a minor member of the Schumacher family. Stuart's old partner, George B. Douglas, and his wife Irene bought this holding for $25,000, the first break in the Schumacher invulnerability.

As word spread among financiers of the internecine warfare in Akron, a group of Cleveland promoters saw a possible opportunity to seize the corporation and promote it into a milling monopoly. They too began to buy stock. Their names were impressive: Myron T. Herrick, later Governor of Ohio and U.S. Ambassador to France; James Parmalee, a moneyman friend of the iron-ore Croesus, Mark Hanna. To disguise their identities, they operated through Arthur J. Eddy, a Chicago corporation lawyer who had assembled combines in carbon and linseed oil. Ironically, the Clevelanders were fed their knowledge of American Cereal by Will Christy, the Schumacher-appointed director. From his insider position, Christy recognized Schumacher's rule as inept, and studied with admiration the Crowell–Stuart techniques which had built the mills into a dominant industry position in half a decade. Crowell discovered suddenly that the Cleveland crowd was on his side, though its members' motives were different—consolidations of grain-milling capacity into a giant powerful enough to control the trade.

Herrick revealed his intentions in a secret meeting with Crowell and Stuart in Cleveland. He outlined a new corporation with sufficient capital to buy or squeeze every important oat miller in the nation, using American Cereal as a nucleus. Crowell would be president, Stuart general manager, with the full backing of the promoters to discard all brand names except Quaker and build for Quaker a world domination of oatmeal traffic. Stuart and Crowell listened but did not commit themselves. From their experience in the old Consolidated, where new millers had arisen faster than they could be bought out, Stuart and Crowell doubted that any monopolistic trust was possible or even desirable, in milling. But they accepted the support of the Clevelanders in a proxy fight to overthrow Schumacher.

The Oatmeal King was undisturbed. He watched the purchase of available floating stock by the Cleveland financiers and assumed that they were buying for investment on the recommendation of Will Christy. The logical assumption was that Christy's friends were Schumacher's allies. To strengthen its position, Herrick's group began to bid for more stock. The price advanced to $50 a share, then within a month to $95. At that value, Ferdinand Schumacher, pinched for cash because of the failure of another venture, sold in Cleveland 3000 shares of his own holdings. He had lost his absolute control.

When news of this event circulated, Herrick announced quietly that his syndicate supported Stuart and Crowell. Instantly the bid for American Cereal stock dropped back to its normal $40 a share. Schumacher, seventy-three years old and weary, saw himself beaten at last. Outvoted but still in possession of a large bloc of stock, he clung to his holdings and blustered until the syndicate bought him and his family out at $95 a share. Schumacher then retired voluntarily.

Three days before the annual meeting of 1899, Arthur J. Eddy released publicly the news of his latest amalgamation, a $33,000,000 New Jersey–incorporated holding company already oversubscribed. Its purpose, he said, was to consolidate the American Cereal Company and twenty-one other millers who aggregated 95 per cent of the nation's oat-milling capacity into a giant combine, run by the most capable brains in the industry, the Stuart–Douglas–Crowell–Andrews–Cormack combination that had developed American Cereal; chairman of the Board of Directors would be Myron T. Herrick. At the organizational meeting, Crowell was elected president. Characteristically, Stuart was installed as treasurer. James H. Andrews returned as a director and as manager of the Akron mills.

The giant trust never developed, however. The president and treasurer suggested to the Cleveland investors that brisk competition, nurtured by large advertising efforts, soon would shrivel all except local competitors, a course more acceptable to government and the public than the odious trusts against which Theodore Roosevelt was then inflaming the nation. Herrick conceded the logic of this position. On March 2, 1899, Robert Stuart recorded in his diary: "The American Cereal deal fell through."

Quickly the new leadership entrenched itself. In 1900, Stuart repaired Schumacher's capital-expense retrenchments by spending $340,000 for new production facilities. This reduced the net profit for the year to $262,000 (before interest or dividends), but it prepared for the first $1,000,000 net-profit year, in 1901 on sales of $15,-793,000. At the end of fiscal year 1900, an audit showed a flourishing company. Its store of grains was worth $1.058 millions, its inventory of manufactured goods was $474,000, its total assets $9.314 millions, up $2.425 from January 1897. To prove its modernity, the company's stock of packages, valued at $107,000, exceeded by $29,000 the value of its barrels and bags, and expenditures for advertising were at an all-time high of $513,000.

A new structure, The Quaker Oats Company, identifying directly with the now world-famous brand, was set up as a holding company in 1901. By now all brands had been consolidated in the Quaker name and all odd-sized, unstandardized packages and shipping units dropped. Quaker's stated assets had risen to $11.407 million. The new enterprise had $7.3 million in preferred stock, $3.9 million in common stock, and outstanding bonds from the original amalgamation carried at $1.2 million. When these bonds were retired in 1906, The Quaker Oats Company became the operating entity of the business, and has remained so ever since.

To insure continuity of their management, Stuart, Crowell, and several friends formed a voting trust in which they deposited 20,800 shares of stock in the new Quaker Oats Company. This holding was pledged to vote for the management at the annual meetings, with control thus perpetuated in the enterprising founders.

Chapter 6 * Growth
and Growing Pains

TWENTY YEARS of uninterrupted growth followed the return of Robert Stuart to the management and Henry Crowell to the promotion of the Quaker milling enterprises.

The achievement was impressive. Far from specializing in oatmeal, Quaker milled more than two million barrels of white flour a year, and was the world's largest manufacturer of livestock feeds. Its price list proclaimed a score of diversified products.

An idea of the growth is reflected in this table:

Year	Total Sales	Oatmeal Sales	Operating Profit	Net
1901	$15,793,876	$4,787,252	$1,196,294	$1,046,546
1905	16,735,000	4,566,000	1,045,000	1,002,188
1907	22,077,802	6,302,965	1,365,165	1,213,753
1910	25,565,220	5,641,689	1,401,117	1,224,343

In 1911, when the net profit approached $2,000,000, Stuart extolled his management modestly by pointing out in the annual report that the profit represented a 24.8 per cent return on the common stock, despite the fact that the nation had suffered seriously from a business recession. In 1912, net profit crossed $2,000,000 for the first time, despite capital expenditures of $213,000.

World War I greatly enhanced production and profits.

The Quaker management, however, refused to increase prices despite the highest grain market since the Civil War. A public statement proclaimed that the company would not take advantage of world-wide food scarcities to profiteer on the war crisis. Even so, increased business volume kept the profit consistently above the $2,000,000 mark, reaching a wartime peak of $4,900,000 in 1917. Sales in the year of American participation in the war totaled $123,000,000, an artificial top not reached by normal growth until 1926.

The company's net worth, as a result of earnings reinvested in the enterprise, also made impressive gains. The stated assets passed $20 million in 1911, exceeded $26 million in 1915 and $40 million in 1917, leaping temporarily to a war-swollen high of $59 million in 1918.

Cash returns to shareholders were equally gratifying. The first dividend on common stock was paid in 1906, beginning a payout that has continued uninterruptedly since that time. The following year, dividends totaled $869,000, equal to 6 per cent on the preferred stock and 8 per cent on the common. In 1911 the disbursement crossed $1 million; by 1915 the common stock returned 10 per cent annually, and in 1918 reached a transient 15 per cent. From 1906 through World War I the company had no funded debt, financing its acquisitions and expansions from retained earnings.

The expansion was lively and imaginative. Pettijohn's wheat cereal made its first contribution to Quaker gross sales in 1904. In that year also, acknowledging competition from the swiftly rising dry cereals, Stuart and Crowell opened a plant at Battle Creek, Michigan, to create such ready-to-eat experiments as Zest, Apetizo, Brittle Bits, and Corn Flakes.

Also, as will be described later, Quaker originated

puffed cereals with an eight-gun salvo of puffed rice at the St. Louis World's Fair. By 1907, Quaker's animal feeds were contributing one-third of the company's net profits. In 1916, spaghetti and macaroni were added to the line and, with typical Crowell audacity, were marketed successfully in Italy, the home of *pasta*—just as in 1893 Crowell had carried his oatmeal to its most discriminating market, Scotland.

Competition was vigorous, not only in oatmeal, but from ready-to-eat cold cereals of other manufacturers. Mother's Oats sales rose gradually until by 1911 they accounted for 88 per cent of Great Western's $5.3 million gross annual sales. Another competitor was the National Oats Company, which made wheat and oat breakfast foods. Sixteen large independents undersold Quaker in their local markets, but Crowell's aggressive advertising programs and Stuart's expansion were decisive. By 1911, after acquiring Great Western's Mother's Oats, Quaker owned 46.4 per cent of the oatmeal-producing capacity east of the Rocky Mountains, a figure raised to 49.5 per cent by 1915. So important now was Quaker's diversification that this figure of nearly half the oatmeal-production facilities, at 7000 barrels daily, was less than one-third of the company's total milling operations of 23,000 barrels daily, and Quaker Rolled White Oats yielded no more profit than did the animal feeds.

Quaker's familiar canister had been reduced in size to a volume of 20 ounces in order to retail at the psychologically advantageous price of ten cents. This coin had been established as a bargain symbol by the "dime" stores of F. W. Woolworth and others and Crowell, ever alert to social trends, capitalized on the situation. Crowell the philosopher was not one to miscalculate the sales value of a symbol, nor did he ever hesitate to adapt sound merchandising evolutions to his own operations.

During these two decades there appeared on the scene a new service industry—the creative advertising agency. Brands and catch phrases proliferated. The Gold Dust Twins, Armour's "ham what am," Van Camp's Twins, pork and beans, "Children cry for it" Castoria—these and many others adorned the American scene by 1905. But the first decade of the twentieth century had almost ended before Crowell made use of an advertising agency to create sales ideas and programs for Quaker products. He and his associates had been writing all the copy, preparing the artwork, and then, at a cost of about $10,000 a year, commissioning placement agencies to distribute his advertising; the promotional ballyhoo was also an intracompany operation. The success of an agency with the puffed cereals finally proved to Crowell, in 1909–1910, that the advertising agencies had come of age and could sell as well as he himself, or—demonstrably in the case of Puffed Rice and Puffed Wheat—better. From then on Crowell, no diehard who insisted on doing every job himself, relied on advertising agencies.

Crowell also brought in an expert in the new specialty, sales management. This man was James H. Douglas, a cousin of Robert Stuart's old partner and uncle-in-law. Douglas helped organize the National Biscuit Company, and as its chief sales executive gained considerable reputation for scientific techniques.

Crowell introduced the packaged premium in 1900 in an obscure asset of the American Cereal Company named Banner Oats. The lure was one piece in a set of dishes. Repeated purchases—and much swapping among friends—were necessary to collect the entire set of chinaware. The volume of these premiums was enormous. Purchases in fourteen months from November 1900 to March 1902 totaled 200,000 dozen *sets* from the pottery manufacturer. When all the company products were consolidated under the Quaker trademark, the premiums for a time were offered in Quaker Oats packages in such numbers that in 1904 the supplier built twelve new kilns to accommodate Quaker orders. Other giveaways were gaudy finger rings for children, spoons, aluminum kitchen gadgets, and coupons redeemable for double boilers or even for two-cents cash reduction in the purchase price of other Quaker products.

Meanwhile the steady bombardment of advertising continued. The celebrated Mr. Dooley, a syndicated newspaper funnyman of the period and forerunner of the comic-strip character, commented on the phenomenon to his friend Hennessey in the dialect his generation thought humorous:

"What's a breakfast food?" asked Mr. Hennessey.

"It depinds on who ye ar-re," said Mr. Dooley. "In ye'er case it's annything to ate that ye're not goin' to have f'r dinner or supper. But in th' case iv the rest iv this impeeryal rapublic, 'tis th' o'y amusement they have. 'Tis most th' advertisin' in th' pa-pers. 'Tis what ye see on th' bill boards. 'Tis th' inspiration iv pothry an' art. In a wurrud, it's oats."

Under all the Quaker-induced pressure from many directions, the Great Western Cereal Company, which had been organized for the avowed purpose of destroying Quaker, was unable to compete. For some years it fought Crowell with his own techniques, advertising Mother's Oats with as large an appropriation as its competitor spent. But the only result was that Great Western showed no profits; as early as 1905 it needed refinancing. During the sharp recession of 1911 its directors decided to abandon their oat-milling capacity of 3425 barrels daily (616,500 pounds) at Fort Dodge, Iowa, and Joliet, Illinois, to save their profitable business in wheat flours. They offered all their oat assets, including the two mills, and the Mother's Oats brand (which sold a volume of $5 million a year) to Quaker for $1 million cash plus the market value of the grain inventory.

Quaker accepted the offer; the company could pay the price from surplus in a single year. Stuart welcomed the handsome additions to manufacturing facilities, acquired at less than replacement cost. Crowell could understand Great Western's necessity to liquidate: he had just bested them soundly by promoting National Quaker Oats Month—the first of the endless parade of special merchandising "months" or "weeks" that have followed. He had organized the nation's largest dairies to leave at every doorstep with the morning milk bottles a brochure extolling the "perfect" diet of Quaker oatmeal plus milk or cream for breakfast. The impact of this promotion alone might have discouraged a much more solvent competitor than Great Western. Crowell also was running four-color advertisements in magazines, illustrating delicious strawberries and other fruits in the gleaming oatmeal bowl. None of his competitors could afford such displays.

"What the artist is to the picture," said the Quaker employee magazine in retrospect of the Crowell period, "or the sun to a growing plant, advertising has been, is and will be to Quaker Oats. . . . After it became the fixed and settled policy to continuously advertise Quaker Oats everywhere, the business all but leaped ahead." Great Western, National Oats Company, and other competitors lagged behind.

The federal government took a jaundiced view of the acquisition of the only valuable trademark in oatmeal that competed against Quaker. It filed suit against The Quaker Oats Company under the Sherman Anti-Trust

Act, accusing the oatmeal manufacturer of swallowing its only serious rival in order to gain monopolistic control of the market. The U.S. Attorney General contended that Quaker was an offspring, born in sin, of the Consolidated Oatmeal Company, the old pool of 1888. Other complaints were that Quaker and Great Western had acted in collusion in the transfer of property, and that since its inception Quaker had made secret price agreements with competitors.

The trial was held in Chicago in 1915 before three federal judges, the prosecutor being U.S. Attorney James H. Wilkerson. Most of the officers and directors of Great Western appeared as government witnesses, but they denied that there were any blood ties between the companies. The accusation of collusion to fix prices fell when the principal witness contradicted himself and discredited his own testimony. The two principal officers of Great Western denied any agreement between the companies: indeed, they said, the cause of their ruin was the sum spent on advertising in an unsuccessful effort to compete. A complaint that the price paid by Quaker for Great Western's assets bilked the latter's stockholders was refuted by proof that the company would have gone bankrupt except for the transaction. Quaker then proved that it was not the chief beneficiary of the merger. National Oats Company, the biggest remaining rival, had picked up three-fourths of the Great Western business without spending a dime.

At this point the federal case collapsed, in the eyes of two of the judges. They held for Quaker in a decision dated April 19, 1916. Wrote Judge Mack in concurring with Justice Baker in the majority opinion: "In no sense has the competition been restricted, so far as I have been able to apprehend, by the union of Mother's Oats and Quaker Oats as against the rest of the world."

The third justice was not convinced. "It is clear to me," he wrote in dissent, "that it [Quaker] purchased the business extinction of the oatmeal trade and the commercial status of its greatest and most powerful rival, thus strengthening the purchaser's already strong grasp upon the entire industry."

The government's action was dismissed by the majority for want of equity. The government appealed the decision to the United States Supreme Court but withdrew the case in 1920. By that time the political popularity of "trust-busting" had waned. The public no longer feared the "soulless corporation" which, curbed of excesses by federal law, had become the major impetus of the American economy. By 1920 even school children were aware that mass production, made possible by mass communication to mass markets, had reduced the cost of almost everything found in the American home, and had provided highly rewarding compensation to millions of employed citizens.

From the acquisition of the Mother's Oats trademark until after World War I, the Quaker management's problem was to balance expanding sales with adequate productive capacity. As early as 1912 the stockholders were advised: "We thought we had made generous provision for a reasonable increase in business in the mill plan outlined in 1911, but . . . the Sales Department is insisting that we prepare for a larger output." The following year: "Additional room is necessary if we are to urge our Sales Department to do its best." In 1915: "Record volume on all products manufactured." In 1916: "A year of unprecedented success." In 1917: "The best balance sheet we ever offered." 1918: "Steady upward trend in our business." 1919: "Our volume is thoroughly satisfactory."

Even the normal growth rate, phenomenal in itself, was outstripped by the demands for food production during the war. Quaker was required to expand its inventories of raw materials to match each new plateau of sales volume. Particularly, the company could not be caught without adequate grain inventories during the war, when most grains except oats were government-regulated.

This circumstance concerned the conservative Scots-bred management of the enterprise. Wild speculation in grains further disorganized orderly buying processes, greatly complicating Quaker's purchases. At that time Quaker's management owned five seats on the Chicago Board of Trade and one on the Minneapolis Grain Exchange. A European correspondent sent daily flashes on grain prices in such prominent world markets as Amsterdam, these cables arriving before the opening of the Chicago exchange. Due to its large feed business, Quaker actually bought more corn than it did oats, both purchases running to millions of bushels, plus substantial quantities of wheat. About half of the company's oats were bought by field men who ranged the states of Ohio, Illinois, Iowa, and the Dakotas, searching for grains of processing quality. To store these purchases, Quaker as early as 1902 bought into the Wells-Hord Grain Company, which operated a string of midwestern country elevators; in 1912, Quaker absorbed the operation entirely.

The war risk was not so much in oats—a relatively stable market in which Quaker buyers often did not even bother to hedge their purchases—as in corn and wheat, which Quaker bought entirely on the open market and which were highest in war demand. The system at that time was for farmers to sell their harvest to a country elevator, which in turn sold to a terminal elevator in one of the big milling cities such as Minneapolis, Omaha, Sioux City, or Chicago. Quaker's purchases of corn and wheat were chiefly at the terminals, the risk covered by hedges on grain exchanges.

The following description of hedging against price decline was taken from a publication of the Chicago Board of Trade. The grain buyer makes four separate transactions to effect a hedge:

On the CASH Market	On the FUTURES Market
	On September 1	
He BUYS	He SELLS
5000 bu. of wheat shipped from country elevator at $2 per bu. (delivered Chicago)	5000 bu. of December wheat futures at $2 per bu.
	On October 20	
He SELLS	He BUYS
5000 bu. of wheat at $1.85 per bu. (delivered Chicago)	5000 bu. of December wheat futures at $1.85 per bu.
For a loss of 15¢ per bushel	For a profit of 15¢ per bushel

In 1920, sellers were permitted to buy back their contracts at any time before the delivery date. Instead of producing the promised grain if the market was higher, they had the option of holding for a better price and making a cash settlement with the buyer for the differential. Quaker often made purchases to fill its war-soaring needs, only to find on contract date that the seller had exercised his option and made a cash settlement, thus forcing Quaker to buy elsewhere—usually at a higher price.

Another difficulty for Quaker was that first-quality oats were becoming more difficult to find and often a stiff premium had to be paid. The pioneer oat seeds imported from Europe had long since become adulterated by use year after year without adequate screening of the trash from the harvests. Weed seeds, particularly dock and mustard, and barley, which is almost impossible to screen out, so infiltrated the plantings that in some areas (such as central Iowa) trash equaled 10 per cent of the total volume. There was also much recidivism to wild grain types. Quaker ranged as far away as North Dakota and Pennsylvania for Number One grade clean oats, increasing its transport charges to the Ohio, Illinois, and Iowa mills.

The puzzle, for a company which purchased grains far in advance of delivery, was when would the war-bloated market and speculative fever end, returning grain prices to normal. Retail prices for finished commodities were based on the anticipated cost of the raw materials and not easily changed. Injudicious inventories at high prices could cost the company millions of dollars in writeoffs if it were caught with bulging elevators in a declining market. Who could say when the deflation would occur? Quaker must supply its needs, even at perilous risk. So the Quaker buyers watched with apprehension.

The war's end did not immediately cause deflation, because of the pent-up demand for war-scarce consumer merchandise. Accumulated savings from war savings bonds and high wages created easy money. A false economy in consumer goods existed throughout 1919. With the armistice of November 1918, the public urge to spend its savings caused wild consumer demand that lasted for a full year.

Counterforces in the economy, difficult to observe and ones nobody wished to note, began to erode the prosperity. Foreign trade balances declined. Unfulfilled defense contracts were canceled, causing unemployment. Huge tonnages of war-built shipping now imported a flood of cheap foreign goods to saturate the American market and reduce American mill output. Enlarged industrial production, adjusting to peacetime demand, cut back payrolls sharply. Oversupply caused tighter credit. The money market dried up.

As 1920 began, the impact was not yet measurable. The Quaker Oats Company's directors, following the annual meeting in February, declared the usual dividends on common and preferred stocks, nearly $2 million, and announced themselves "hopeful and conservative."

But there had been little cutback in grain plantings by the American farmer, who in 1917 and 1918 had thrown thousands of marginal acres into wheat and other grain production in response to the patriotic slogan *Food Will Win the War!* The bumper harvest of 1920 could not be absorbed. In August 1920, a sudden world economic depression coincided with the oversupply in grains. The Federal Reserve Board increased the rediscount rate, shortening the supply of money in circulation, making credit purchases more difficult and causing banks to clamp down on once-good loans, which now suddenly had become risky.

Waves of factory shutdowns cut employment as much as 50 per cent in such big industries as automobiles and steel. Merchants, loaded with expensive inventories and few buyers, themselves pressed for payment by their creditors, were caught.

Wheat at Chicago dropped from $3.50 to $1.58 a bushel. Corn declined from $2.17 to 67¢, oats from $1.29 to 46¢. Those who had extensive holdings of futures at the top prices unhedged with offsetting sales contracts were heavy losers. Many of Quaker's dealers who had overbought on flour and feeds, hoping to realize a speculative gain on a price rise, refused to accept delivery at the original contract price—to have done so would have meant bankruptcy. Quaker was struck critically in this area: almost all of its contracts with flour and feed dealers were repudiated. Quaker took further severe inventory losses on grains and commodities on hand or bought for future delivery. And there were smaller, though serious, shrinkages in such materials as India burlap bags, ordered in advance for delivery six weeks later at 30¢ each. By the time they arrived, the open-market price was 7¢ a bag—the loss to Quaker: 23¢ a bag. A Minneapolis concern had contracted to supply Quaker several carloads of linseed meal, an ingredient in livestock feeds, at $90 a ton. By the delivery date in October, the open-market price of this commodity was $30 a ton. However, knowing that Quaker was good for the money, the suppliers refused cancellation, insisting on delivery at the full contract price. William Suits, Quaker's manager of feed sales, in December 1920 wrote his salesmen, "We have tons of scratch grain here at the mills. It cost us $27 a ton. Get what you can for it." Only a few weeks earlier, this feed had been $90 a ton. Nor could Quaker store the merchandise against ultimate price stability, since feeds in those days were largely by-products of the milling process and accumulated daily. The company had no storage capacity for such volume.

This was the greatest crisis in the history of The Quaker Oats Company. The refusal of buyers to accept delivery on their contracts left Quaker the alternative of enforcing sales through court action or of renegotiating the terms of purchase. Robert Stuart, calmly realistic in the emergency, took the long view and as a result probably saved the enterprise. To sue a customer was to lose him forever; to keep him in business was an investment in a client gratefully loyal henceforth. During the critical autumn of 1920, some of Quaker's management suggested suing at least those dealers who had defaulted due to speculative greed. Stuart rejected this policy. "There's no use wasting good money on lawsuits," he told his sons. "In a period of this kind, if you take the feed dealers to the country courts, you haven't a Chinaman's chance. What country jury will give a judgment to a big corporation against a friend and neighbor?"

Renegotiation became the order of business in The Quaker Oats Company. The management called on Myron J. Aubineau, Frank Farley, Harry Murfey, Paul Guse, William T. Cunningham, and other trusted executives personally to contact each dealer who found himself in trouble. When the beleagured merchants found themselves unable to meet deliveries, the men on the renegotiation team worked out settlements to keep their distributors in business.

One of the company negotiators later wrote of this period: "If we had tried to collect the amount of the market difference, we would have lost a good 50 per cent of our dealers. Instead, in order to keep the man in business, we renegotiated his contract at the new market price plus, in the case of feeds, a cancellation charge of one or two dollars a ton. Quaker's way of taking care of the trade was in contrast to the procedures of other mills." Quaker held the loyalty of its customers.

During this flash crisis, the company had little money coming in. The surplus of more than $1,500,000 built during the first half of the year was wiped out quickly, and Stuart now faced a crisis with his bankers. "Several banks," John Stuart recalled of this day, when he was first assistant to his father, "had been extending rather liberal lines of credit to the company. My father thought it likely that the bankers would be considerably less open-handed when they learned of the company's circumstances. The two of us visited the offices of these bankers, explained the company's problem and told them how we hoped we could keep our customers in business until they got back on their feet and were able to pay us. Every one of those bankers assured us that their commitments to the company were as good as ever. I remember James B. Forgan, of Chicago's First National, simply asked, 'How much money did we say we'd give you?' My father named a figure. 'All right, that's the amount of credit you have with us,' Mr. Forgan replied."

The economic hurricane was costly. The year 1920 showed the only operating loss in the Company's history. Further worsening the picture, the directors had voted $2,000,000 in dividends on the basis of the bright outlook early in the year, which had to be charged to surplus when the year turned in a net loss. The market collapse which came late in the year cost millions more in inventory losses and contract renegotiation. The annual statement for 1920 showed the final score, a shrinkage in assets of $10,000,000.

During the first two decades of the twentieth century, Robert Stuart, the careful manager, had trained a man-

agement succession against the day of his own retirement. With the fury of 1920 survived and prosperity
restored, the architects of Quaker's development as the
first great national miller and breakfast-food supplier
relinquished their command. In 1923 Robert Stuart
stepped out of the treasurership to the post of chairman
of the executive committee, which he occupied until his
death three years later. In 1922 Henry Parsons Crowell
took a newly created position, that of chairman of the
Board of Directors.

Robert Stuart was a man of precise mind. He even
split his long-distance telephone calls into fractions,
charging off each to the operation involved, and he handled larger matters with the same conscientiousness.
Once, shortly after the new century had begun, a Chicago speculator sought to corner the wheat market on
the Chicago Board of Trade. Long several million bushels, he needed storage space for his accumulating grains
and sought temporary use of a large elevator at Stuart's
Imperial Mill. Oats is a lighter grain than wheat, and
Stuart, writing the rental contract in his own hand without legal advice, specified that the elevator was "for the
storage of grain for an amount it would safely hold." The
lessee so overfilled the storage that the elevator burst,
spilling wheat across Dearborn Street and inundating
the tracks of the Belt Railroad. The speculator declined
to pay his rent or damages on grounds that the structure
was faulty. Stuart took him to court. The judge read the
contract, and that ended the case. "The judge said," an
eyewitness reported later, "that it was the simplest and
clearest contract the Court had ever seen, and there was
no question but that the lessees were liable." Stuart collected.

His meticulous diary revealed a wide curiosity and
activity. Even in his late years his golf score was in the

eighties. He skippered a sailboat proficiently, was a zealous participant in the Scottish sports of lawn bowling and ice-rink curling. Rugby football, sandlot baseball and billiards found him capable, and for hard exercise he bicycled before breakfast. With his wife he attended opera, the theater, the circus, Buffalo Bill's Wild West Show, political rallies, and the Presbyterian Church. One of Chicago's first motorcar enthusiasts, he owned one of the city's pioneer gasoline-powered automobiles. He played a canny game of eucre. Contrary to the American Presbyterianism of his time, he liked a wee dram at bedtime, following the Scottish custom of crackers, cheese, and a stomach-warmer of whiskey as a nightcap. These viands were offered as a late-evening ritual off the dining-room sideboard. As his sons matured and joined this ceremony, he gave them brief words of advice: "Never talk unless you have to. Live by your convictions. You'll never get yourself in trouble by talking too little."

When he stepped down, the City of Cedar Rapids, Iowa, which owed him much—his great mills on the bank of the Cedar River being the town's most prominent and most depressionproof industry—sent a representative to Chicago with an idea. The fiftieth anniversary of the founding of Stuart's mill was approaching. The city wished to honor the company and pay well-earned tribute to its founder and longtime manager. His son John Stuart was consulted on the matter. "Let's go in and talk to Father," he suggested. All that the visitor's eloquent presentation earned from Robert Stuart was a genial smile. Outside, John explained, "I think the reason Father does not go for your plan is that he's afraid he'll have to make a speech."

Henry P. Crowell continued as chairman of the board until 1942. He also had other interests besides oatmeal.

From 1904 until his death forty years later, he was president of the board of the Moody Bible Institute, a position to which his son succeeded. The Hereford Cattle Breeders Association of America acknowledges Crowell as one of its great benefactors. On a ranch near Cheyenne, Wyoming, Crowell as a hobby developed some of the great blood lines of the breed. Ultimately he endowed the operation as a continuing center for Hereford improvement, a trust managed by the Association.

Crowell was an evangelist in everything he did, selling oatmeal or stoves, raising prize bulls, or converting the heathen to fundamentalist Christianity. At times, he carried his religious zeal to unlikely lengths. For thirty years one of the most celebrated early advertising agency men, Albert Lasker, had Quaker as his best account. A mutual association of admiration and affection grew between the two creative advertising geniuses. One day Crowell, over lunch, looked wistfully at Lasker and suggested seriously that he become a member of Crowell's Presbyterian Church in Evanston. Lasker smiled and agreed to do it—provided Crowell would join Lasker's synagogue on Chicago's near North Side.

The end of a thirty-year relationship between The Quaker Oats Company and Albert Lasker occurred in 1938, when Quaker's advertising department signed up for the Townsend Plan, a service supplied to advertisers by two brothers Townsend for evaluating advertisements in advance of their release for publication. For a fee scaled to the size of the company's advertising appropriation, the Townsends installed a 27-point checking system in Quaker's advertising department by which the advertising agency's creative product was judged. The laws of the Townsend Plan were precise and inelastic, with little room left for the play of creative talent.

This was too much for Lasker. "I mark your papers," he used to say to Lord & Thomas writers. Lasker finally resigned from his oldest client. He appeared in the Quaker executive offices, along with David M. Noyes, his chief lieutenant on the account, and in a final meeting made his farewell, saying that he would not impose on his creative people the obligation to write advertising to the Townsend formula. In time, Quaker dropped the Townsend Plan. Like other hopeful schemes to reduce advertising to an exact science, it fell of its own weight and disappeared from advertising circles.

Crowell's only son followed his father's religious causes rather than The Quaker Oats Company. Robert Stuart's two sons, however, were attracted to careers in management of The Quaker Oats Company. The elder, John, was born in Cedar Rapids in 1877. After graduation from Princeton University with a degree in civil engineering, he entered the Cedar Rapids mill as a sweeper at fifteen cents an hour in 1900. He was much like his father; they even looked alike. "If you walked down the street behind them," an associate observed, "you could not tell the two apart."

Robert Stuart did not coddle his sons. Their apprenticeship was calculatedly rugged. In 1900, the mill foremen at Cedar Rapids were rough, tough, and proud, sons of strong-backed Bohemians who had settled the farms of the vicinity after their migration from Europe. Among the miller's prerogatives was the right to tote a whiskey bottle and nip during his work. Law and order on the working floor was enforced by the iron fists of the foreman.

There is no record that the boss' son was ever slugged, but John learned the business from the milling floor up. Upon his transfer to Chicago, he and his father worked together with extraordinary warmth. "My father," said John, "was my best friend." The pair visited company installations together, the father tutoring the son in the details and philosophies of management. By 1922, John was second vice-president and a director, actually the first management assistant to his father. He was forty-five years old, with twenty-two years of experience in the company. His apprenticeship had been thorough. He was elected president at the directors' meeting of May 23, 1922, which elevated Crowell to the chairmanship.

Crowell had been a strict, authoritarian taskmaster, supremely confident in his judgments and unyielding in his decisions. His brilliance earned him the respect of his associates, but they were more awed than warmed by his righteousness. John Stuart was another sort entirely. He could, when he thought the occasion required it, affect the stern no-nonsense air supposedly typical of business executives. Through his apprenticeship he had learned to mask his natural warmth and gregariousness, modeling himself on his elders and remembering his father's advice about talking as little as possible. He could indeed be snappish and impatient with sloth, sham, carelessness, extravagance, and similar offenses. When thus outraged he bristled with anger, his pale blue eyes glinted with indignation, and to the shaken offender he seemed far taller than his five feet, four inches. He was good at business, and serious about it; he was the embodiment of personal integrity, no less so than Crowell. But he was at bottom a friendly and totally unpretentious man, with a sparkle of humor he was incapable of repressing. "He brought an air of benignancy to the company's affairs," one veteran recalls.

John Stuart's first policy decision was to revamp the company's inventory control so that no repetition of the crisis of 1921 would be possible. In the booming prewar years of rising prices, Quaker's sales policy, like many another's, had been to encourage "loading" the trade by high-pressure selling. The hero was the Quaker salesman who sold in carload lots—one had a reputation for selling by the trainload—scorning small orders. Hence, when the 1920 panic developed, many of the dealers were caught with inflated inventories and in self-defense were forced to repudiate agreements. John Stuart changed all that.

His policy encouraged optimum rather than *maximum* sales, asking buyers to stock only their immediate needs, with faster turnover. This line of thinking anticipated the modern trend in food marketing, signaled by the rapid expansion of the innovative Piggly Wiggly self-service chain. Turnover was the key word of the new sales generation, and John Stuart conformed Quaker to the new fast-in fast-out merchandising system. The chain, then the supermarket, soon changed the buying habits of the nation's housewives, and with the advent of self-service, the retailer lost control of his customers at the point of sale. Thenceforth, the consumer's mind more than ever would be made up by influences exerted before she ever got to the store through advertising and promotion.

John Stuart's presidency was a period of enormous world-wide expansion for Quaker. By the time he ascended to the board chairmanship in 1942, he had taken the company into such collateral lines as pet foods, chemicals, and ready-mixed pancake flours. Building on his domestic diversification, which had generated $90 million in annual sales by 1942, the company would climb to a gross of $277 million on 200 different products by 1956, when he retired as chairman and chief executive officer.

After the economic collapse of 1921, John Stuart quietly determined that so far as he could plan it, The Quaker Oats Company would never be without plenty of ready cash. He decided to make arrangements for standby credit as a hedge against the day of tight money. As Quaker grew into a business giant financing its daily operations, not to mention further capital expansion, required ever-increasing amounts of money. John Stuart, therefore, contracted with banks at firm rates of interest for sums of money subject to call in the future. The first program of this kind involved $20 million. Cash was to be made available over ten years at 2¾ per cent interest, Quaker to pay only ¼ of 1 per cent a year for the unused credits still subject to call. The plan worked to Quaker's advantage, since its bank loans were available for a decade at interest charges substantially lower than the prevailing rates. More important, the cash was there on demand in emergency.

"Let's look on it," he told his colleagues at the inception of the plan, "as a form of insurance. Now you know for certain that you can get bank loans at a future date and for what rate. The trouble is that if you wait to borrow until you need to, then maybe a lot of other people will be needing money at the same time, and the cost of borrowing goes up."

Robert Stuart would have approved his son's foresight. It was in the founder's tradition.

As his first official act as president in 1922 John Stuart promoted eight of his own management generation to vice-presidencies. Among them was his younger brother, R. Douglas Stuart, who became vice-president for advertising. No man had a more difficult assignment than the younger Stuart—he had to succeed the originator of national food advertising, Henry Parsons Crowell. Douglas was nine years his brother's junior, with a temperament too restless for the long Princeton University training John had found so much to his liking. Douglas Stuart, like Henry Crowell, matured while on his own in the western states, engaged in the rugged outdoor life. He was successively Canadian logger and Nevada gold-mine prospector before he returned home where "the old oats company looks pretty good." His father sent him as a mill hand to the Peterborough, Ontario, factory in 1906. He followed his brother to an executive desk in Chicago, where he understudied Crowell and supervised the advertising. He, too, was ready for leadership by 1922.

"Doug" Stuart was one of the first corporate advertising executives to embrace the policy of hiring more than one advertising agency, a practice now almost standard in American business. He believed Quaker's diversification policy, through both new-product development and acquisition, called for a greater spread of talent than any one agency would provide. He also was first to take to Quaker sales offices all over the country advance presentations of advertising and selling plans, which helped Quaker salesmen educate the grocery trade on the value of rapid turnover and the role of advertising in bringing it about.

During R. Douglas Stuart's years some of Quaker's most memorable advertising appeared, such as the campaign featuring the Dionne Quintuplets. Group photos of the girls, headed by an announcement from Dr. Alan R. Dafoe that "Today our Dionne Quintuplets ate Quaker Oats," attracted nationwide attention. Indeed the diet and health of the Quints seemed to be of personal interest to millions of people and amounted to one of the most dramatic clinical tests ever performed on a food.

The discovery of Vitamin B-1 in oat grain in the 1930s presented Quaker Oats with an advertising opportunity most large companies dream about. Full-page advertisements of the vitamin richness of Quaker Oats appeared in magazines and newspapers across the country. Traditionally not given to wide, sudden swings in its sales curve, Quaker Oats responded to this campaign with a 35 per cent sales increase. The bulk of Quaker's expenditures for advertising has been spent on educating generations of housewives on the merits of Quaker products.

In 1942 R. Douglas Stuart succeeded his brother John as president and later served as vice-chairman and chairman until his retirement in 1962.

Chapter 7 ✶ *Food*
Shot from Guns

IN SAINT LOUIS the day was muggy with cloying humidity that rises from the Mississippi River during the hot season. But the enervating weather was no deterrent to the clamorous Labor Day crowd that jammed the Word's Fair of 1904. A sensation was in prospect.

After several seeks of well-publicized delays, a battery of eight bronze cannons, each five feet long and with a muzzle eight inches in diameter, had actually been mounted at the Quaker Oats exhibit and were to be fired with rice ammunition which miraculously would explode into a succulent confection.

Henry Parsons Crowell and the American Cereal Company already were known to almost every state fair and regional exposition in America. They gave away free samples of cooked Quaker Rolled Oats, to the delight of snacking children, and a welcome meager lunch for thrifty adults. Thousands of suitable-for-framing, handsome four-color chromos of famous sights such as Niagara Falls and Independence Hall had been passed out on the Fairgrounds; on the reverse side were printed instructions and a map spotting the location of the Quaker tent, where the oatmeal was ladled from glistening copper double boilers by pretty attendants. So everyone knew what was going on and how to get there, including a cousin of the Mikado of Japan, attracted by any demonstration of a palatable new use for Oriental grain.

The cannons were Spanish-American war pieces, among the first breach-loading artillery to be equipped with recoil mechanisms. The muzzles were capped with an easily removed plug. To music and fanfare they were loaded with rice. Then they were rotated for forty minutes in gas-fired ovens, while the crowd was told that the 550-degree heat was converting the moisture in the grains into steam under tremendous pressure. Removed from the heat chambers, the guns were wheeled rapidly on a narrow-gauge railroad track to an enormous cage forty feet wide and two stories high. With suitable *éclat,* at the command "Fire!" attendants knocked the caps from the muzzles. With the roar of a military fusillade the artillery barrage spewed myriad fluffy puffs like little cocoons in a shower from which the cage protected the crowd. The steam had caused about 125 million explosions within each grain of rice, bulging the kernels to eight times normal size and giving the grain an entirely new texture and flavor. Covered with a caramel coating the puffs were boxed and sold to the gaping onlookers.

The demonstration was the introduction of a new Quaker product, *Puffed Rice.* The event was one of the great sensations of the autumn days of the Fair, and the rice-candy confection sold six thousand packets a day— a sellout. Even President Theodore Roosevelt, visiting the Fair, sampled the unique novelty at the Quaker booth and recognized the cannon as perhaps veterans of the artillery used at San Juan Hill.

Having launched his new product so auspiciously, Crowell's imagination for once failed him. He did not realize that here he had a ready-to-eat breakfast cereal that could compete successfully against the Kellogg Corn Flake.

He looked upon the puffed rice as a novelty and contracted to sell the Company's entire production at the Fair to a candy-maker. After the exposition, the battery of guns was installed in Stuart's Empire Mill in Chicago. The product, packed in barrels or sacks, was offered to the candy trade.

Ever since Labor Day, 1904, the Quaker management has received a rather steady accumulation of letters from incredulous buyers, all asking the same question:

Dear Sirs:
I am writing to ask an extremely foolish question. But in order to settle a standing disagreement between my husband and myself, I want to find out whether or not, in the manufacture of Puffed Wheat and Puffed Rice, are the grains actually shot from guns? I have always believed that they were—ever since I was a child. My husband finds my belief very amusing. He says that shot from guns is only a slogan, that the grains are exploded in some entirely different process. Can you tell me—is there actually a form of gun used? Do you have any pictorial evidence to prove this? Please excuse this silly letter, but I have to settle this once and for all, even if I'm wrong, which I probably am.

Sirs:
Our family is having a dispute over your cereals. Please tell us are Puffed Wheat and Puffed Rice really shot from guns? I think they are and I sure hope you can prove me right. Please send a rush answer.

Dear Quaker Oats:
I would like to know if Puffed Rice and Puffed Wheat is really shot from guns. If they are I want to know how. Our class is arguing about it. Our teacher says it is and the

class says it isn't, so please answer before school's out in June. Thank you.

The answer to all such inquiries is basically the same. Quaker Puffed Rice and Puffed Wheat actually are made by shooting them from guns. The unwieldy early cannon has yielded now to an automatically loaded, self-firing, multiple-barrel device; but it is still a gun, the kernels are shot from it, and they erupt with a noisy roar.

The originator of the puffing process and the inventor of the first puffing gun was a biochemist named Alexander P. Anderson. Doctor Anderson looked the public concept of a theoretical scientist. Gaunt, thin-faced, ascetic, his head spread above the ears to present a broad forehead, his wide expanse of cranium covered by unkempt hair. His hands were long-fingered, gnarled, and bony, his blue eyes preoccupied. The professorial attitude was accentuated by octagon-shaped rimless spectacles. The sum of his face was recognizable to any Nordic as of Swedish antecedents: he was as Swedish as Minnesota, which had been his birthplace.

As a graduate student at the University of Minnesota, searching for a doctoral thesis in plant chemistry, Anderson focused on the cellular structure of starch. He sought a method to break up starch granules so that the human digestive juices would react upon them more quickly and more effectively. Reading the literature, he discovered a monograph by specialists at the University of Munich, describing a technique whereby rice grains could be expanded by heat for better study under the microscope. Anderson went to Bavaria in 1895. He watched the Germans heat rice in a test tube until steam pressure expanded the grains to several times their normal size; the cereal then could be cut apart easily and examined. Anderson was warned not to seal the end of the test tube or the generated steam pressure would shatter it.

Intrigued by this statement, Anderson borrowed the use of a Munich laboratory, put some rice in a test tube, sealed the tube, screened it with a wire mesh, and heated the tube slowly over a Bunsen burner. After nearly an hour, the test tube was shattered by a violent explosion. Said Anderson later, "That was as good a puffed rice as was ever puffed anywhere."

His studies completed and doctorate in hand, Anderson received an appointment to teach at Columbia University in New York in 1901. An attractive feature of the assignment was faculty encouragement for Doctor Anderson to continue his starch-cell studies in the laboratory of the New York Botanical Gardens. One day he filled three test tubes with cornstarch, sealed them hermetically, put them in an oven and heated them to about 500 degrees—a somewhat safer procedure than his Bunsen-burner experience with the rice in Munich. There was no explosion in the oven. Anderson then withdrew the hot tubes, placed them behind a protective wire screen, and cracked one with a hammer. A sharp blast sprayed the laboratory with glass and with cornstarch expanded to ten times its normal volume, now a porous, puffed (and presumably more easily digested) mass.

Dr. Anderson was a practical sort of scholar. He knew at once that he had discovered a process with possible commercial implications. He patented the exploding process in 1902, and the product—puffed rice and puffed wheat—in 1904. An improved method of steam processing to superheat the tiny cells was similarly protected in 1912.

His original patent secured, Anderson returned to Minneapolis to seek financial backing for the development of his invention. Nobody seemed to know quite what to do with it. Ready-to-eat cereals were then just becoming popular and consisted of boxed flakes of corn and wheat; they were almost as great a novelty as Professor Anderson's invention. Robert Stuart and Henry Crowell, however, were interested. Even though their stake was in hot cereals, they recognized the ready-to-eats as a labor-saver for the housewife and therefore important to any cereal manufacturer. The two men journeyed to Minneapolis to examine Anderson's primitive puffing gun, then under development at the Minneapolis Steel and Machinery Company. They met Anderson. The upshot was an agreement whereby Doctor Anderson would work for Quaker and would assign his patent, and any future patents on the process or product, to his employer.

A secret laboratory was built and equipped in a grain bin at the Empire Mill in Chicago. The space was about ten feet square and three stories high, hoppered at the bottom to discharge the stored grain. A floor was built over the hopper and a door cut in the wall—Quaker's first research center. Anderson broadened his puffing experiments to all the common grains to discover which were most responsive to the steam-expansion treatment. This early work was with glass tubes, metal tubes, and finally with an improvised cannon. At the critical moment of every experiment, Anderson's life was actually in danger. "It's a wonder," said John Stuart, one of the select few permitted to observe him, "that he didn't blow himself up."

The laboratory was placed under strict security. Not even Quaker personnel who worked in Chicago knew what Anderson was doing. The inquisitive got nothing from the scientist himself. "He was the most quiet and reticent man," one of them remembered later. "In the early stages everyone wanted to know what he was doing, of course. But he scarcely spoke to anybody, and as far as the management was concerned, it was a deep secret."

Meanwhile Quaker's milling engineers had no success developing a puffing gun based on Anderson's patent that was either commercially practical or safe to use. The original guns had no recoil mechanism, and the steam pressure loosened their riveted foundations with every explosion. The machine shop at Akron, under James H. Andrews' aggressive and ingenious direction, worked on the puffing-gun problem during the last half of 1902 and well into the spring of 1903. Several of the explosions tore out the floor. Workmen refused to go near the shop while the experiments were in progress.

One day Myron T. Herrick, then Governor of Ohio and also a director of Quaker, dropped in, curious to see the problem which was causing Andrews so much trouble and peril. Herrick reportedly said, "This is a gun, so what you need is an expert in ordnance. There are effective recoil mechanisms for artillery; maybe you can use the same idea." He put Andrews in contact with a U.S. Army artillery officer in Cleveland, who adapted an artillery piece as a puffer, using a cannon from the Spanish-American war. This cumbersome unit was so heavy that it was pulled on a small flatcar on narrow-gauge railroad tracks. When the closure on the gun muzzle was knocked loose by a man swinging a huge wooden mallet, a prodigious explosion, accompanied by an ear-splitting blast, reverberated amid a hail of puffed grains. For some time thereafter, a practical joke in Akron was to ask visitors if they would like a close look at the secret puffing gun. The unsuspecting victim was placed just outside the collecting cage. Seldom did the curious request a second demonstration.

By now Crowell had decided he had merely a novelty confection, not a ready-to-eat cereal. The production problems were too great. The cumbersome guns, even in multiple batteries, could not produce sufficient puffed grain to justify national distribution. With limited production, no campaign to introduce so unusual a cereal to the public was economically feasible. For ready-to-eats, he turned his attention to the development of toasted corn and wheat flakes, similar to those of several fast-rising competitors in cereals whose production was entirely in the ready-to-eat lines. These novelty cereals were gaining acceptance as health foods, and Quaker's Apetizo had attained considerable success as The Great Hemoglobin Producer and "physiologic food." However, while these dozens of new and competing new products were still in development, Andrews produced a substantial improvement in the puffing gun. He devised a stationary gun which discharged its puffed grains into an expansion chamber. The gun's rotating barrel cut the heating time from forty-five minutes to three and a half, and the cannon did not have to be wheeled into a cage before firing. Now, with eleven times the original puffed-grain production in hand, a capacity that could be expanded indefinitely merely by the addition of new units, Crowell introduced Puffed Rice—but not to the consuming public. He sold it in barrels or sacks to candy manufacturers. The volume was insignificant.

Meanwhile, Professor Anderson had been experimenting with puffing of wheat grains. After many a costly trial, he produced another puffed grain, which the Company named Wheat Berries, also for the confectioner trade.

But Crowell had not forgotten the ready-to-eat business. His Toasted Corn Flakes and Toasted Wheat Flakes, introduced in 1907, had failed to establish a market. To recoup, the two confections, now called Puffed Rice and Puffed Wheat, were packaged in 1909 for the grocery trade and were a nationwide sensation. Quaker's operating profit that year advanced nearly a half-million dollars, rising above $2,000,000 for the first time in 1912. The puffs were responsible for much of the increase.

How this development ensued is controversial, although there is no doubt about the promoter. He was one of the first truly creative advertising copy writers, a working demon who late in life admitted that he had never taken a day off during his entire career, and often had toiled until midnight. His name was Claude C. Hopkins.

Son of a Wisconsin small-town newspaper publisher, orphaned at ten, Hopkins was a house-to-house salesman, a theological student, and then, after attendance at a business school, a clerk for the Bissell Carpet Sweeper Company, then a small manufacturing concern. By improving the design of the sweeper for eye appeal and devising a mail-order campaign, Hopkins sold 250,000 sweepers in three weeks. From then on he was in demand, working days for a meat packer or patent-medicine maker, nights on a free-lance basis to anyone who sought his services. In 1898 he joined the advertising agency of Lord & Thomas, which another pioneer named Albert D. Lasker was in the process of developing toward a creative agency. Now Hopkins evolved the Van Camp Twins to sell pork and beans, inviting the public to compare the product with any other brand. This attack was an ethical heresy, since manufacturers by tacit agreement did not deprecate each other.

Ten years later Hopkins was generally conceded among advertisers to be the most imaginative advertising writer living.

In his autobiography Hopkins related that he was called to Crowell's office alone, his work was praised, and he was offered a $50,000 account (large for that day) to exploit any Quaker product not then being advertised. After some study, Hopkins said, he became intrigued with the two puffed confections and the dramatic manner in which they were shot from guns. Visiting Akron, he talked with Professor Anderson. Then, changing the name *Wheat Berries* to *Puffed Wheat* to give double impact to a single campaign advertising both puffed grains, Hopkins wrote advertisements highlighting the personality and prestige of the learned college professor who had produced a scientific and nutritious ready-to-eat cereal shot from guns.

Lasker's memory of the incident is substantially different. His tape-recorded memoir recalled that in 1908 Crowell wrote to nineteen advertising agencies soliciting their ideas for a campaign to launch his Puffed Rice and Wheat Berries as ready-to-eat cereals. Lasker responded by arranging an interview with Crowell, taking his star copywriter Hopkins with him. Crowell showed them an advertisement, already in preparation, of a Chinese eating rice.

"That's no good," Lasker says he replied contemptuously. "Nobody cares what a Chinaman eats. The housewife is concerned over what she feeds her family, and it's a long way from her kitchen to China."

Crowell was impressed. Lasker states that he then recommended on the spot that the two puffed cereals have companion names, so that they might be promoted "as a package." Crowell resisted this concept, seeing the two as entirely separate sales items. Lasker urged that the consumers be exhorted to put both puffs on the pantry shelf for variety. At this vision of doubled sales, Crowell reportedly succumbed. Lasker then suggested that the price of ten cents contemplated for Puffed Wheat be raised to the fifteen-cent retail charge for Puffed Rice, otherwise the products could be promoted adequately only at a loss. He walked from the office ten minutes later, he asserted, with the account in his pocket, and kept it for thirty years. Hopkins also takes credit for the pricing, which added $1.25 a case to the billing revenues from Puffed Wheat.

Hopkins exploited the American respect for educators. His advertisements built a distinguished character in Doctor Anderson, complete with his photograph, and made much of the intriguing idea that the food was detonated from a cannon. Pushing dual sales, he wrote "Get both. They differ vastly. Let the children decide which they want. Don't wait until tomorrow—order them now. For you are missing a food that's better than any you know."

Hopkins believed in the magic persuasive power of words. He minimized illustrations because pictures took space away from his precious copy. Nor did Hopkins use color, which might divert the eye from the sales message. To insure exposure of the advertisement to the reader, he laid out his ads in fractional pages and specified that his paid space must abut important reading matter. He believed that humor had no place in advertising. His copy was earnest and direct, with none of the lightness and whimsy Crowell often had employed.

For the decade during which Hopkins promoted the puffed cereals (he also campaigned for the hot cereal Quaker Oats from 1911), the annual reports of The Quaker Oats Company showed consistent advances in gross sales and net profit. World War I, of course, contributed greatly to this gain, but the contribution of Hopkins is acknowledged. From the second year of his promotional effort, Quaker's annual profit was never under $2,000,000 except in the economic depression year of 1920. In the year puffed grains were introduced Quaker had an operating profit of $1,401,000; in 1911, $1,977,000; in 1912, $2,429,000; in 1913, $2,287,000; in 1914, $2,367,000.

The war pushed the puffed cereals, and oatmeal too, to new highs. Reported Hopkins, "All of us were urged to eat meat substitutes and the study of calories became a fad. The calories in Quaker Oats showed conspicuously. The cost per 1000 calories was about one-tenth the cost of meat. We doubled the Quaker Oats sales on that calorie presentation." The sales of the puffed cereals surged upward year after year, giving Quaker a toehold —though not an impressive position—in the total ready-to-eat market. Oatmeal remained the company's premier consumer product.

Doctor Anderson's original patent on the puffing process expired in 1919, his improved steam-injection process patent in 1929. The basic product patent had run out in 1921. No imitators appeared then, however, since the process could not be duplicated without infringement. The Quaker management was well aware that after 1929 anyone might make a puffed rice or wheat. But it relied upon its twenty years of established brand following and the important trademarks Puffed Rice and Puffed Wheat to maintain the company's position. It was not prepared, therefore, for the flood of competitors beginning in 1930. The chain stores were saturated with cellophane bags full of cheap merchandise labeled "puffed rice" and "puffed wheat." A suit to preserve these titles for Quaker was instituted, but the company abandoned the litigation after the Supreme Court decided, in another case, that "shredded wheat" was a generic term and not protectable as part of a trademark.

A tremendous promotional battle followed in the 1930s to retain the puffed-goods market for Quaker. Manufacturing as well as promotional devices were employed. The two cereals were enriched with vitamins and iron through a process which showered the puffs with a misty spray of a solution containing thiamin, niacin, and iron. The advertising called this Vitamin Rain. For a time the pair were rechristened Quaker Puffed Rice Sparkies and Quaker Puffed Wheat Sparkies, in an effort to set them apart from competitors' puffed products. Simultaneously, someone decided that Claude Hopkins' celebrated "Shot from Guns" slogan should be played down after almost continuous use for a quarter-century. The consumers rejected these departures from tradition. When sales of the puffed cereals dropped, Quaker quickly restored the old names and the advertisements were soon again thundering "Delicious breakfast shot from guns. There is nothing else like food shot from guns—nothing even half so good." Professor Anderson's name was back again, too, now billed as "formerly of Columbia University." Sales picked up. Nobody has ever again tinkered either with the name or the basic advertising cannonade. By 1939 the imitators were no longer serious competitors, a result partially of a prewar shortage of cellophane.

Comic strips, Sunday supplements to newspapers,

and network radio were the big carriers of the Quaker puffed-cereal message in the 1930s. Babe Ruth and prominent male and female movie stars, headed by super-moppet Shirley Temple, testified to the tastiness and healthful properties of the exploded grains.

The Babe, still at the peak of his baseball career, led off in 1934 with a heavily advertised campaign. He appeared in comic strips "knocking another one out of the park," and also in nonbaseball sequences. He climbed a mountain on the pep supplied by Puffed Rice. He helped a tired vaudevillian to success in the big time by prescribing a proper breakfast for him. At the National Air Races he urged Puffed Wheat on a pilot-pal who had lost his energy with the big race coming up.

"You have to stay in condition to stay in the Big League—and that means you have to eat right," The Babe advised his readers. "My secret for starting the day right is Quaker Puffed Wheat or Rice with fresh fruits and milk." To the children he spoke directly: "Live right, get plenty of sleep and eat right—if you want to make good in sports or in business. Eat lots of Puffed Wheat and Puffed Rice—they taste swell, and they're good for you. I'm telling you straight because I eat 'em myself. I like 'em best with strawberries and cream. They're a real dish."

The Babe told much the same story to radio listeners on the National Broadcasting Company network, as he handed out anecdotes and tips on how to play the games of life and baseball. He had a natural appeal for children, particularly little boys, who hung on his radiocasts and, at his bidding, developed long-time habits of Quaker puffed-cereal breakfasts.

The Sunday comic pages were equally effective. They showed Babe Ruth in action at the plate and at the cereal bowl. He offered premiums for boxtops as head-lines shouted, "I've sent a million kids these swell base-ball gifts . . . Free! One boxtop will get you a Babe Ruth Championship Badge. Wear this swell badge. Made of oxidized bronze, with the Babe's picture on it!" Eight boxtops were good for a baseball, and literally millions of them were sent in response to the offer.

The 1934 promotion using Ruth was so successful that it was repeated in 1935. Lured by the tremendous attraction of the baseball star, 200,000 grocery stores had tied into the initial campaign with window displays showing Ruth swatting on energy gained from Puffed Rice or Puffed Wheat. The second year, more emphasis was placed on news stories supplied by Quaker's adver-tising agency. The Babe was pictured as boyhood's bountiful benefactor, giving away trainloads of baseball equipment so that deprived boys (with access to box-tops) could learn America's national sport.

This campaign appealed chiefly to children, but their mothers were not ignored. In one newspaper display, Mrs. Babe Ruth asked, "Do you have the same trouble with your husband that I have with mine?" She con-fessed that George Herman needed constant watching due to his tendency either to skip breakfast entirely or eat enough for three men. A doctor friend had advised puffed cereals, and the Babe was doing fine now.

Big Hollywood box-office names glittered for Puffed Wheat and Puffed Rice from 1935 to 1938. In straight testimonial ads, George Brent told readers that he kept fit easily on puffed cereals. Anita Louise withstood hot weather by ingesting those light, nourishing cereals. Ralph Bellamy, Ida Lupino, and June Travis kept cool, fit and either lovely or handsome on the same diet. Bing Crosby confessed that his favorite breakfast was Puffed

Wheat with berries, plus cream cheese. Fred MacMurray went along with the cereal, but wanted grilled mushrooms instead of the cheese.

An unusually successful puffed cereal campaign, one of the most imaginative in modern cereal advertising, was used to promote the two Quaker ready-to-eats in 1955. It evolved, as do most successful advertising ideas, from creative agony.

At the time, Quaker was sponsoring on television a successor to its radio-network hero, Sergeant Preston of the Yukon. Preston, a Simon-Pure good guy with a Simon-Pure good dog named Yukon King, both of whom were infallible and at all times virtuous, was a Northwest Mounted Policeman who defended law and order in the vast wilderness of the Canadian Northwest during the wild Yukon gold rush of the 1890s. For the American moppet market he had to be an American-born red-blooded boy, so the script had his father murdered during the gold rush while Our Hero was at college. He became a Canadian citizen and joined the Mounties to track down his father's killer. A supreme woodsman, naturally, he had the usual good-guy-vs-bad-guy adventures. The dog was a Husky nurtured by a she-wolf. Preston had rescued the puppy after the foster mother had been killed defending her charge from a bobcat. Preston made Yukon King into a lead dog who could do no wrong.

The script was no problem. It ground itself out year after year. But the merchandising offers by 1955 had begun to pall. Everything that seemed appropriate had been tried: boxtop and coupon lures had included a compass, a skinning knife, a fire-lighting prism ring, and other goodies. These were popular and suited to the Sergeant Preston theme, but not entirely distinguished from the premium offers of other manufacturers, and Quaker had asked its agency to come up with something not only inexpensive but "different," and worthy to compete against the campaigns of all the other 67 ready-to-eat cereals marketed by competitors.

Thus the suffering started.

Premiums were in such great currency that every conceivable idea had seemingly been exhausted, either by Quaker or by some other merchandiser appealing to the child consumer. The trick was to find an impelling premium that would draw huge business without draining from two to five cents each away from other forms of advertising.

"It all started," its creator Bruce Baker wrote later, "with that sickening feeling one has when one is smoking two cigarettes at the same time . . . at home at three o'clock in the morning, with the horrible realization that by noon the next day one has to be at the Quaker Oats Company with the *idea,* period."

Half awake, his subconscious dredged up the recollection of a scheme of which he had read some years earlier, wherein tiny bits of land had been given away in Oklahoma. Why not, he asked, offer a deed to a square inch of land right in Sergeant Preston's own Yukon Territory? The cost should be negligible. The result might be sensational. Just as the program itself gave youngsters a mysterious faraway setting for an adventurous relief from afternoon chores and schoolwork, actual ownership of a bit of Gold Rush Country might set millions of young imaginations tingling.

By mid-morning Baker had sold the idea to his agency, and by noon to Quaker's merchandising department—but not to its lawyers. The legal complications seemed insurmountable. But rather than abandon what to every-

QUAKER ALBUM OF FAMOUS ADVERTISEMENTS

*Chromo in color promoted
west coast campaign 1891*

*24-page premium inserted
in oatmeal cartons 1893*

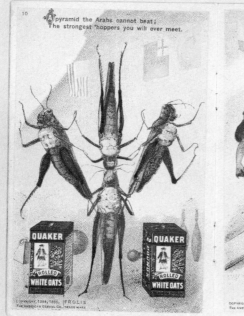

*First of millions of Quaker comic books, 16-page
grasshopper circus giveaway was distributed 1894*

THE
EASY FOOD
·
EASY
TO
BUY
·
EASY
TO
COOK
·
EASY
TO
DIGEST

QUAKER

ROLLED
WHITE OATS

Ceres, fair goddess of the harvest fields,
Now to the world her choicest treasure yields.

AT ALL GROCERS IN 2-LB. PACKAGES ONLY.

Very daring for its day: from McClure's Magazine 1897

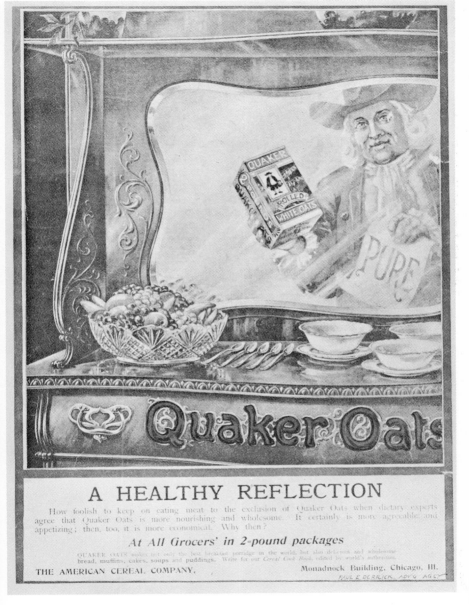

A milestone: Saturday Evening Post's first full page back cover ad, also its first ad in two colors, 1899

This Radio

$1.00

With 2 Quaker Oats trade-marks cut from packages

Get YOURS now—supply is limited

MANY who own complicated radio sets, with expensive tubes, batteries and chargers, complain that reception is not what they expected.

We experimented with a simple crystal set that would eliminate the bother and expense of bigger sets, and give more perfect clarity, sweeter tone as well. That would positively end distortion. Two years ago we offered this set for the first time, and many thousands obtained them. Last year still more radio fans got our simple Quaker Oats set. Demand came for more, but we couldn't supply them all.

Now we offer you, this Christmastime, a simple and practical crystal set that will receive for about thirty miles. Perfect in every detail. Clear, with pure tone, this set has delighted the thousands who have owned it.

We offer it again this year to advertise the remarkable new kind of Quaker Oats—Quick Quaker, which cooks in 3 to 5 minutes, and makes steaming, flavory oats not only the world's best breakfast, but the quickest, too.

Remarkably simple to operate
This new radio outfit is a facsimile of the Quick Quaker package. Simple to operate and absolutely foolproof. They're going like hot cakes. Get YOURS before the supply is exhausted.

Go to your grocer—get two packages of Quaker Oats, either regular Quaker, the kind you have always known, or Quick Quaker. Then cut the Quaker trade-mark (the picture of the Quaker) from each, that is all.

Do not delay—act now
Bring or send these trade-marks and amount of cash according to which outfit you want to the address given below, and get your radio at once.

Act quickly! The supply is limited. First come, first served.

An Ideal Christmas Gift!

Boys and Girls!

Tell your mother and father about this chance to get a real practical radio. Ask them to let you get the Quaker trade-marks necessary.

Radio and Parts
This is the complete Radio Outfit for $5
(and 2 Quaker trade-marks)

Radio Machine.
50-foot coil insulated wire for lead-in or ground.
2 porcelain insulators.
1 set of headphones, 2400 ohms.
100-foot coil, 7-strand copper wire.

The Quaker Oats Company

407 Louisiana Bldg.
NEW ORLEANS, LA.

---

*First radio set in a quarter-million U.S. homes
was this ingenious Quaker Oats premium in 1921*

THIS MORNING
THE DIONNE QUINS
HAD QUAKER OATS

FOR a few pennies, your children may have the very same brand of oatmeal selected by the experts in charge of the Dionne 'Quins.' They got Quaker Oats even before their first birthday, because it does children such a world of good.

Doctors say everyone, young and old, needs the precious Vitamin B stored so abundantly by Nature in Quaker Oats, to combat nervousness, constipation and poor appetite due to lack of Vitamin B.

ALL PHOTOS WORLD COPYRIGHT 1935, N. E. A. SERVICE, INC.

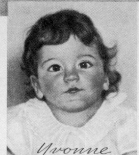

Yvonne

Marie

Annette

Emilie

Cecile

WE SHOW DIONNE PICTURES TO PROVE WHY QUAKER OATS HELPS EVERYONE KEEP FIT*

QUAKER AND MOTHER'S OATS ARE THE SAME

THE same reasons why specialists pick Quaker Oats for the Dionne Quins, apply to you.

For nervousness, constipation, poor appetite know no age limits. They prey on the energy of thousands, young and old, because their diets do not contain enough of the precious 3-purpose Vitamin B so richly supplied by a Quaker Oats breakfast. That's why the whole family should eat Quaker Oats and milk every morning. It supplies plenty of wonderful 3-purpose Vitamin B to combat three symptoms everyone dreads — NERVOUSNESS, CONSTIPATION AND POOR APPETITE due to lack of Vitamin B. And also supplies amazing amounts of food energy! Order at once from your grocer. Either 2½ minute quick-cooking or regular. Quaker and Mother's Oats are the same.

* Where poor condition is due to lack of Vitamin B.

SEND FOR DETAILS OF FREE $10,000 DREAM HOME OFFER!

ASK YOUR GROCER, OR ADDRESS THE QUAKER OATS CO., BOX L, CHICAGO

Tie-in with celebrated Canadian quintuplets in 1935 emphasized Company's educational campaign on vitamins

Billboard was big in 1903

SEND NO MONEY.
SAVE THESE COUPONS

BEAUTIFUL SILVERWARE FREE

An exact reproduction of the teaspoon of our new "Glenwood" silverware which we give free for coupons like this

This is a new method of introducing and advertising our famous cereal foods. It is the most liberal and attractive plan ever placed before the people, and is sure to meet with the hearty approval of every consumer of our products. It gives every person who buys our cereals an opportunity to secure high grade table silverware without cost. Under this offer there is no money to pay and no conditions to comply with, except to send the number of coupons specified.

On the other side you will find a list of our cereals which contain these coupons. There is a coupon in every package and EVERY COUPON HAS A VALUE.

"GLENWOOD SILVERWARE," in design and workmanship, is the equal of the finest silverware made. It is a dainty floral pattern with the popular French gray finish, heavily plated with pure silver, 999 fine, and will last for years. You will be more than pleased with the quality and beautiful design of this ware.

OUR OFFER
1 Teaspoon for 6 Coupons
1 Butter Knife for 12 Coupons   1 Table Fork for 12 Coupons
1 Tablespoon for 12 Coupons   1 Table Knife for 24 Coupons
1 Sugar Shell for 12 Coupons   1 Pickle Fork for 14 Coupons

Save these coupons until you have the required number for the article you want and mail them to us. Be sure to state which piece you want and to write your name and address plainly. All these premiums will be sent absolutely free, charges prepaid.

This coupon is good only in the U. S. A. and expires December 31st, 1907.   (OVER)

Address **The Quaker Oats Company**
1755 Railway Exchange, Chicago, Ill.

Return coupon offer 1907

Quaker Cooker Offer

We have this made for users of Quaker Oats. It is pure aluminum, large and extra-heavy. It cooks the flakes perfectly, while retaining all the flavor and aroma.

Send us our trademark—the picture of the Quaker—from 50c worth of Quaker Oats. Send one dollar with them and we will send this Double Cooker by parcel post.

Cereal Capacity 2¼ Qts.

This is one of our efforts to make this dish the dainty of dainties in every home.

This present cooker offer applies only to the United States. Address The Quaker Oats Company Railway Exchange, Chicago

Quaker Oats
The Luscious Vim-Food

He Invented the Foods Shot from Guns

You owe these puffed foods, and all your delight in them, to Prof. A. P. Anderson.

He was seeking a way to break up starch granules so the digestive juices could get to them.

He was aiming to blast the starch granules to pieces by an explosion of steam.

When he did this, he found that he had created the most enticing cereal foods in existence.

Note the curious process

This drew 700,000 replies   *Used in 1909 and 1933*

Big radio promotion 1934

Movie star tie-in 1936

Huge success: 21 million youngsters received deeds
in 1955 tie to TV show, Sgt. Preston of the Yukon

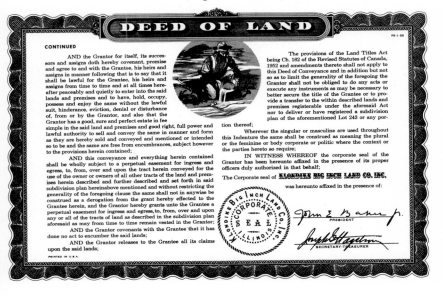

By mid-1960s 80% of Quaker ad budget was in television with Cap'n Crunch the star. Note the giveaway offers one looked, indeed, like an idea with sure-fire customer appeal, Baker, accompanied by a Quaker representative and an attorney, flew next day to the Yukon by chartered plane.

They had no conception of what the country was like. Clad in Brooks Brothers suits and bench-made shoes, but with no adequate overcoats to shelter them from the Arctic winter, they reached Dawson, the once-proud capital of the Territory, after three changes of plane. The few old sourdoughs remaining in the virtual ghost town, scanning this city-slicker elegance, concluded that someone must have found the mother lode. This touched off a rumor that occupied the Territory and part of Alaska the rest of the winter.

Baker had made an appointment with a Queen's counsel by telephone. The barrister had never heard of such a proposition as free one-inch deeds to gold-rush land, and he was not sure that he wanted to waste his time on it. But convinced of the men's sanity—a difficult enough undertaking—he and the Chicago lawyer worked out the details so that the offer would be legal in the Territory and safe in the United States from various state laws against the promotion of questionable securities. From a map they selected a 19.11-acre plot on the Yukon River 12 miles north of Dawson and acquired it for $10,000, passing title to the Big Inch Land Company, Inc., a new corporation that would disperse the land by subdivision. All went well until the Chicago lawyer insisted on seeing with his own eyes what he had bought. Baker agreed that they should visit the property and take motion pictures of it for the enlightenment of Quaker executives, and possibly for advertising and promotional purposes. The river was filled with floating ice, and the Indians had long since put up their canoes for the winter. But now the Northwest Mounted Police came to the rescue. The resident Mountie fancied hmself rather the prototype of Sergeant Preston, and even had a Husky named Yukon King. Since the days of the old radio show he had enjoyed a certain prestige in the Territory. Introduced to the creators of Preston, he volunteered to escort the trio to their land in an open skiff equipped with an outboard motor. There was ice in the river, but it was not yet solid.

"How long," Baker asked as they started north half-frozen, "would a man last in this water?"

"You about thirty-two seconds," the Mountie responded, eyeing the ad man's natty but unprotective garb, "me about eight minutes."

"And what's the temperature now?"

"About ten below zero."

An hour later, approaching the river bank at the new purchase, the outboard struck a submerged rock and sheared a pin. The boat almost swamped. The men climbed ashore with frostbitten feet. They began to take movies. The camera froze. Now they began to drift downstream, hoping to reach Dawson before they froze to death. They had one five-cent candy bar, which they split four ways. At Dawson, the constable thawed them out with 160-proof rum, served as a hot toddy. Leaving Dawson by car, the Chicagoans were about halfway to Whitehorse, some 200 miles, when the car stalled. In trying to repair it, they burned it up. They had all concluded that their adventure was fatal when, in the murky twilight, a gasoline truck appeared—the last vehicle over the road that winter. From Whitehorse, none the worse for their exposure, they went by narrow-gauge railroad to Skagway, then by plane to Juneau, Seattle, and home. Quaker's marketing committee approved the Big Inch promotion.

The land was divided into twenty-one million parcels, each an inch square and properly designated by individual letter and number to differentiate each parcel from its neighbors. The recipient of each deed acknowledged the right of every other owner to an easement permitting him to cross his inch at will. No mineral rights were involved, since the Canadian government reserved all such assets to itself.

Altogether, 21 million deeds were enclosed as free premiums in Quaker Puffed Wheat and Puffed Rice boxes during the spring of 1955. The giveaway was promoted, of course, on the Sergeant Preston show.

A followup promotion cost very little more. Dirt from the Yukon was kedged to Whitehorse, then transported up the Alcan Highway to an orphanage near Anchorage. There the children earned money by making tiny pouches, each filled with an ounce of bona fide Yukon dirt. Twenty million of these were offered as premiums, a fitting complement to the land deed. These also were sold out.

In 1965 the Company received occasional inquiries about the land and whether the deeds had any actual value. To all these the legal department wrote that the "real value of the deeds was based on the romantic appeal of being a property owner in the Great Yukon Territory rather than on any intrinsic value of a one-inch-square piece of property." One correspondent claimed that he had collected 10,800 deeds which he reckoned represented a piece of land 75 feet square. He asked how he might consolidate his holdings into one piece, preferably with riparian rights. The lawyers humorlessly discouraged his attempt. They would have to see the serial numbers to each deed, they replied, to discover whether even two of the inch bits were contiguous. Further, they doubted he could swap parcels with any other owners, since there were 20,989,200 of them, none of whose names or addresses were in possession of the Company.

In the mid-1960s the Claude Hopkins slogan "Shot from Guns" was still in use to advertise the puffed cereals. With great fanfare, the Quaker exhibit at the 1965 New York World's Fair featured the Zacchini Troupe. Four times daily Nancy Zacchini or her husband George was shot from a cannon, soaring above a mammoth Quaker Puffed Cereal package into a net. Henry Crowell might have envied that one.

Chapter 8 * *The Incredible World of Selling*

IN the autumn of 1961 The Quaker Oats Company introduced to the American housewife a new ready-to-eat cereal. Before the first gaily colored package appeared in a single store, Quaker had invested $7 million in the product. Before national distribution was achieved, the gamble—the biggest risk in the company's history to that time—had reached $11 million. Yet nobody really knew whether this expensive infant had stamina enough to survive in the fiercely competitive battle in which 6000 new consumer products appear annually and 80 per cent or more disappear in less than 12 months.

There were scientific indications, of course, that the entry would be a winner. But the Quaker management had the chilling vision of the "scientifically designed from user preference" Edsel automobile, which presumably had been failure-proof, as a reminder that public fancy did not always concur with its proclaimed desires. The new cereal had been created especially to catch the trend toward high-protein-but-low-calorie breakfast foods: zip and go without fat. It had been taste tested, eye-appeal tested, bite-sensation tested, nutrition analyzed, aroma savored: the entire spectrum of sensational and emotional impacts upon the public acceptance of a breakfast food had been analyzed scientifically, and corrections made to overcome every conceivable fault. The container in which the young hopeful was to appear had been virtually psychoanalyzed for color and shape appeal; there were built-in safeguards to protect the cereal against damage in shipping or from shelf deterioration, and carefully devised package dimensions to insure the best possible display on the supermarket shelf. The name had been pretested, sampled, submitted to batteries of consumer interviews in eight different geographic regions to be sure that it was confidence-building, habit-forming, and easy to remember. All these operations required four years of intensive effort within the Company and on the part of hired experts from the outside.

But nobody could say whether Quaker would ever get its $11 million back, let alone a profit on the investment, or whether the cereal would do what it was supposed to do—give Quaker for the first time a really significant place among the leaders in the ready-to-eat cereal market. The sales of the old reliable Quaker Oats still held up—in fact, with the population increase sales expanded about 4 per cent a year—but the rate of growth of the ready-to-eats was faster. Until 1947, hot cereals commanded more than half of the U.S. breakfast-cereal market; by 1965 this had been trimmed by the ready-to-eats to only 40 per cent. So Quaker was anxious to move with the times. The Company had, of course, marketed the very first ready-to-eat puffs in 1905. Most of the ready-to-eats were made from a mixture of ingredients that were the exclusive formula of the manufacturer but actually differed very little one from another. The infinitesimal difference, however, was everything. A batter was cooked, toasted or baked, and then milled into assorted sizes and shapes simulating stars, balls, pillows, alphabet letters, flakes, biscuits, or any other shape somebody thought might sell. Hence the astonishing variety, some to survive, most to succumb quickly.

Quaker had taken into this jungle a number of safaris that ended in frustrations—Toasted Wheat Flakes in 1907, Corn Puffs in 1912, Quaker Quakies in 1921, Crackels in 1924, to name the most significant. It also had acquired by purchase a steady seller in Muffets, a shredded wheat, during 1927. But in 1961 Quaker, for all its leadership in the puffed-cereal line, was essentially a minor factor in ready-to-eats. Its big market, and far more than half its income from cereals (though by no means half its total income) was in the old hot perennials—Quaker Oats and Mother's Oats.

Further, as a matter of policy, the Scots-bred management was committed to modest launching fees for any new endeavor. Despite its tradition for aggressive advertising of an established line, Quaker had never put up big risk capital on a new trademark. The business had grown through the years by aggressive—but reasonably frugal—merchandising and selling, and by the acquisition of established brand names such as Aunt Jemima, Muffets, Ken-L Ration, and Puss 'n Boots, all of which had been brought along to leadership in their respective fields. Management policy required any new product—cereal, cat food, or chemical—to pay its own way, to earn sufficient acceptance market by market to warrant further expansion. Thus the original budget for the new high-protein cereal was an unheard-of $5 million. When expenses passed $7 million, Quaker's management had begun to experience the facts of life about the intricate science and outright speculation of product introduction. When the total cost had crossed $11 million, even the most optimistic advocates of keeping up with the battle for survival on the supermarket shelf were appalled at the commitment Quaker had undertaken. Old-timers remembered a few disasters of the past, when whimsical vagaries had knocked out expensive promotions. Even the early master, Claude Hopkins, had erred. His first campaign for Quaker Oats had assumed that Quaker controlled most of the trade and therefore he needed only to convince users to consume more of the product. The assumption was wrong and the program failed. His next argument adjured users of other brands to switch to Quaker Oats, with great success. Also well-remembered was the razor edge of difference between acceptance and rejection of a brand name. When new milling methods permitted Quaker to introduce a fast-cooking oatmeal after World War I as Two-Minute Oats, it did not sell, but as Quick Quaker Oats it was a hit.

Fortunately for everyone, the new cereal, named *Life*, performed as hoped. It was an instant success. By the end of the first year it had achieved a significant share of the total national market for ready-to-eats and was returning a profit on the promotional investment.

Times had changed since the successful launching of Quaker Puffed Rice on a total budget of $50,000 and the recovery of the development costs in a single year. When Life was born, there were 300,000 food stores in the United States, but the 37,000 (12 per cent) classed as supermarkets did two-thirds of the total business. Thus the supermarket was crucial to the existence of any cereal, and most supermarkets then carried between 6000 and 8000 items. Their shelves jam-packed, managers were reluctant to find space for anything new except a proved winner. The first sales of any new product were no clue to acceptance. Resale was the measure.

What the supermarket required was a constant flow in and out fast enough to warrant restocking in full-case quantities thirty or forty times a year. Only with such volume was the precious shelf space justified. To achieve national distribution of Life, Quaker had to prove in key tests that Life was a fast repeater. Hence the exhaustive safeguards against failure, the endless market analysis.

As related earlier, Quaker's second generation of management had in 1922 devised its own fast-turnover inventory system, anticipating the new marketing trend. John Stuart's motto, after the catastrophe of 1920, was simple: avoid inventory gluts. The day of loading the trade was ended. The trend was revealed in 1916 when in Memphis, Tennessee, the Piggly Wiggly chain had eliminated clerks, imposed cash-and-carry self-service, displayed goods on open shelves after the fashion of the dime stores, and moved the cash register to a checkout point near the door. The result of these economies was cheaper retail prices. Piggly Wiggly was by no means the first chain: The Great Atlantic and Pacific Tea Company had begun the specialty trend in 1859 with tea and spices, expanding to general groceries in 1865. Others followed quickly. But they were much like the privately owned stores of their era until 1912, when A & P went cash-and-carry, cutting out the middleman and establishing central purchasers and regional warehouses. The independents fought the trend with associations and cooperatives, but gradually lost the battle of price.

Then in 1932 The Big Bear, a catch-all with eleven departments which sold everything from gum to go-carts and had a turnover of $3,800,000 annual sales on a total capital investment of less than $100,000, launched the age of the supermarket. The scheme mushroomed, forcing most independents and small chains to adopt supermarket self-service methods. With the flight of millions of young marrieds to the suburbs after World War II, the supermarkets followed the population. They installed huge parking lots and designed their markets with shopper convenience in view. New postwar products in endless streams filled display cases designed for frozen foods, ready-mixes, prepackaged meats and vegetables, the shelves arranged to encourage wives to depart from their grocery lists and fill the new shopping carts with "impulse" purchases. The supermarket shopper became known as "a woman with $20 and 20 minutes, a baby in the shopping cart and two more in the car outside." Embroiled in child care, the PTA, politics, the bridge club, or a full or part-time job, women demanded fast, fast relief from kitchen drudgery. The meal that cooked itself—or that the kids might cook—was what the housewife wanted. And the same for her dog and cat.

No longer would a helpful clerk look in a reference book and tell his customer what a pimento was, or the difference between tuna and albacore, and certainly not how to bake a TV dinner. The merchandise sold if the customer had been presold by advertising or promotion before entering the store, or the package—or the novelty of its display—induced its purchase on a sudden impulse. Without advertising and promotion, then, it was dead. A manufacturer rash enough to change the shape or color of his box, or the identifying trademark, risked having the shopper's eye pass over the unfamiliar newness in the rush of sweeping her gaze over 6000 to 8000 items. For the store manager, any item that did not sell fast was replaced by a more popular money-maker: he could not afford loyalty to any supplier or salesman.

Claude C. Hopkins, when he was creating Quaker Oats advertising, made this appeal in *Ladies' Home*

Journal in 1911: "The love of oats is a life long asset. It should be started early, nurtured continuously, encouraged and fixed." For the sophisticated housewife of 1966, Hopkins might have amplified his formula to reassure her on the cholesterol count, amino acids, trace minerals, vitamins, and calories. Moreover, how to prepare it in two minutes flat; or, better yet, how to get Junior to fix it for himself.

Premiums in the package, boxtop or label offers, coupons to be mailed for valuable or useful goods or kiddy gadgets, have been the lifeblood of Quaker merchandising from the company's earliest days. Ferdinand Schumacher's double boiler and Henry Parsons Crowell's huge pottery distributions have already been mentioned. The big deal in 1901 was a "fortune telling calendar in fourteen colors" for 5¢ in stamps and a Quaker Oats label. The double-boiler offer, repeated in 1915 for $1 plus five cutouts of the "man in Quaker garb" sold 700,000. By 1928, the annual chinaware premiums had reached 155 carloads of 7500 sets each; by 1939, more than 5 per cent of all the chinaware manufactured in America was used as giveaways. A significant evidence of the power of sets of dishes, which must be accumulated one at a time, is revealed in the promotion of Mother's Oats. In-the-box chinaware offers have for fifty years been almost the only sales stimulant given this product, yet it continues to sell in large quantities.

After World War II, due to the high exposure of television, almost every American family had joined the boxtop bonanza, which had some elements of a national pastime like the collection of trading stamps. Quaker's harvest of boxtops sent by the American public in response to premium offers numbered 2,500,000 a year. These "send for" premiums were usually designed to be self-liquidating, since experienced advertisers have long diverted as little of the promotion dollar as possible away from consumer product advertising. The cash asked for the premium paid not only for it but also the cost of postage and handling. It had to be a tremendous bargain, however, or people did not send for it. The successes were those premiums offered at a much lower price, because of the huge quantities purchased by the advertiser, than a housewife could possibly buy the same thing for in a store.

A celebrated Quaker promotion of 1921, when radio was an infant, was a crytal set made to be mounted on the round Quaker Oats carton. This paraphernalia cost $1 plus a boxtop. For $5 plus two labels, a kit complete with earphones was supplied. These were the earliest radios to enter thousands of American homes.

To be effective, a premium should be a novelty unavailable at the stores and preferably have an association with the product, such as the Aunt Jemima rag dolls and chinaware cited in Chapter 9.

Network radio from the beginning cultivated the children's market as its very own. Cowboy star Roy Rogers got into the act when he sang "The giant of the cereals is Quaker Oats" and galloped his horse Trigger through several years of Quaker-sponsored Western radio dramas. "Delicious, nutritious, makes you feel ambitious," the lyrics further advised. During the 1930s the air was filled with Quaker "Hey kids!" appeals, since then transferred to television without appreciable change. A radio show based on the famous dog, Rin Tin Tin, extolled the puffed cereals. Heavyweight boxing champion Max Baer flexed his muscles in comic strips and carried over into radio a three-boxtop offer of a "How to Fight" booklet with which 200,000 youngsters worked off their aggression. Collateral premiums on the Baer show were a body-measuring tape for one boxtop, an iron-grip hand exerciser for three tops, a wrist protector, an elastic muscle builder. These attractions unfortunately promoted a ready-to-eat cereal called Crackels, which failed to take hold, proving once again that ingenious promotion alone is not enough. The product must have essential value in its own right.

Among particularly successful premiums (although not with mothers) was a boxtop-plus-25¢ offer of a box of "Crazy Rings." They were crazy all right, and so drove mothers. The novelty rings mounted whistles, sirens, and bells, the joy and bedlam of 300,000 homes. Mothers also recoiled at a snap cannon, made as a cutout in puffed-cereal boxes in 1964, which made a sound like a pistol shot. Another success was a set of cookie cutters which stamped out famous motion-picture animated-cartoon animals. Over 500,000 were distributed.

The affluent society of the post–World War II years led to a more expensive line of premiums. An electric coffee maker required a certificate from a package of Quaker Oats or Mother's Oats, plus $5.50, and drew one of the greatest returns in history for higher-priced items: 400,000 responses. An electric griddle brought 250,000 returns to Aunt Jemima in 1959 at $10 plus a coupon. But a simple stove-top pancake griddle for $1 plus label was so ignored that 30,000 unused premiums were warehoused. A big item was a bathroom scale ($4.95) promoting Puffed Wheat and Rice, emphasizing the diet characteristics of these cereals. A huge success was a 1964 booklet on how to treat a baby sitter and what to expect of the sitter. But the biggest puller, in terms of dollars, was the offer, just before Christmas 1961, of a $25 Lionel electric train set for $11.95 and two Quaker or Mother's Oats tops. It drew 500,000 responses in less than a month. Since coupons, boxtops, contests, and premium offers for all U.S. merchandising had become a billion-dollar-a-year business by the 1960s, companies sprang up to specialize in this market alone.

The mechanics of promotions were expensive but simple, from Quaker's point of view. An outside agency was employed to conduct all contests and audit all boxtop returns, except cash coupons. Contest winners' entries were never published, lest a deluge of letters claim to have submitted identical or superior entries. The mere mechanics of giveaways by the mid-1960s cost The Quaker Oats Company around $800,000 a year.

Money coupons were the responsibility of Quaker's own controller. His office processed about 5 million redemptions in 1965. After auditing, checks were sent to the grocers for the redemption cost, plus handling fees and postage. To big stores, these checks may total hundreds of dollars in a single month. The Quaker coupons, ranging in trade value from five to fifty cents, were printed generally in newspapers and magazines or inserted in the product packages. Often the container carried a notice of the saving to be found inside, called a "spotmark" in the trade. These marks act as silent salesmen at the retail outlet.

Premium offers occasionally have their lighter side, though not for the legal department. In 1964, a woman wrote complaining that she had waited several weeks for an ordered premium. During this interval, she stated, she had become very nervous, and her peace of mind could be restored only if the company sent her $5000 by return mail. This letter, like every other complaint, was investigated by the lawyers, but no payment was made.

After three-quarters of a century of experience with give-aways, The Quaker Oats Company's counsel had encountered almost every type of eccentric.

Women in search of a bargain sometimes would react in odd ways at the supermarket. Scientific studies showed that cans marked 6 for 99¢ (16½¢ each) actually outsold the identical merchandise shelved at 15¢ each, or a "bargain" offer of two for 31¢. Women took more goods from an untidily loaded shelf heralded by a crayon-scribbled sign that said "Special today" than from a neat pile proclaimed by a printed placard, although the two were equally "special." Successful merchandisers cater to these quirks.

The best display of merchandise was found to be in the center of an aisle, where the shopper must detour around it. Next best was the end of a busy aisle near the checkout counter. Any location that broke the monotony of the long lines of shelving held the shopper's eye. Quaker salesmen sought such prime locations, allocated sparingly by supermarket managers, to give needed display exposure to laggard items and to introduce new products. It was found that when a shopper pushed her cart down the aisles of a supermarket, her eyes were on any one item for one-fifth of a second, then passed on—unless something about a package or display held her gaze long enough for the buying impulse to operate. How the merchandise was displayed; more important, how it was presold by advertising were the differences between success and failure.

To get merchandise onto the shelf in the first instance required another kind of sales procedure: convincing the central buyer for the chain or the local store manager with the sales results in test markets. Seasonal extra-profit temptations, trade allowances for local advertising costs, a bonus of free goods with a large order were all part of the repertoire, and incentives offered to one customer must be available to all.

Speed of turnover exposed the manufacturer to risk that his products became out of stock through slow reordering techniques. To prevent such, Quaker installed strategic central warehouses within a few hours by truck of most of its customers. The largest—the central buying warehouses of supermarket chains—bought on an automatic reorder schedule, knowing to within a few cases how much of any Quaker product sold in their stores in a given time. Quaker supplied its products in these precise amounts at regular intervals, minimizing storage space and time required at the customer's end. The automatic reorder procedure provided Quaker a steady flow of cash, since most retailers pay promptly in order to get the 2 per cent discount offered for cash within ten days of receipt of invoice. In most cases, it is the supermarkets' margin of profit.

Most of the food industry's new products were developed in the laboratory and then taken over by the merchandisers for naming, packaging, promotion, and marketing. The Quaker Oats Company's most successful promotion in the decade of the 1960s reversed the order. A promotion was evolved and a cereal developed to match the specifications marketing men drew up.

The trend of the early 1960s toward presweetened ready-to-eat cereals for the children's market eliminated the sugar bowl from the breakfast table, pleasing mothers who were inclined toward low-calorie foods for the adults in the house. Quaker had no pre-sweetened product designed to appeal directly to the whimsies of the under-ten age group which, with the population explosion, had become a market of 40 million hungry mouths.

Market researchers determined that the under-tens much preferred a crunch food. At the same time, the advertising department was developing a trademark strong in juvenile appeal; a salty, bumbling comic old sea captain, an animated-cartoon character surrounded by a fascinating coterie of friends, both human and piscatorial. They named both the central character and the product he represented *Cap'n Crunch*, the ultimate in identity between trademark and product virtue. All that remained was development of a product to live up to the name preceding it. Research and Development took over and proceeded to find the optimum of flavor and crunchiness in a ready-to-eat. What evolved was a corn-oats extruded, pillow-shaped kernel. Toasted and lacquered with sugar, it stayed crisp in milk.

As the first experimental batches of Cap'n Crunch cereal were emerging from the extruders, out of Jay Ward's animation studio in Hollywood came an animated-cartoon commercial featuring the antics of Cap'n Crunch, the comic sea captain conceived by Quaker's advertising men. In September 1963, a cartoon commercial featuring the visage of the animated hero appeared on local stations in six cities. The critical period of test marketing was under way. Sales took off so rapidly that pilot-plant production lagged. A full-scale Cap'n Crunch plant was constructed in Quaker's huge mill at Cedar Rapids, and marketing was expanded to a national scale. By 1965, Cap'n Crunch was number two in the pre-sweetened market of under-ten-agers—in New York and Chicago it was number one.

On the supermarket shelves, Crunch outsold 55 competitors. Cap'n Crunch Fan Clubs sprang up all over the country—an unexpected windfall. Youngsters wrote The Quaker Oats Company to confess that the cereal was their favorite "secret snack," to be smuggled into school and eaten surreptitiously. What mother could possibly resist it at the supermarket?

Chapter 9 * *The First Ready-Mix*

THE place is Disneyland, California, the year 1965. The building, large and imposing, replacing an earlier structure erected in 1955, is southern colonial in style. Its doors open onto a bright patio, and from the comfort of this terrace diners watch the hordes of youngsters relive the days of Tom Sawyer on Disneyland's reproduction of a segment of the Mississippi River. The *Mark Twain*, a giant stern-wheeler, and its companion the frigate *Columbia*, course the waters with teeming cargoes of tourists. River rafts roll in the steamboats' wakes. The diners on the patio are eating Aunt Jemima's famous pancakes, almost as much an American institution as Tom Sawyer.

Nearly three-quarters of a century separates the opening of the sparkling kitchen at Disneyland (the original restaurant on the same site had served pancakes to 1,600,000 guests in eight years) and the day in 1889 when two men who knew practically nothing about cooking hovered over a kerosene stove in Saint Joseph, Missouri, to experiment with the first packaged pancake flour, the first ready-mix of any kind ever developed. Ingenuity created the product. But sheer inspiration is responsible for its having been named Aunt Jemima, thereby laying the groundwork for a series of advertising campaigns which created a legend, endowed the product with an appealing warmth, and established for the pioneer pancake mix generations of customers. Early-day advertising men literally brought Aunt Jemima to life, and chose the sparkling Nancy Green to impersonate their trademark. She gave herself completely to the role, and for three decades she *was* Aunt Jemima, both to the public and in her own mind. In thousands of personal appearances she embroidered the romantic legend, captivating audiences with her tales of the past and transforming the slave-born Nancy Green into Aunt Jemima Green who, according to the legend, had also been a slave. Recalling her own girlhood, Nancy Green spun countless anecdotes of Aunt Jemima's early days on a plantation "somewhere in the Deep South." She became one of the world's best-known women, and Aunt Jemima Pancake Mix became a staple item in kitchens throughout America. The trademark meant quality, friendliness, good will, and good eating. Aunt Jemima's pancakes weren't just pancakes. They had personality, and that personality was in great measure attributable to the imaginative Nancy Green.

The American Negro has always represented in American life the acme of the culinary art, respected as in France are the chefs who belong to the Société Gastronomique. Traditional southern hospitality in slave times was made possible by the legendary genius of the Negroes as cooks and chefs. Long before the Civil War the Negro had become entrenched in folklore as the ultimate expert in cookery. From its first days, Aunt Jemima pancake flour capitalized on this identity so rooted in the American culture. And in each generation, Aunt Jemima has reflected the advancing status of the Negro. The first Aunt Jemima, as portrayed by Nancy Green, took pride in being the white man's valued servant. In the next generation, the overweight, good-humored but unsophisticated Anna Robinson established the Negro cook as a personage in her own right. She carried forward the tradition from the Chicago Century of Progress Exposition in 1933 to the days of television, and was the dinner companion of celebrities at New York's El Morocco and the Waldorf. In the mid-twentieth century, Edith Wilson and other show personalities completed the transition. They were singers, entertainers and gracious hostesses like Arlene Lewis at Disneyland, far removed from the days of servitude and lending fresh dignity to the image of the Negro as America's unrivaled culinary expert.

Together the three generations of Negro women who have personified Aunt Jemima span the entire history of processed foods and represent vividly the emancipation of the American housewife from the drudgery of virtual slavery in her kitchen to the ease of food preparation in today's wonderland of easy-to-cooks, ready-mixes, ready-to-serves, and frozen prepared foods at prices every housewife can afford. This emancipation begins with Aunt Jemima.

More accurately, the first ready-mix begins with Chris L. Rutt, an editorial writer on the Saint Joseph, Missouri *Gazette,* and a friend in the milling business, Charles G. Underwood.

Saint Joseph, Missouri, had many claims to grandeur before the arrival of Aunt Jemima. The frontier community had been for a generation the jumping-off place for the covered-wagon caravans that crossed the Oregon, Mormon, and Santa Fe trails to populate the West. The town had been the eastern terminus of the Pony Express, which galloped the mail to California in eight days. Great cattle pens were there, and the homestead of the children's poet Eugene Field. And because of the grains which teemed on its rich Missouri River Valley bottomlands, Saint Joseph had long been one of the most important milling centers on the frontier. The earliest mill (about 1858) used the water power of Black Snake Creek to grind a flour carried by the pioneers on their way West. Thus the town prospered and by 1888 the mill had expanded into a modern plant with capacity of 800 barrels a day. But now overproduction, and the abatement of western migration via wagon, had caused evil times and several mill reorganizations. All this would be unimportant here except that in one of its critical moments, Chris Rutt, the newspaperman, hungry for a better life, bought the property with Underwood and organized the Pearl Milling Company.

Local competition soon convinced the partners that they could not survive merely on the sale of conventional milling products. They needed something exclusive and novel. What did almost everybody eat? Pancakes. What consumed a lot of flour? Pancakes. What was difficult to mix with any consistency from one batch to the next? Pancake batter. Therefore, the partners reasoned, their fortunes would be made if they developed a self-rising pancake flour that even a bride could use to make good pancakes every time. The fact that nobody had ever heard of such a thing gave the inquisitive newspaperman all the stubbornness he needed to persevere in the face of many disappointments. Batch after batch of experimental batter was griddled on an old kerosene stove in Rutt's home on Sylvanie Street. Finally a recipe was evolved that seemed to the inventors to make light, fluffy hotcakes from hard wheat flour, corn flour, phosphate of lime, soda, and a bit of salt.

Anxious to confirm their hopes by the opinion of a

disinterested third party, they undertook one of the earliest consumer research programs. They approached Purd B. Wright, the town librarian, known locally for his wit—and also for his candor—and asked him to taste the product.

One afternoon, as Wright described the event later, he was escorted by Underwood to the Rutt kitchen. A ready-mixed concoction lay in a bowl. As Wright and Underwood watched, Rutt added milk and beat the mixture quickly into a batter. By now the griddle was hot, and circles of bubbly yellow batter were ladled out and browned evenly on both sides. A neat stack, laced with melted butter and sugar syrup, was set before the tester.

"I ate the first perfected Aunt Jemima pancake," Purd reported, "and pronounced it good." His enthusiasm was so hearty, in fact, that Rutt was moved to break out a bottle of Missouri corn whiskey with which the trio toasted the world's first self-rising pancake.

The first commercial batch of Aunt Jemima was packaged in paper sacks. The run used the following ingredients: 100 pounds of hard winter wheat white flour, 100 pounds of yellow corn flour, 7½ pounds of phosphates, 2¾ pounds of baking soda, 2 pounds of salt. The Aunt Jemima name had not yet appeared, and the novelty had no name at all except the generic description of exactly what it was: self-rising pancake flour.

Now Chris Rutt set out to find a trademark. He wanted the name to reflect the festive spirit that had always been associated with the pancake. One of the very earliest forms of human food, the pancake was known to man in the Stone Age as a simple ground grain cake cooked on hot stones. With the advent of voluntary Lenten shriving observances in A.D. 461, the pancake became associated with the celebration preceding the holy season of Lent. When in the ninth century canon law prescribed the Lenten fast for all Roman Catholic Christians, the pancake became even more popular as a substitute for meat, and in eleventh-century England the Shrove Tuesday tradition developed. At the toll of the church bell, townspeople went to confession to shrive themselves of their sins before the holy days, the act preceded by a rollicking feast. By the thirteenth century the Shrove Tuesday pancake feast had become a tradition in Britain and, with variations, in parts of Germany and Scandinavia. Many rhymes and jingles accompanied the feasting, among them:

> Shrove Tuesday, Shrove Tuesday
> 'Fore Jack went to plow
> His mother made pancakes,
> She scarcely knew how.
> She tossed them, she turned them,
> She made them so black
> With soot from the chimney
> They poisoned poor Jack

With its religious connotations, the shriving cake soon became imbedded in religious custom and took on symbolic emphasis. The egg in it represented rebirth, the flour was the staff of life, the salt represented wholesomeness, the milk innocence.

The symbol Chris Rutt sought for his self-rising pancake flour was an identification with the best tradition of southern cooking. One evening in the autumn of 1889 he attended the local vaudeville house. On the bill was a pair of black-face comedians, Baker & Farrell, a characteristic of that day. This was the era of the minstrel show, with dialect which then passed for humor, and of teams of white entertainers blackened with burnt cork who cracked alleged Negro jokes. This era survived into the 1930s and reached its demise with singer Al Jolson and the team of Amos 'n Andy. The show-stopper of the Baker & Farrell act was a jazzy, rhythmic New Orleans style cakewalk to a tune called "Aunt Jemima" which Baker performed in the apron and red-bandanna headband of the traditional southern cook.

Here was the image Rutt sought! Here was southern hospitality personified. He appropriated not only the song's title for the name of his pancake flour, but also the likeness of the southern "mammy" emblazoned on the lithograph posters advertising the Baker & Farrell act. He put the name *Aunt Jemima* on a one-pound paper sack as a trademark, along with a wide-eyed, grinning caricature of Aunt Jemima in what today would be described as living color. Now he was in business.

Unfortunately, other elements of a merchandising success were not within Rutt's means or those of his very silent partner, who evidently was an expert miller but no promoter. The Pearl Milling Company invited the public to see its display at the New Era Exposition in Saint Joseph that autumn, but there was little or no additional advertising. The exposure was not broad enough to introduce the product even locally. Rutt and Underwood soon ran out of capital and the Pearl Milling Company expired.

The partners, however, retained their valuable asset in the failure and, a few months later, with renewed optimism and a new moneyman, they organized the Aunt Jemima Manufacturing Company, with Underwood's brother Bert as financier and promoter. Rutt meanwhile had returned to his job on the *Gazette,* and Charles

Underwood had found employment for his skills with the R. T. Davis Milling Company, the largest flour miller in town. Bert Underwood registered the Aunt Jemima trademark, but had no better luck than the originators in promoting the pancake flour. The novelty, about the beginning of 1890, passed by sale to the Davis mill, which had large manufacturing facilities, money, and a reputation throughout the Missouri Valley with the wholesale and grocery trades. R. T. Davis was a fifty-year veteran of milling in Saint Joseph at the time he acquired Aunt Jemima, and he knew what to do with his acquisition. First he improved the flavor and texture of the product by adding rice flour and corn sugar, then he simplified the ready-mix principle by adding powdered milk—an extremely significant simplification. The housewife needed to add only water.

Davis was a master at fashioning publicity. It was he who envisioned a living Aunt Jemima to advertise his wares. He sent requests to all his food-broker friends to be on the lookout for a Negro woman who might exemplify southern hospitality, and who was a sufficiently poised and talented actress to demonstrate the self-rising pancake mix at fairs, expositions, and festivals. If the public saw a replica of the trademark alive and charming, they might be persuaded to try the newfangled product on the strength of its apparent origin in a famous southern kitchen. Here was a new advertising concept: to bring a trademark to life. Since that moment of Davis' inspiration, scores of advertisers have introduced living impersonations of their trademarks, particularly since the advent of animated television commercials.

Davis' request to the food brokers met a response from Charles Jackson, a Chicago wholesaler. A Negro woman in the employ of his friend Judge Walker, he wrote, was probably exactly what Davis had in mind. She was a magnificent cook, an attractive woman of outgoing nature and friendly personality, gregarious in the extreme. Her name was Nancy Green. She had been born fifty-nine years earlier on a plantation in Montgomery County, Kentucky, a slave. Utterly unself-conscious, she loved crowds and loved to talk about her own slave days, her stories no doubt partly apocryphal but nonetheless entertaining. Here seemed to be the Aunt Jemima image brought to life.

Davis called on her, confirmed Jackson's appraisal, and made a contract whereby Miss Green worked exclusively for Aunt Jemima the remainder of her life. Her role in the company was so effective and so important that she survived several changes of management, company bankruptcies, and reorganizations. Her debut in her lifetime role took place at the Columbian Exposition, the Chicago World's Fair of 1893. She presided over a pancake demonstration which proved to be almost as gala an attraction as the flamboyant Midway's belly dancer Little Egypt.

Accompanying Davis to the Fair was Purd Wright, the original one-man test panel and librarian, now advertising manager for Aunt Jemima. He built a display booth for the company's milling products in the Fair's food building. The booth resembled a giant flour barrel, 24 feet long and 16 feet in diameter. Doors were mounted in the side of the barrel, and the interior was fitted out as a reception parlor in which to entertain visitors. Outside, near the barrel's front door, Aunt Jemima presided at her griddle, cooking pancakes for the crowd, trading greetings, singing songs and telling stories of the Old South. Her routine was a lively combination of folklore, wisdom, and fun. Some of her script was drawn from the words of the old vaudeville Aunt Jemima song, some from memories of her own plantation days, and much from her imagination. From this complicated patter emerged the image of a wise old cook from the Deep South of Civil War times, who had brought her secret pancake recipe to a benighted northland through the courtesy of the R. T. Davis Milling Company. The crowds loved the fantasy and many took it for gospel.

Wright devised a souvenir lapel button to pass out to visitors who jammed the aisles for a glimpse of Aunt Jemima. On this emblem was the likeness of Aunt Jemima with the caption "I'se in town, honey." Her audience took up the phrase and it became the catchline of the Fair. Wherever Miss Green went, crowds followed her. Special police had to be recruited to monitor the exhibit. Davis claimed later that more than 50,000 orders for his pancake flour were placed at the Fair by merchants from all over the world.

In recognition of her triumph, Fair officials awarded Aunt Jemima a medal and certificate, lauding her showmanship as Pancake Queen. The personality of Aunt Jemima completely absorbed the identity of Miss Green. She was Aunt Jemima the remainder of her life. When not on tour, she lived on Chicago's South Side, where she was also a celebrity, and helped found Olivet Church, now one of the largest Baptist congregations in the world. On September 24, 1923, Nancy Green was struck by a car on East 46th Street on Chicago's South Side and died of her injuries.

After the 1893 Fair, Davis decided to capitalize on Aunt Jemima's triumph by publishing a souvenir booklet. Purd Wright was the creator of this pamphlet, entitled "The Life of Aunt Jemima, the Most Famous Colored Woman in the World." He prepared an organized narrative from the apocrypha told by Nancy Green concerning her plantation life in the Old South, along with more factual material on her personal triumph at the Fair, the resulting honors and medals bestowed upon her and on her self-rising pancakes, and copies of the tributes of press and public. One anecdote explained how Aunt Jemima had saved the mustache and the dignity of her employer, one Colonel Higbee, whose plantation stretched along the banks of the Mississippi River. When the Union Army arrived, the northern villains were about to tear the colonel's handsome mustache out by the roots when Aunt Jemima offered the troops her pancakes, and in the excitement the colonel was able to escape. Another story: a southern officer and his adjutant, separated from their troops after a battle, reached Jemima's cabin door dejected and exhausted. She served them her pancakes, miraculously restoring their strength. They spread the word and hundreds of soldiers came by to sample her wares, carrying away the story of her skills. One of these tasters returned after the war with some friends from up North to prove to them that Aunt Jemima made the most delicious pancakes in the world. They persuaded Aunt Jemima to go north and share with the world her celebrated formula.

Salesmen for the Davis Company drummed the grocery trade in the principal cities, booking orders for Aunt Jemima Pancake Flour and arranging for one of the earliest organized campaigns of sales promotion. When the trade was stocked, billboard posters heralded the arrival of Aunt Jemima in person with the caption—"I'se in town, honey." Her demonstrations in grocery stores of how to cook a self-rising mix taught an entire generation of housewives that some forms of cooking could be simple and made them clamor for others, thus starting the procession toward ready-mixes and other prepared food products. The era of "convenience" foods had begun.

Nancy Green carried her crusade against kitchen drudgery back and forth across her native land but she refused to go to the Paris Exposition of 1900, fearing the ocean voyage. "I was born in this country," she demurred, "and here I'll die, not somewhere betwixt here and somewhere else."

Davis followed the lead of other cereal-product manufacturers by offering boxtop premiums, one of which became the most famous in merchandising history. For one trademark off the carton and twenty-five cents, which paid for all the costs, customers received an Aunt Jemima rag doll. Literally almost every city child owned one. The rag doll evolved from an earlier stunt of 1895, when Aunt Jemima began to be distributed in cartons rather than in one-pound sacks. To popularize the new container, Davis printed on it a cutout paper doll of Aunt Jemima. The promotion was tremendously successful. A decade later, when the company was rising from one of its bankruptcies, the Aunt Jemima rag doll emerged, renewing itself year after year until an entire family of rag dolls had been created, featuring Uncle Mose and twin moppets Diana and Wade. Just before The Quaker Oats Company acquired Aunt Jemima, the rag doll was offered again in an advertisement in a women's magazine. The flood of requests almost swamped the sponsor. Almost every woman who answered the advertisement said that she had been raised on the Aunt Jemima dolls and now wanted them for her daughter.

Latter-day promotions have distributed four million sets of Aunt Jemima–Uncle Mose salt and pepper shakers in polystyrene, and 200,000 dolls in vinyl plastic. A cookie-jar premium shaped like Aunt Jemima sold 150,000. Another premium sought by more than a million housewives was a plastic syrup pitcher.

The Aunt Jemima merchandising plan lost its master hand when R. T. Davis died in 1900. His death almost proved the end of the enterprise he had organized with such devotion and skill. For the next twenty years, the Aunt Jemima business no sooner recovered from one disaster than another came along to engulf it. First, R. T. Davis' immediate heir soon found the company in bankruptcy. Then the receivers for the defunct company, seeking to realize some quick cash, sold quantities of spoiled pancake flour and lost still more money making good on their mistake.

In 1903 Robert Clark, former general manager of the R. T. Davis Milling Company, came in as the head of a reorganization. Clark in time put the business back in order and in 1914 it was renamed The Aunt Jemima Mills Company; just prior to World War I, sales were the highest in its history. As a wartime measure, the government restricted the domestic use of wheat flour. The Aunt Jemima management resorted to an emergency blend of flours unacceptable to the public. Sales declined alarmingly and Clark realized that unusual efforts would be required to restore Aunt Jemima's prestige. A legion of new customers was sorely needed for the postwar Aunt Jemima product, restored to its traditional quality.

The advertising campaign that achieved this goal came from the gifted pen of James Webb Young, manager in Chicago for the J. Walter Thompson Company. The series became known as the legend of Aunt Jemima, with each advertisement a fascinating narrative, spinning out a choice bit of Aunt Jemima lore. This exciting departure made its debut in national magazines in the fall of 1919 and deeply influenced future creative technique in American advertising.

Jim Young was born in Covington, Kentucky, the son of a Mississippi riverboat captain. His father's sympathies were with the North, and he had helped transport Federal troops at the siege of Vicksburg. His mother, on the other hand, was a fiery partisan of the Confederacy. From both parents Young acquired a sense of the uniqueness of the South—its traditions and its folklore. Above all, he acquired an intimate knowledge of its people. His father's stories, which often revolved around what he called the "western waters," the Mississippi and Ohio rivers, roadways Mark Twain celebrated in *Life on the Mississippi* and *Huckleberry Finn*, invariably involved the fascinating lore of the southern Negro. "I decided," Young has remarked, "to develop a series on what you might call the Americana of the Deep South. I think I can say that the series was the first of what I could call 'the romantic school.' It was a departure from nearly all the advertising of the day."

Young's advertisements were illustrated by N. C. Wyeth, an eminent artist, and reproduced in four colors. One carried the heading "The Night the *Emily Dunstan* Burned" and showed an awe-stricken Aunt Jemima watching a Mississippi riverboat burn to the water's edge. The text told how the grateful passengers found their way ashore to her cabin where they were delighted by Aunt Jemima's pancakes. Another told of "The Visitors from the North," and revealed four enterprising gentlemen threading their way to Aunt Jemima's cabin door to negotiate with her for her famous pancake recipe. Finally, another in the series told how Aunt

Jemima became convinced and went North to begin a new career working for the Yankee millers and thus came to belong to the whole United States.

Young's arresting advertisements, completely novel in approach, were an immediate success. Millions of new customers responded by welcoming Aunt Jemima's pancakes to the family table. Young's creations continued to appear long after his retirement in 1929.

Disaster, seemingly never far off from this enterprise, occurred again with the commodity market collapse of 1920. The trade refused delivery on commitments made at the higher price levels, and the company had to write off millions in losses, draining off all of the working capital of the Aunt Jemima Mills. It did not have reserves comparable to the ones that enabled The Quaker Oats Company to weather the same storm.

Robert Clark tried to rescue his company by attracting new investors. Many with faith in the enterprise, including people in its advertising agency, invested fresh capital. But the flood of demands from creditors and other stockholders could not be contained, and the shareowners elected George E. Porter chairman of the board and gave him complete control of finances. Robert Clark was permitted to remain as president, though his actions were subject to approval of the board of directors. It was an intolerable situation for Clark, an entrepreneur of vigor and imagination, then in his later years. The unhappy situation continued under this dual control with Robert Clark nominally in charge but actual control exercised by a three-member finance committee led by Porter. Virtual control of the company and its finances had been vested in their new committee, a member of which was Milton J. Tootle, president of the Tootle-Lacy National Bank of Saint Joseph, Missouri. The new ar-

rangement brought some improvement, sufficient to
warrant a five-dollar dividend to the common stockholders of record June 1, 1925, the first and last common
stock dividend to be paid by the Aunt Jemima Mills since
its 1920 reorganization. The personal tensions in the
divided management continued to mount; family feuded
against family. The only thing they could agree on was a
sale of the company at the proper price. In June 1925,
John Stuart and his brother, R. Douglas, paid a visit to
Milton Tootle, member of the powerful finance committee, at his home on Mackinac Island. Tootle assured the
Stuarts that a proposition to acquire the Aunt Jemima
Mills would be seriously entertained, particularly since
The Quaker Oats Company was the interested party.
Later, a meeting was held in St. Joe among the two
Stuarts, Milton Tootle, Robert Clark, and George E. Por-
ter. Negotiations, largely concerning the purchase price,
went on for several months. Finally, the sale of Aunt
Jemima Mills to The Quaker Oats Company for $4,202,-
077.28 was ratified by the Aunt Jemima stockholders on
January 15, 1926. The preferred shareholders in Aunt
Jemima Mills received $110 per share and accrued divi-
dends for their stock, and the common stockholders received $80 per share in the final liquidation. After the
contract of sale was formally signed at the offices of
Aunt Jemima Mills, the principals involved adjourned to
the Robidoux Hotel, St. Joseph's traditional center of
hospitality, where proprietor Chris Neipp played host.
Guests included the leading businessmen of St. Joe, officials of Aunt Jemima Mills, John Stuart, and R. Douglas
Stuart. The best in the house was served, including some
treasured reserves of the Robidoux's famous wine cellar.
John Stuart said later, "They made us feel right at home.
It was a very cordial welcome." Robert Clark continued

at St. Joe in a managerial capacity until he retired in 1937.

Quaker's selling organization quickly proceeded to expand Aunt Jemima's spotty and limited representation in grocery stores to a truly national distribution. Traditionally, most of its business came from a handful of metropolitan markets in which unusually good broker connections represented the brand. Quaker's wholesale distributors put Aunt Jemima into retail stores all over the country for the first time. Soon the annual volume of business under Quaker ownership came to exceed the best years of the Aunt Jemima Mills.

For a decade following the acquisition of Aunt Jemima, the brand enjoyed a healthy growth. In the depression years of the 1930s, pancake flours suffered along with other foods of marginal necessity, and a way was sought to revive the public's interest in pancakes. Recollecting the success of Aunt Jemima's personal appearance at the Chicago World's Fair, the advertising planners decided to bring Aunt Jemima back to life in an exciting new contemporary background. A living Aunt Jemima, dressed in her gay traditional costume, would circulate among people and places which were making the news of the day. Everything needed for the project was at hand except an Aunt Jemima as well suited for the role as Nancy Green had been. To find her, want ads in Chicago papers invited aspirants to auditions at a commercial photographer's studio. This was deep in the depression of the 1930s and Chicago's South Side, with its unemployed, seemed to be filled with Aunt Jemimas seeking a job with good pay. The audition was overrun with hundreds of hopefuls. One stood out among all the rest. She was a massive woman with the face of an angel. Her name was Anna Robinson. Like

Nancy Green, she remained on the Company's payroll until her death, which occurred in 1951. Never to be forgotten was the day they loaded 350 pounds of Anna Robinson on the Twentieth Century Limited and sent her to New York in the custody of Lord & Thomas advertising agency people to pose for pictures. There, personal appearances were arranged for her in celebrated places— El Morocco, "21," Sherman Billingsley's Stork Club, the Waldorf. Backstage at theaters she hobnobbed with stars of Broadway's hit shows. Everywhere pictures were taken of Aunt Jemima serving her pancakes to happy recipients, famous people in the news of the day. The resulting advertisements ranked among the highest-read of their time. So magnetic was the smile Anna Robinson projected from the new Aunt Jemima advertisements that the likeness which had been on the package for years suffered considerably by comparison. To resolve this problem, Haddon Sundblom, a front-rank commercial artist who later modernized the Quaker trademark, was commissioned to paint a portrait of Anna Robinson. The Aunt Jemima package was redesigned around the new likeness. Sundblom's portrait captured the magnetism of his live subject and has been the Aunt Jemima trademark ever since.

An Aunt Jemima promotion of international scope takes place annually on the day before the Lenten season. According to legend, a fifteenth-century British matron in Olney, England, was making her Shrove Tuesday cakes in a skillet when the church bell rang, summoning the faithful to the shriving. Rather than be late, the aproned housewife seized her skillet full of pancakes and ran to the church, flipping her cakes enroute. Ever after, certain of the young women of Olney participated in the Olney Pancake Day Race. At 11 A.M.

on Shrove Tuesday, contestants race a 415-yard zigzag course from the town pump to the church steps, flipping a skillet of pancakes as they run. The winner's reward is a kiss from the vicar.

In 1950 a Quaker public relations man persuaded the Junior Chamber of Commerce of Liberal, Kansas, to promote a challenge race between the damsels of Liberal and those of Olney, the times to be compared by long-distance telephone. To a fanfare of international publicity, the women of Olney won the event, their fastest sprinter running the distance in one minute, ten and two-fifths seconds. The promotion was such a success that it became an annual festival, publicized world-wide, with the previous year's winner acting as Pancake Queen.

For all Aunt Jemima's success under the Quaker standard, her life has not been an unbroken chain of triumphs. New, easy-to-prepare foods were flourishing in the years immediately following World War II, and Quaker jumped into the field of packaged cake mixes, putting into limited distribution two flavors bearing the Aunt Jemima trademark. For reasons still debated, Aunt Jemima's magic didn't dent the cake-mix market. Ten years later Aunt Jemima baking mixes were launched again in the form of ultra-convenient preparations for cornbread and coffee cake. Each package contained its own foil baking pan, with the mix in a plastic bag into which the housewife could pour milk and egg and then knead for a few seconds before squeezing the batter into the pan.

Aunt Jemima also led the company into the thriving frozen foods business. Her waffles—crisp, brown, and ready to eat after a minute in the toaster—were joined in the middle 1960s by frozen corn sticks, cinnamon twists, and other toaster products. Hot breads, out of favor with housewives who had long since forgotten whatever their mothers had taught them about baking, were coming back to popularity in a form which reduced preparation time almost to zero. Aunt Jemima had traveled a long way from the steamy plantation kitchen of the legendary Colonel Higbee to the automatic griddles and the blast freezers of the new bakery in Evanston, Illinois. By the 1960s Quaker was recovering each year more than its original investment.

In recent years, Aunt Jemima restaurants have been franchised to independent operators in various parts of the country. Factors of size, location, and possible integration with motel sites are being carefully scrutinized for the ultimate formula on which to build a nationwide network. The one in Disneyland produced a unique success story. The Aunt Jemima Kitchen originally built when Disneyland opened in 1955 proved to be more of an attraction then expected. Its capacity was inadequate for the crowds of customers. Disney and Quaker agreed to start all over again. The original building came down and in June 1962, a spacious and elegant new colonial building opened for business. Rodney C. (Bud) Coulson, a personable and enterprising executive in the Walt Disney Studios, and his wife Betty were made proprietors of the new Aunt Jemima Kitchen. As a Disney executive, Coulson had been observing the popularity enjoyed by Aylene Lewis in her role as the Disneyland Aunt Jemima, both with the thousands of men and women who run the Disneyland Park and the tens of thousands more who come to visit. She had reigned for five years as hostess in the original Aunt Jemima Kitchen at Disneyland and Bud Coulson made certain that this gracious lady with a warm heart and magnetic smile would preside over his new establishment.

Aylene Lewis loved Disneyland. "I'm the happiest person in the world," she said when interviewed. Like her counterpart Nancy Green at the Chicago Fair seventy years before, Aylene with open friendly manner enchanted an endless parade of people who came to her kitchen door. Pictures of Aylene Lewis by tens of thousands have been snapped by camera-happy visitors to Disneyland. Indian Prime Minister Nehru's normal calm turned to animation as he posed with Aylene's hand clasped in his. She received before her death in 1964 letters from all over the world, in all languages and from all races and creeds. She was greeted by name by people of all ranks and all age groups. Strolling through Disneyland in her traditional costume, smiling at the crowds, someone with a camera invariably asked her scores of times a day, "Aunt Jemima, how about getting my picture taken with you?" Even in front of the television camera she was completely at ease. One night she performed an astonishing bit of impromptu routine, serving pancakes to a delighted Benny Goodman on a nationally televised pickup from her patio in Disneyland. Aylene Lewis' love of Disneyland was matched by her admiration for Walt Disney himself, a feeling shared by many of those who observe the work of this tireless perfectionist. "Most times," she related, "when he drops in here, he's wearing work slacks and a sport shirt, and has mud on his shoes from walking around some new thing he's starting to build, seein' how they pour the concrete and nail the nails."

The cycle had now come full turn in the story of Aunt Jemima. As Nancy Green, the first Aunt Jemima, and her biographer Purd Wright, no doubt talked over events of her triumphant days in 1893, so did Aylene Lewis talk to her biographer under a golden California sun seventy years later on a spring day in 1963. The interview was brought to a close typically by a smiling visitor to the park who came up to the table where Aylene Lewis was seated and said, "Aunt Jemima, how about letting me get my picture taken with you? You can get back to your friend with the notebook later."

Chapter 10 * Adventure
in Chemistry

O N a Saturday morning in the spring of 1921 the customary staff meeting of the Miner Laboratories, consulting chemists for The Quaker Oats Company, was about to convene. At the conference table were Carl S. Miner, founder of the organization, and several of his research associates. Miner was a midwestern industrial research consultant in chemistry and a missionary in his field, since at that time only the big chemical specialists such as duPont, the manufacturers of steel, soaps, and drugs, and the oil men paid much attention to chemical research. For Miner to have The Quaker Oats Company as a client was considered something of a breakthrough, so unprecedented was it for a grain miller to be embracing chemical research.

When the meeting began, a report was expected from Harold J. Brownlee, an associate assigned to the project of converting the cellulose in oat hulls to sugar to enhance their value as a livestock-feed ingredient. Instead, he placed a small bottle of amber liquid on the table and announced, "Here's some furfural. I made it from oat hulls."

Miner, Brownlee remembered afterward, almost fell from his chair. Furfural, a scientific curiosity, sold for $1.25 an ounce. "How do we know it's furfural?" Miner asked. One of those present recalled that a bottle of German-made furfural lay on a stockroom shelf, and sent for it. "Fortunately," Brownlee commented later, "my stuff smelled and looked enough like the German product to convince Miner that I really had furfural."

Before World War I American industrialists had depended upon the advanced research of German firms in deriving such valuable materials as alcohols, resins, sugars, adhesives, solvents, and medicines from plentiful, inexpensive source materials such as straw, sawdust, and coal. World War I cut off this supply of chemistry know-how, and a crash program by American industry to duplicate the German capability was financed by the U.S. government. After the war, to satisfy the few manufacturers daring enough to embark upon the mysterious sea of chemistry, consulting chemists like Miner Laboratories were organized. These independent experts contracted to do client research for a stipulated fee. In time, companies—including Quaker—built and staffed laboratories of their own, but in the earlier era, Miner and others indoctrinated skeptical manufacturers with the concept that economies and improvements could be derived from chemistry. In fact, Miner contended that the new frontier for American industry was in chemistry. By using his facilities, Miner argued that a company need not invest its own assets in such unestablished values as scientists and equipment.

The date of this eventful meeting is significant in Quaker history for what it reveals of management foresight. The year 1921 was a crisis time at Quaker; the commodity market collapse of 1920 had given the Company a huge loss for the first time. In 1921 Quaker reported to its stockholders a shrinkage of nearly one-fifth of its total assets. Yet not one penny had been trimmed from the research budget designated for Miner Laboratories. Quaker's managers maintained their investment in the future.

The weekly meetings in Miner's office amounted to clinical sessions at which various staff members reviewed progress made during the week on research objectives assigned to them. One of these projects especially intrigued Carl Miner. He had learned sometime earlier of the German success in improving by chemical treatment the digestibility of straw, thus increasing the importance of this inferior roughage as a livestock feed. Straw and oat hulls have in common a high cellulose content. Miner had been inspired to approach The Quaker Oats Company with a proposal to improve through chemistry the feeding value of oat hulls, an inevitable byproduct of the milling operation. At that time, more than 50,000 tons of oat hulls a year were disgorged by the Cedar Rapids mill alone. During World War I, with practically all foodstuffs in short supply, a ready market existed for oat hulls as livestock feed at a price as high as $25 a ton.

When the commodity market collapsed in 1920, even the choicest grades of oats and corn became so cheap that the demand for hulls evaporated. With typical ingenuity, Robert Stuart found a use for some of them. He made a deal with the Iowa Light & Power Company to swap hulls for electricity and steam-treated water. Thus the huge industrial complex that had mushroomed from the original Quaker mills on the banks of the Cedar River could be sustained without the large capital expense and maintenance costs of a private power plant. Since oat hulls have 60 per cent of the heat-energy value of soft coal, the utility company also profited by the exchange with Quaker. The hulls provided a much cleaner and cheaper fuel than coal without the costly removal problem of ashes and clinkers. The utility plant was only 1500 feet from Quaker's Cedar Rapids location. The contract stipulated that Quaker would blow oat hulls to the power company through a pipeline, and in return would receive its power and steam-treated water—a deal that enabled Quaker to trade a waste for two vital necessities. Incidentally, this contract was so satisfactory to both parties that it is now a firm agreement to the end of the year 2003, without a single change from the terms of the original covenant.

Quaker also had other mills and other hulls in abundance and was receptive to Miner's proposal that oat hulls might be made a valuable feeding ingredient with the help of chemistry. He was therefore authorized to research a chemical process for converting the cellulose in oat hulls into sugar, making a more digestible and better assimilated feed.

Miner's first attempts had involved the treatment of oat hulls with an alkali, but this process proved both unsatisfactory and costly. The project then was assigned to a newcomer in the Miner organization, Harold J. Brownlee, a graduate in chemistry from the University of Kansas with a master's degree from the University of Toronto. He joined Miner in 1920 after employment as a research chemist with a synthetic resins manufacturer. Miner asked Brownlee to pursue the oat-hull-sugar project, this time by acid treatment; results again proved disappointing. The sugars induced in the hull were of negligible feed value, and the cost of the treatment, to Brownlee's dismay, was $5 per ton of hulls, twice the value of the hulls in the depressed markets of the early 1920s. What was more, feeding tests indicated that cattle didn't savor the treated hulls.

This failure caused Brownlee to digress from his assigned task to investigate the possibility oat hulls might have an even more important use than as cattle feed. At the time, the mysterious chemical called furfural was gaining attention in the scientific journals. Brownlee had known of it from his work in resins, where furfural could be substituted in the manufacturing process for formaldehyde, except that its cost was prohibitive. Furfural had been discovered in 1821 by a German scientist named Dobereiner, who published his findings in 1832 to almost complete disinterest of the scientific world. The substance appeared to have no practical use. U.S. governmental agencies became interested in furfural as a possible derivative of value from wasted agricultural byproducts. "I recalled," Brownlee said later, "seeing an article on 'The Preparation of Pentoses from Agricultural Waste Materials,' published by the National Bureau of Chemistry. Research on agricultural wastes had increased greatly during the war years. In one inquiry, corncobs were examined as a possible source of furfural. With all this work, it was only natural that I would sooner or later become exposed to it. Probably what triggered my interest was the article by K. P. Monroe."*

At that time, corncobs were the usual source of the cellulose material from which furfural was derived; Brownlee discovered that oat hulls were also a source. Until Brownlee's work, the standard chemical analysis of oat hulls stated merely the amounts of protein, carbohydrate, and crude fiber contained. Brownlee broke down his analysis of carbohydrate into chemical fractions that included the pentosans from which furfural was derived. He discovered that the pentosans in oat hulls compared favorably with those in corncobs. His

* "Preparation and technical uses of furfural," *Journal of Industrial and Engineering Chemistry* (1921), No. 13, p. 133.

extraction of them into a sample was laid before the Miner Laboratories meeting.

Again the significant question was asked: "What is the stuff good for? What use could Quaker make of it?" Brownlee was supposed to be working on a different project altogether. How could the costs of his work be justified to a client whose critical need was an improvement in its livestock feeds, not an esoteric chemical?

Furfural was sold by drug supply houses and imported from Germany, where it was made only in laboratory quantities, hence the prohibitive price. And such firms as Stokes and Smith of Philadelphia had patents on industrial applications of furfural, particularly as substitutes for formaldehyde in the manufacture of phenolic resins. During World War I, the price of formaldehyde had climbed to $1 a pound, so there was demand for a less costly substitute. If, Brownlee told the meeting, Quaker could make furfural from oat hulls and sell it profitably at ten or fifteen cents a pound, the company might have a lucrative sideline. He said he would pursue the economics of manufacture, but was reminded by Miner not to let his new enthusiasm interfere with his basic task, which was to break down the cellulose in oat hulls into digestible sugar.

That summer, still pursuing oat-hull digestibility, Brownlee visited the Forest Products Laboratory in Madison, Wisconsin. This laboratory had several unusually large cookers, in which Brownlee experimented with digestibility processing at a volume approaching commercial quantities. The condensates from these distillations were sent to Chicago for further research. Later, Brownlee discovered in the distillates enough furfural to equal 2 per cent of the weight of the original oat hulls. A ton of hulls at this rate would make forty pounds of furfural—approximately eight times the entire world's visible supply of the chemical at that time. Quite possibly, furfural could be developed to compete against formaldehyde. Now the Quaker management expressed an interest and financed Brownlee in further work. Brownlee was installed, like his predecessor Anderson with his puffed-grain experiments, in the abandoned grain elevator at the Imperial Mill on Dearborn Street.

A ton of furfural was accumulated at Cedar Rapids— more than had ever existed before. At this proof of ability to ship in quantity, Stokes and Smith began to buy for use in synthetic resins manufacture. At the price paid, this made oat hulls worth nearly $40 a ton.

But Quaker was not yet ready to organize a sales force of chemical specialists. It therefore assigned sales of furfural to Miner Laboratories. At the Chemical Exposition in Philadelphia in June 1922, Miner exhibited a 500-pound drum of furfural to prove to the astonished scientists that such a quantity actually existed, and that The Quaker Oats Company had solved the problem of mass production.

Quaker now had a product in which there was very little commercial interest. Despite widespread curiosity, a consuming market was negligible. One day's byproduct of oat hulls at Cedar Rapids would make enough furfural to supply the world demand for a year. Previously, the short supply and high price had discouraged even industrial research, let alone application. Miner realized that arduous missionary work among industry's technicians would be necessary before furfural became a commercial success. He suggested that Brownlee— furfural's chief American enthusiast—leave his research bench and become a salesman. Brownlee demurred and eventually, in 1928, transferred to The Quaker Oats

Company's research department to continue his development of furfural. Later he became manager of Quaker Oats Limited at Southall, England.

Miner appointed another member of his staff, John P. Trickey, to the post of furfural missionary to industry. For seven years Trickey wrote, published, preached, and demonstrated furfural. As sales agents, Miner Laboratories advertised in chemical journals, inviting experimentation with the substance. Limited usage was won when Hercules Powder Corporation revolutionized the wood-resin industry by manufacturing, with the aid of furfural, an economical pale wood resin from the wastelands of pine stumps in Georgia. Quaker management was encouraged on the day Hercules ordered its first railroad tank car of furfural. This industry never developed into a significant furfural customer, and there remained the old problem of finding new uses if the development was to become an economic success.

In 1925 Fredus N. Peters, with a doctorate in chemistry from the University of Wisconsin, joined the Miner organization. His task was to produce such esoteric but useful furan derivatives as tetrahydrofurfuryl alcohol, which seemed to offer even greater opportunities than furfural itself. Thus began a research project that did not pay off for two decades, but in World War II produced a bonanza. The extensive use of furfural as a substitute for formaldehyde did not materialize—the early patents on furfural-phenol resins were closely held. Inability to obtain licenses discouraged much research at a time when formaldehyde-phenol resin technology developed rapidly. As an alternative, Peters turned to the alcohols, hoping to discover commercial uses for these derivatives of furfural not covered by patents.

But he, too, was destined to become a salesman. In

1927, discouraged with the failure of furfural to warrant the organization of a subsidiary corporation, John Trickey resigned his missionary task, and the assignment went to Peters.

Between 1928 and 1930 Peters roamed the nation searching for furfural customers, continuing his researches at the same time. He sought markets in the oil industry after the development in 1925 of a patent by Egon Eichwald of Hamburg, Germany, for a process using furfural to convert lower-grade oils into superior lubricants—equal in many respects to products from the Pennsylvania-type crude oils then considered the world's best. The American rights to the Eichwald patent, held by Royal Dutch Shell, were for sale at $25,000. But inquiry among three big American refiners drew the same answer: no interest in solvent refining. No effort was made to secure the Eichwald assignment either by Miner or Quaker—a large oversight, as second-guessing proved. Doctor Peters also abandoned this possible outlet for furfural in his salesmanship. He concentrated, without much tangible result, on the big chemists such as duPont, the shoe and textile dyers, powder companies, and abrasives manufacturers.

By the beginning of 1932, seeking ways to cut costs during the economic depression, a Quaker executive in Chicago sent a directive to Cedar Rapids. The prospects for furfural were so poor, the letter said, that the mill management was to fill the storage tanks with furfural and then cease its manufacture. "It is quite likely," the instruction concluded, "that we will never make furfural again."

On the contrary, however, there was shortly a race to keep the furfural tanks refilled. Soon after the shutdown order reached Cedar Rapids, Peters received a telephone call from a duPont subsidiary in Niagara Falls, New York, inviting him to a secret meeting. On his arrival, they discussed in vague terms whether there might in the future be available a steady supply of furfural, and what estimate of price Quaker could make based on a multimillion-pound volume per year. Peters staggered under the implications of such a huge potential, and assured the duPont chemists that Quaker could supply furfural in any desired amount, at prices which, in enormous quantities, would be under ten cents a pound. The scientists thereupon began to buy small quantities of furfural for experimental purposes. But not until twelve years later did Peters learn that the product for which furfural was needed was a synthetic fiber named Nylon.

Then, on New Year's Day, 1933, while Peters relaxed at his home, he was summoned by telephone to an urgent meeting in New York with top executives of The Texas Company, as it was then known, refiners of Texaco products. Management, he learned the next day, had committed Texaco to a venture in solvent refining—a venture destined to give Quaker a world market for furfural. "The Texas people told me," Peters recalled after his retirement, "that they had bought the American rights to the Eichwald patent. They were building a new unit at Lawrenceville, Illinois, for solvent refining. They, of course, wanted to know whether we could supply furfural in large and steady quantities. I said we could." From this beginning, furfural by the trainload eventually was needed to supply the processing lines of 60 oil refineries.

Soon after war with Japan began in 1941, the Far East sources of natural rubber were shut off. The government gave top priorities to the development of synthetic rubber. A method of quantity production had already been developed by the Phillips Petroleum Company—a process that involved a chemical reaction between two petrochemicals, styrene and butadiene, the latter a derivative of crude butane. However, to achieve a successful union into a basic substance for synthetic rubber, the butadiene had to be almost absolutely pure. Furfural was found to be the most effective agent for recovery of high-purity butadiene during the refining process. National interest thus demanded furfural in large quantities.

A surprised Fredus Peters received a long-distance telephone call from Washington one day in March 1941. The caller identified himself as a representative of the Reserve Rubber Corporation, the wartime agency responsible for obtaining rubber for military and civilian uses. The conversation, as Peters remembered it, went about as follows:

WASHINGTON: We need 40 million pounds of furfural right away for the synthetic rubber program. How soon can it be shipped?

PETERS: It can't be shipped. There isn't that much furfural in the world.

WASHINGTON: We've got to have it. If your total production is allocated to us, how soon can we have 40 million pounds?

PETERS: Possibly three years.

WASHINGTON: That's far too long. We must have it within the year.

PETERS: The only possible course is to build a new furfural plant and find a new raw material. There aren't enough oat hulls in America to make that much furfural, and it will take at least a year to build a plant.

WASHINGTON: You'd better get down here right away. I can see we can't settle this thing by phone.

Peters' visit to Washington led to a contract between the federal government and The Q. O. Chemical Company, a new subsidiary, for Quaker to design, supervise, and operate a new plant at Memphis, Tennessee, large enough to produce 24 million pounds of furfural a year. The U.S. Defense Plant Corporation completed construction of the giant new chemical installation in nine months. Operations started in July 1943 and continued to the end of 1946. For its supervisory services, The Quaker Oats Company was paid a service fee by the government to cover the salaries and expenses paid to its own executives assigned to the project. "Our only interest," said the report to stockholders, "is one of providing management for the government."

This demand for furfural exceeded the entire reservoir of oat hulls. Moreover, a wartime shortage of feedstuffs also made oat hulls valuable once more as livestock feed. Cottonseed hulls furnished a temporary source of raw material until a larger and cheaper fund of raw material was found in corncobs lying waste in American barnyards. Since most cobs were shelled on the farm and thrown away, Quaker had little difficulty organizing a system to collect this waste.

Furfural now became a primary product of the Quaker company. At the onset of the rubber program, the Memphis plant worked 24 hours a day to charge up the refineries in the oil fields with sufficient furfural to start operations. Each unit required a two- to three-million-pound supply. After the processing lines were filled, only an occasional replacement of furfural was necessary to compensate for leakage and mechanical loss. In 1946, the crisis ended, Quaker bought the Memphis plant as surplus. By then Quaker needed a second plant, since the wartime developments in chemistry had caused a fivefold increase in industrial uses of furfural.

When duPont announced its development of Nylon, furfural acquired a new significance as a basic organic chemical, a raw material in itself with an infinite range of uses in manufacturing synthetic products. The duPont company needed such quantities of furfural that Quaker built at Omaha a third manufacturing unit, the largest producer of furfural in the world. The use of furfural in Nylon was discontinued for a time, then resumed. In the interim, new vistas in the synthetic-fibers industry were opened by the Quaker Chemicals Division for furfural and its derivatives. Elastomeric fibers of the spandex type were produced from tetrahydrofuran, a latex derivative.

The list of products in common use today utilizing furfural technology includes lubricating oils, resins, pharmaceuticals, abrasives, synthetic rubber chemical-resistant pipe, ducts, vats and flooring, foundry-core binders, antifreeze, charcoal briquettes, vinyl plastic garments, textiles, flavoring agents, plastic bottle caps, buttons, furniture, glue, and antiseptics.

Many other applications for furfural and its derivatives in industry have been discovered. Andrew P. Dunlop of Quaker's research staff commented on future trends: "The depletion of fossil fuels will some day be complete. Minerals do not multiply. They bear no reproductive seed. It is now clear that man will then derive his energy requirements from the atom and from the sun. But what will be the source of his organic chemicals—those building blocks of ever-increasing necessity to the perpetuation and advancement of the complex social structure he has achieved, and which he is obligated to pass on to his posterity? I submit that products available, now and potentially, from annually renewable farm and forest sources will be the prime organic chemicals of that future day."

Prominent in the technical literature on furfural produced by scientists are the first writings by Harold J. Brownlee and Carl S. Miner. Furfural Bulletin #1 from the Miner Laboratories was the first compendium of bibliographical references on the subject ever printed. The American Chemical Society saluted the twenty-fifth year of furfural in American industry with a symposium in New York. Four of the papers read before this scientific group were delivered by Quaker staff members. Similar papers have been delivered by Quaker personnel before the Royal Institute of Chemistry in London and the Chemical Institute of Canada. The most comprehensive single publication in furfural literature is a monograph of nearly 900 pages published in 1953 by Andrew P. Dunlop and Fredus N. Peters under the auspices of the American Chemical Society. Entitled *The Furans*, this work was the first comprehensive compilation of the chemistry and technology of furfural ever published in any language, and is the standard reference. The Q. O. Chemicals technical bulletins are the current literature for keeping world-wide industry informed on new developments in furfural technology.

As to furfural's future, Dr. Homer E. Duffy, vice-president in charge of Quaker's Chemicals Division, had this to say in 1965: "We see three promising areas for further growth of our chemicals business: continued intensive development of world markets for our products through either export or local production; development of new specialized products to fill specific needs; and acquisition of companies or products which would fit into Quaker's operation. In all three of these areas, the key to success is research on products, on processes, on markets. We expect that intelligent selection of research projects, effective use of our research manpower, and intensive market development will enable us to make new worthwhile contributions to the world's chemical needs."

New industrial uses for furfural and its chemical offspring kept turning up, and by the 1960s the basic chemical was in such short supply that Quaker could not keep up with demand. Established customers were being allocated less than their desired shipments and new customers were being turned away, a necessity that irked Dr. Duffy and his sales force. In 1966, construction of a fourth chemical plant was begun at Belle Glade, Florida, on a site adjacent to a sugar-cane refinery. The new plant utilized as raw material the conveniently nearby fibrous sugar-cane residue called *bagasse*.

As the plant in Palm Beach County took shape, new uses for furan chemicals were still appearing. Furfuryl alcohol had established itself in the foundry industry, having unique properties as a binder in cores from which castings were made. Tetrahydrofuran was being used in the manufacture of synthetic foams for cushions and mattresses, as well as for the spandex fibers from which lacy foundation garments and other lingerie are woven. From tetrahydrofuran, Quaker also made a new chemical with applications in plastics manufacturing. Its full name was polyesteramethelyne glycol ether, sold under the mercifully abbreviated trade name, QO Polymeg.

Harold J. Brownlee's speculative oat-hull research in the early 1920s had borne astonishing fruit. The "Daddy of the Furans," as his scientific contemporaries called him, had now retired, his name secure in chemistry's hall of fame.

Chapter 11 * The
Pet Foods

PET FOODS are big business. Within a single generation, this new industry's sales volume grew to more than a half-billion dollars a year. Quaker, a leading manufacturer of farm-animal feeds, now has similar leadership in pet foods with its Ken-L Ration for dogs and Puss 'n Boots for cats, the first canned foods for pets ever offered to the public. P. M. Chappel introduced the first canned food for canines to the American market in 1923; Sam Hornstein performed the same service for felines in 1932. The two brands were perpetuated through acquisition by Quaker.

There is no record that Chappel, who pioneered pet-food history in Rockford, Illinois, and Hornstein of Los Angeles ever met. Their early struggles were similar, as were their battles to win acceptance for a new idea of prepared pet food in tin and their struggle against competition, once they had created the new market. In both enterprises, the second generation of management encountered much the same problem, the prohibitive cost of marketing a single product in competition with others whose promotional costs were spread over an entire "line." In both instances, the problem was solved by alliance with the Quaker organization. From Quaker's point of view, the two properties offered opportunities to diversify into collateral branches of the food industry.

P. M. Chappel started his business life as a procurer of horses for the United States government and its allies during World War I. The horse was a prime combat necessity for General Pershing's American Expeditionary Force. Civilian horse owners, however, refused to part with sound animals, since the inflated wartime economy had boomed the country's agriculture and industry. Work horses on the farm and dray animals in the city were at a premium. Chappel and his group searched farms and villages, city livery stables, police departments changing over to motorcycles, and any other place in which a "hay-burner" might be found. Through their diligence, Chappel and his associates furnished approximately 117,000 horses to the United States during World War I.

The French military authorities, to whom the United States allotted part of Chappel's equine export, pointed out to him the opportunity to ship horse meat to Europe for human consumption. Chappel said later, "I came in contact with a number of French officers who were very much interested in horse meat for their country, as the French people had been accustomed to horse meat for centuries. With that thought in mind, I went to France after the war to check into the possibilities of trading with that country, and found a very good market available, not only in France, but in Holland, Norway, Sweden and Denmark."

Before Chappel could trade in horse meat with foreign markets, he had to obtain changes in laws and regulations on both sides of the Atlantic. First he received the promise of the French Minister for Agriculture that if the United States would put horse meat under government inspection, French authorities would change their laws to lift the restrictions against import of horse meat except on the hoof. With this assurance in his portfolio, Chappel returned to the United States and persuaded Congress to permit the packaging of horse meat for human consumption under the supervision of U.S. government inspectors. Thus protected, the French, Scandinavian, and Netherlands governments permitted the import in any form of Chappel's horse meat bearing a U.S. inspection seal.

Soon Chappel and his brother had a profitable business in the export of pickled horse meat. Chappel, however, wanted much more a market for horse meat in the United States. The American public had no tradition for this protein and apparently no desire to change its habits. Chappel then began to experiment with a canned dog food, an entirely new idea.

His first experiments were not a technological success. An absolute condition imposed by the U.S. meat-inspection authorities was that any canned meat must be sterilized. This presented no problem with beef. But Chappel's experience was that extreme heat from the sterilization process produced in his product a dark, unappetizing appearance. After three years, during which he sought advice from the New York State Veterinary College and other sources, he solved this problem.

The Chappels then sought a canning plant, and acquired an abandoned packing house in Rockford, Illinois. The trademark *Ken-L Ration* was registered and applied to the first commercial dog food, recognizing that dogs, like humans, need a balanced diet to maintain excellent health. The corporation, Chappel Bros., showed a profit in its first year. Within a few years, a dry dog food called *Ken-L Biskit* was manufactured—first for boarding kennels, breeders, and veterinarians, then gradually extended to national consumer distribution. The reputation of Ken-L Biskit with the professionals led to ready acceptance by pet owners and became known as the "Food of Champions."

By 1930, when the great depression struck, Chappel Bros. was showing an annual net profit of more than $500,000. Then hard times caused acute pressures from big distributors. Large meat manufacturers, seeking new sources of income, were unable to resist the lure of the fast-growing new market for canned meat developed by Ken-L Ration. The exclusive Chappel empire was invaded by powerful competitors. Attractive new names and labels appeared on cans of beef-based dog foods in the grocery stores. Competitive advertising and aggressive merchandising diverted generous amounts of Chappel's business to the new brands. During the early 1930s the public was extremely price-conscious, and some competitors sold their goods at half the Ken-L Ration price.

Chappel decided to bring out a beef-based Ration with which he hoped to compete against the new competition from the Chicago stockyards. Chappel said, "Our competitors made so much capital of our horse meat product that it was necessary for us to produce a beef Ken-L Ration in order to take away their ammunition." He predicted that "within the next year of two, horse meat Ken-L Ration sales will have been reduced to a point where it will be advisable to discontinue the manufacture of horse meat and confine ourselves to the manufacture of the beef product." His move to beef was as great an error in judgment as his prediction. Beef Ken-L Ration was just another nonentity in the grocery stores, smothered by the weight of advertising and promotional pressure from the big packers. As to Ken-L Ration's established identity with horse meat, time would prove this an asset, not a liability. Skilled research later would discover such great nutritional virtues in horse meat as to make this brand again the most popular with dog-lovers. But none of this was foreseen by Chappel. Throughout the 1930s, the company steadily lost money; worse, its market position collapsed. Chappel abandoned the fight in 1937, surrendering the management to other members of his family.

The company was now heavily in debt to its suppliers, the arrears running to several hundred thousand dollars. Investors and creditors alike stood to lose if the enterprise failed. Chappel's board chairman, Robert W. Green, one of the original Chappel backers, met creditors early in 1938. Unanimously they decided that the only possible salvage lay in keeping the company in business to work off its debt. An experienced hand was clearly needed for such a formidable task.

To Green fell the problem of finding a man who could restore health to the sick corporation. He selected Frank Warton, an enterprising executive of Swift & Company. Warton was in his late forties, had made a reputation in meat packing, and knew a good deal about horses. He had restored a reorganized Allied Packers to robust health and disposed of it on terms highly satisfactory to Allied's stockholders. Then, as president of a Swift subsidiary, Warton had liquidated a number of ranches in Wyoming owned by Swift or members of the Swift family. Two of these properties were sold to Chappel Bros., and in this way Warton met Green. Later, someone in Chappel proposed stocking the Wyoming ranches with plump work horses from midwestern farms in the hope they would crossbreed with the wild mustangs native to the mountain wilderness, the goal being a self-renewing crop of horse meat for the Rockford cannery. The result was altogether unexpected. Resenting invasion of their province by strange horses, the mustangs killed off the immigrants.

Following Green's invitation to become president of Chappel Bros., Warton studied the company. He noted that the $250,000-a-year loss was the result largely of costly efforts to deploy beef-based Ken-L Ration against similar products of the Chicago packers, while the cheaper horse-meat Ken-L Ration had been allowed to drift. Quality control had lapsed. Even the label had become nondescript, a conglomerate of twenty-four dog pictures. One grocery chain after another had dropped Ken-L Ration and distribution was alarmingly small.

Warton's first move was to discontinue the manufacture of a beef dog food. Accurately, he assayed the valuable franchise in the horse-meat base and worked this advantage aggressively. Then he hired John S. Williams, a marketing expert qualified to repair the damaged distribution in the larger grocery chains, and appointed him vice-president for marketing. Professional research was started with three famous scientists—Dr. John Wesley Patton, who operated a biological laboratory in Lansing, Michigan, Dr. C. A. Elvejhem, noted authority on nutrition and later president of the University of Wisconsin, and Dr. Clive M. McKay of Cornell University. These experts set nutritional standards for dog food. From their studies emerged the first common knowledge of the importance of Vitamin B-1 to dogs as a specific for certain canine neurological disturbances and for maintaining a generally agreeable disposition in breeds inclined to be high-strung.

Warton immediately fortified Ken-L Ration with added Vitamin B-1 and introduced precise quality controls in manufacturing. Professional endorsement of the new formula was secured in the form of seals of approval from the Good Housekeeping Institute and the American Veterinary Association. Advertisements were prepared demonstrating the improvement in the behavior of a vitamin-deficient canine after feeding of Ken-L Ration with Vitamin B-1.

All Warton needed now was time for his rehabilitation program to work down to the consumer level, but time was denied him. What might easily have been a fatal mishap struck the struggling, money-tight company. With the onset of World War II, government conservators placed pet foods on the nonessential list of users of tin, and the supply of Ken-L Ration's familiar container was cut off for the duration of the conflict. Even this disaster Warton converted into an asset. Ingeniously, he advertised that patrons now could *see* Ken-L Ration's new product superiority in glass before they bought.

The glass jar caused a monumental problem: where to get the money for the packing equipment and glass jars to pack. Manufacturers of food products commonly sought bank loans secured by warehouse receipts for inventories of finished foods. To ask for a loan on empty glass jars was unheard of. Nevertheless, Warton persuaded the Rockford National Bank to grant the loan. Soon 10 million glass jars were in the Ken-L Ration warehouse ready to be packed for national distribution.

From the time he became president of Chappel Bros., Warton had been forced by a lean purse to work with a minimum sales force. He had only twelve men, who covered only 29 of the largest metropolitan markets. With such limited distribution, Ken-L Ration sold only 3 per cent of the total dog-food business in the nation.

Without money to finance expansion of his own organization, Warton sought a distribution arrangement with another company equipped with a strong national sales department. He sent an inquiry to The Quaker Oats Company, but Quaker's management said that it did not wish to risk its reputation selling a product over which it had no manufacturing control. Two weeks later, George B. Whitfield, then controller of The Quaker Oats Company, called on Frank Warton at his office in Rockford. All day and well into the night the two men discussed Whitfield's offer of outright purchase of Chappel Bros. by Quaker.

Whitfield returned to Chicago and on December 17, 1941, made his report to the Quaker management. He recommended the outright purchase of Chappel Bros., notwithstanding, as he put it, "with the war on and a shortage of tin, you may only own a bakery." His reference was to the small plant that produced Ken-L Meal and Ken-L Biskit. John and R. Douglas Stuart inspected the Rockford operation and came to terms with Warton. A call to Chappel Bros. stockholders requested them ". . . to authorize the sale to The Quaker Oats Company of all the property, assets, and business of Chappel Bros., Inc. . . . for the purchase price of $350,000 cash and a further sum in cash representing the inventories." Robert W. Green, as company chairman, in his accompanying letter to the stockholders, said: "Since the entry of the United States in the war . . . the problem of your company in obtaining essential materials, supplies, and transportation for the manufacture and sale of its products has become serious. . . . Because of its financial condition, your company is not in a position to withstand a curtailment of its operation. . . . Your directors feel that they are fortunate to be able to present to you the proposal to sell to The Quaker Oats Company. . . ."

Frank Warton became a vice-president of Quaker, in charge of a new Ken-L Products Division, which remained for the time at Rockford. With the wartime restrictions on tin, Warton's bank-financed 10 million glass jars became a significant asset. Unexpected revenues came from another source. During the war, retail markets specializing in horse meat opened in eastern U.S. cities. These shops catered to persons of foreign origin to whom horse meat was a familiar and welcome item of diet. The profits on sales of horse meat for human consumption helped carry the Ken-L Division through the war. East Coast markets sold as much as five to six carloads of U.S. government-inspected horse meat a week.

After the war, Warton and his associates realized even more fully the advantages of their affiliation with Quaker. Freed from the threat of bankruptcy and with strong new research facilities, marketing machinery, and financial resources, the Ken-L group moved quickly to a position of market leadership. Within a few years, Ken-L Ration became established as the first brand in its highly competitive field, a position it has maintained ever since.

One resource made available to Warton upon his affiliation with Quaker was canny Scottish management. After Ken-L Ration had become prosperous in the early postwar years, R. Douglas Stuart, then Quaker vice-chairman, asked Warton one day, "What are we doing with Kit-E Ration?" At the moment, Kit-E Ration was far from Warton's mind, but such a product did exist, a brand of cat food in the Ken-L line that had never achieved a substantial sale. The executive needle had its effect. Cat food immediately received top priority at The Quaker Oats Company.

Warton conferred with Dr. Fredus N. Peters, the former furfural salesman who by now had become Quaker's research vice-president. Peters recalled of that meeting, "Warton said to me, 'We're going into the cat-food business.' I told him research would develop a cat food." Peters then summoned an assistant, George Hensley, and said, "We've got to get cats." To Hensley was assigned the project of experimental feeding of a cat colony.

"We got those cats from practically anyplace, and while the cats were apparently healthy when they came into the laboratory, each one carried a few germs to which it was immune but the others were not. We soon had the darndest bunch of cat diseases known to man in this laboratory. But we medicated the animals like human beings. Ours was the most carefully attended cat colony anywhere. At first we thought we would experiment with meat products similar to those in Ken-L Ration, but then it was pointed out to us that commercial fish cost about two cents a pound, a lot cheaper than any meat. Also, there was this Puss 'n Boots cat food on the market, made from fish, and it was pretty good."

Peters' research team developed a cafeteria for its test panel of twenty-five alley cats. Samples of all the leading cat foods, plus concoctions from the Quaker laboratory, were offered to the cats simultaneously. At first, the felines leaped to the nearest dish, but they soon learned to be more discriminating. They would pad up the line delicately nosing dishes, perhaps licking a bit off the top, twitching noses and ears, pondering ultimate selection. Then almost invariably they settled down to a meal of

Puss 'n Boots. To this frustration of the laboratory was added another: the technical problem of packing a fish-based pet food of Quaker manufacture in a tin can. A preservative for the fish was required, otherwise the product turned black and presented an unattractive appearance. Puss 'n Boots had solved this problem by a sulfur dioxide treatment Quaker scientists were reluctant to try because of the possible effect of the chemical on the nutritive values of the food. "We had all sorts of troubles," Peters recalled. "For a number of months we tried and tried to make fish products and they went off color, they went off flavor, and we didn't know what was the matter." To which Hensley added, "All along the line the preference tests made on our laboratory cats were in favor of Puss 'n Boots." Reports of this consumer research were made to the Quaker management on June 2, 1950.

Throughout these months of testing, Frank Warton was looking intently over the shoulders of the research group. He sensed that there would be trouble before the secrets of canning fresh fish could be solved. Further, he approximated the cost of the marketing and advertising effort that would be required to unseat such firmly entrenched competition as that provided by Puss 'n Boots. Long before the discouraging feeding tests were completed, Warton began to press his associates in Quaker management for permission to negotiate for the purchase of the Coast Fishing Company, which manufactured and distributed Puss 'n Boots.

After the disappointing research report of June 2, Warton was authorized to explore the purchase of Coast Fishing Company, a thriving enterprise located on the southern shore of Los Angeles Harbor. Seven Japanese nationals had chosen this site in 1914 as the base for commercial tuna fishing in California coastal waters. The Japanese incorporated and proceeded to harvest the rich tuna.

Sam Hornstein had reached San Francisco via Japan at twenty-three. Born in Cairo, Egypt, he was three years old when his widowed mother moved her little family to Tokyo, where she remarried. Sam spent his youth and early manhood learning to speak and read Japanese. At the time, a friend in the food brokerage business was attempting to establish a source of California white albacore tuna for eastern U.S. distributors. He suggested that Sam, conversant as he was in the Japanese language and familiar with Oriental customs, might interest the Japanese fishery in this specialty. In very little time, Sam had arranged a regular supply of choice albacore to his friend's eastern customers. This happy arrangement was threatened when the Japanese owners decided to return to their homeland during World War I. An eastern distributor of Sam's albacore, Seaman Bros., agreed to lend Hornstein $50,000 with which to acquire the capital stock of Coast Fishing and another $50,000 for working capital. Sam became sole owner and operator of the enterprise. Within five years he had repaid all the loans.

Through the 1920s the business thrived on a steady demand for tuna, sardines, mackerel, and anchovies. Then abruptly a crisis nearly swamped the enterprise. As family food budgets were pruned during the economic depression of the 1930s, such luxury items as California canned fish were among the first consumer retrenchments. Sales nearly dried up.

But Horstein saved himself. As a sideline he had taken on, a year earlier, a formula for a feed in demand at fox farms and trout hatcheries. This business was of little consequence until human consumption of Hornstein's products waned, then the little sideline suddenly became the most important item of sale. Hornstein regarded it with new interest and concluded that with some changes in formula he might have an entirely different product: a canned dog food. The sideline was renamed *Balto*. The name came from the famous Husky sledge-dog who saved Nome, Alaska, from pestilence by leading in a sledge team loaded with serum through a ten-day blizzard. (A statue of Balto stands in New York City's Central Park.)

Hornstein released a massive program of newspaper and radio advertising in southern California. The Los Angeles public was invited to a dog show at Loyola High School stadium, featuring personal appearances of Hollywood movie stars, a dog team of snow-white Malemutes, and a competition in which dog-lovers were invited to display their own pets. Within four years, Balto was selling in southern California at the rate of 50,000 cases a year.

But the product had a weakness, which consumer testing might have revealed. A fish product is too rich for a canine's daily diet. The cost of advertising and promoting Balto was far too great for its limited potential as a supplementary food suitable for one or two feedings a week.

Hornstein's future course happily was resolved by a chance bit of intelligence on consumer usage of Balto. Surprisingly enough, a good part of the production had been purchased by cat owners, even though cats had never been mentioned on the label or in the advertising. The irresistible fish bouquet of Balto had transmitted its own sweet message to Los Angeles cats. So the indefatigable Hornstein's Balto became Puss 'n Boots. The name, suggested by a food broker, Walter Randall, capitalized on the story of one of the most famous felines in literature, Charles Perrault's *Le chat botte*, whose tricks and witty remarks won his master, a penniless miller, a medieval princess and a great fortune. No other canned cat food then existed in the American market.

The change was blessed with almost instant success. The first order for Puss 'n Boots "exclusively for cats" was shipped to Ralph's Grocery Company of Los Angeles in October 1934. Hornstein had the new field of prepared feline food entirely to himself. Chain stores clamored to be given exclusive distribution of the item, since cat fanciers instantly recognized that a scientific food gave pets far better nutrition than a homemade diet of table scraps and milk. One of the largest chain groups threatened to discontinue the sale unless it was given sole representation in its territory. "Nothing doing" was Hornstein's answer. "Just go ahead and cry." For the rest of Hornstein's lifetime the sweet smell of success was the predominant odor hovering over his fish cannery. When he died in 1940, Coast Fishing Company was a flourishing enterprise with an exclusive franchise in the pet-food business that one day would realize millions of dollars for his heirs.

Production was expanded with construction of an East Coast plant at Lubec, Maine, in 1948, and by 1950 sales of Puss 'n Boots had reached a level of almost $7 million a year, with a net income to the stockholders after taxes of around $700,000. One morning in October of that year William Hornstein, Sam's principal heir, entered the Coast Fishing Office and told Racey Bivin, the president after Sam's death, "Yesterday I had a phone call from the Bank of America. They would not reveal any names but they said a large eastern food processor was interested in acquiring Coast Fishing Company." Willian Hornstein and his mother thought an inquiry should be initiated, and others in the company agreed. Accordingly, the bank arranged an informal meeting with the prospective buyer, who turned out to be Frank Warton of Quaker Oats.

The Hornstein family owned majority control of the privately held company. No public market existed in the stock. The enterprise had a value running into millions of dollars, hence large federal and state inheritance levies were about to be assessed against Sam Hornstein's estate. Further, the Korean war had begun; restrictions might be imposed on the use of tin for cans. The Hornsteins solved several problems by selling their holdings in the company. Two months after the first interview, Quaker purchased Coast Fishing Company for $7,130,-000. Such was the legacy that had grown from the $100,000 loan in thirty-five years. A Coast Fisheries division of The Quaker Oats Company was formed to manage the enterprise. Frank Warton and R. Douglas Stuart had their cat food.

Almost immediately following the Quaker acquisition, the mackerel, anchovies, sardines, and hake deserted the California coastal waters and did not return for two years. New fishing grounds had to be found quickly. A team of Quaker scouts was appointed to survey all the coastal waters of the continental United States for a new source of supply. The search committee was attracted to the Gulf of Mexico, where fleets of clean little shrimp boats plied. These fishermen told Cliff Yeomans, head of the search party, "Why don't you buy our fish—it's exactly what you need and it's cheap."

These fish were small, mostly croakers, brought up in the nets along with the shrimp. In the trade they were known as trash fish, wholesome enough but not favored for human consumption. The fisherman usually washed them over his decks and back into the sea. Yeomans sent a boatload of the fish to the Ken-L Division cannery at Wilmington, California, where they made up into excellent pet food. Quaker moved quickly to build a cannery in Pascagoula, Mississippi, adjacent to this seemingly inexhaustible source of raw material. Since then, Quaker's purchase of industrial fish for Puss 'n Boots has become an important factor in stabilizing the rather erratic fishing business at several ports on the Atlantic, Pacific, and Gulf coasts. Fishermen at the old whaling port of New Bedford, Massachusetts, found a new market when Quaker opened a plant there in 1963, replacing the Lubec plant, which had grown obsolete and was poorly located in relation to major markets.

As the time approached for Frank Warton's retirement, the management decided to integrate the sales and general management of the Fisheries Division with the company's headquarters in Chicago. In bidding farewell to Vice-President Warton, who retired in 1956 to continue an avocation as a commissioner of the Illinois State Racing Board, an official Quaker spokesman said: "Under his direction, pet foods have continued to be one of the most profitable divisions of our company." Robert D. Stuart, Jr., was elected vice-president of the division when Warton retired. The battle for position in this intensely competitive $600-million-a-year industry was a severe test of management skill, a good training ground for the third generation of Stuarts and future president of the company.

At its research laboratories in Barrington, Illinois, Quaker established in 1962 a luxurious and complete facility exclusively for pet-feeding and pet-nutrition studies. Staff nutritionists, biochemists, veterinarians, and researchers here test improvements in the Ken-L Ration and Puss 'n Boots formulas. Dog and cat taste panels yield data on the palatability preferences of animals which, combined with studies of growth, vitality, and general health, are the basis of pet-food formulas and feeding instruction. Each of the 200 dogs resides in its own private compartment with outdoor patio. Three hundred cats dwell in splendor in a pastel-colored area complete with scratching tree, resting shelf, and screened porch. Expectant mothers in both kennel and cattery are quartered in special maternity wards; puppies and kittens have deluxe nurseries.

As a result of its studies of dogs and cats, Ken-L Ration added chlorophyl in 1952 and polyunsaturates for coat and skin betterment in 1961, the first canned pet food to introduce such improvements.

A change in Puss 'n Boots' formula resulted from an incident with which the scientific resources of the old Coast Fishing Company might have been unable to cope. In 1954 a hospital reported that certain cats fed exclusively on Puss 'n Boots died mysteriously. Research by Quaker's scientists soon turned up a double thievery of Vitamin B-1. A thiaminase enzyme in some fish destroyed B-1 during the cooking process, though the thiaminase itself disappeared before the cooking was completed. Experiments also uncovered the fact that the sulfur dioxide used to keep the fish from turning black drove out Vitamin B-1. Tests proved further that cats deprived altogether of the precious vitamin died in about 45 days. The deficiency was corrected by adding a hard pellet of Vitamin B-1 to the formula late in the canning process, after the vitamin-destroying thiaminase had dissipated itself. The other culprit, sulfur dioxide, had no effect on the B-1 pellet. The contribution of Quaker's research staff in this emergency was of incalculable value.

Since 1961, canned pet foods have been one of the three best-selling categories in the grocery stores of America. The U.S. population of house dogs was estimated at 25 million, the census of pet house cats at 20 million. In these vast twin markets, Quaker was entrenched in both with the leading brand of canned pet food.

Chapter 12 * *Quaker*
and the New Farmer

STAGGERING CHANGES took place in rural America during the middle years of the twentieth century. These changes, so fundamental and so rapid that they amounted virtually to agricultural revolution, directly affected an important area of Quaker's business—the manufacture of feeds for the nation's poultry, livestock, and dairy farmers.

Mechanization and scientific technology combined to create a new system of farming in America and a new way of life for the people engaged in it. No other producer has embraced mechanization so eagerly as has the farmer in his desire to multiply his efficiency by the factor of horsepower. Power machinery had freed the agriculturist from the endless grind of manual work, traditionally the farmer's lot. Expense and uncertainties associated with hiring seasonal labor (migratory or local) have been minimized by the machine. Total man-hours expended in agriculture in the United States were halved by a sixfold increase in power machinery and equipment during the first half of the twentieth century. One man-hour of farm labor now produces three times its previous volume, with much less physical effort.

Inevitably, the new opportunity in mechanization produced a new breed of farmer. The essential challenge was thinking on a larger scale; operations had to be expanded to match the increase in productivity made possible by power machinery. At the same time, a larger line of bank credit was required for purchase of expensive machinery and equipment, and for increased working capital. Finally, education in the new techniques of production and management were essential to capitalize on the scientifically tested know-how available from agricultural colleges, state experiment stations, the U.S. Department of Agriculture, county agricultural agents, and field men for suppliers of feed, fertilizers, pesticides, and machinery. Farming became part of a vast economic complex economists and sociologists term Agribusiness.

The broad outlines of this transformation can be seen in statistics from the Bureau of the Census and the federal Department of Agriculture. About half the farms in the United States have disappeared. This does not mean that the land went out of cultivation; three and a half million farmers simply did not survive the stress of change and surrendered their land to stronger hands. Those engaged in farming once represented more than half the civilian work force. By 1960 farming represented only 7 per cent of total employment, and the figure has since continued to shrink.

The remaining 3,500,000 farms were by and large more profitable than the 7 million farms of the 1930s had been. The value of farm land and buildings in the United States increased fourfold, and in twenty years farm income leaped 350 per cent.

An intimate picture of this change, and the problems and opportunities it created for the feed division of The Quaker Oats Company, is found in a close-up of two farmsteads in the United States, one of a half-century ago, the other under contemporary management.

The old Hamilton farm of 360 acres is located a few miles from New Concord, Ohio, the home town of Astronaut John Glenn. Andrew Hamilton established a homestead there and was rewarded in 1826 with a grant of land by President John Quincy Adams. On his death in the late 1860s his farm descended to four children, a bachelor and three spinsters whose sterile existence reflected the relentless mastery of the individual by the land in an earlier day.

The women on the Hamilton farm tended small flocks of chickens, turkeys, ducks, and geese, and twice a day they milked a few scrub dairy cows, sustained like the poultry by feed grown on the farm. The women made clothes, baked bread, manufactured soap, mixed nostrums for man, fowl, and beast, separated cream, churned butter, put up all the farm's garden and orchard provender in glass against the hard winter, washed clothes, attended to the housework, cooked meals, and fed the lambs after weaning. With a tiny weekly income from butter and eggs they bought calico, needles, thread, and an occasional magazine or stick of peppermint candy.

Brother Henry, the sole man on the place, raised the cash required to meet the mortgage, pay taxes, buy tools and machinery, replace livestock and seed, and if possible to pay the wages of a hired hand during the heavy work months of planting and harvest. The total cash earned by this farm in a year's time was less than $1500. Hamilton's only machinery was horse-drawn and consisted of a single-blade plow, a McCormick reaper to harvest the grain, a mowing machine to cut the hay, and a trip rake to gather the hay in windrows—about $2500 would cover the equipment investment. The value of land and buildings did not exceed another $9000, and the farm operated without a balance of working capital. The only line of bank credit available was through a mortgage on chattel property or land. Both were resorted to in hard times. The crop program included three varieties of grain plus two of hay—clover for the cattle and timothy for the draft horses. Hamilton also tended a feedlot of hogs, made pasturage for sheep, dairy cows, and the horses, maintained a small yard for slaughtering calves, hogs, and sheep for the family's meat supply, had a smokehouse for curing meats, a granary for small grains, and a crib for corn. He repaired his tools, wagons, buggies, and machines, trained his horses, castrated his rams and bull calves, and doctored his livestock. The only feedstuff he bought regularly was salt.

Two world wars made the farming techniques of Henry Hamilton obsolete. The drudgery was too much for the human spirit. War gave the farm boy employment in the city, and the automobile afforded him the means to get there. In both world conflicts, pressures were heavy for increased agricultural production. Mechanization offered enterprising farmers the means by which a profit could be realized from cultivating marginal land with minimum human help. By midcentury there were fewer farms than ever before, yet the total annual agricultural production was billions of dollars larger than in the past.

What manner of man brought about this change? His profile was recorded in a document prepared by Quaker's feed department:

S. V. "Skip" Johnson is a young businessman who lives near Ottumwa, Iowa. His business is farming. His home and farmstead appear, as you drive by, much the same as they did ten or twenty years ago, but that's where the similarity ends.

Today his home has a hi-fi and a dishwasher. He has an office with a comptometer—and he retains the services of a Certified Public Accountant. He gets a weekly livestock market newsletter. He has milk delivered to the door. He has $35,000 in notes at the bank on cattle and hogs. He grows larger acreages of crops. And housed in more utility-type buildings are more machinery and more livestock.

In the two decades between 1940 and 1960 these changes have occurred in "Skip" Johnson's operation. The rate of these changes has accelerated sharply in the years most recent. During the twenty-year span the acres he owned increased from 140 to 500; his crop acres from 80 to 340, the hogs he fed from 250 to 2000, the cattle he fed from 15 to 200, his land valuation from $30,000 to $160,000, his farm machinery from $10,000 to $30,000, his gross income from $25,000 to $125,000, and his annual net income from $6000 to $14,000. "It's been harder to raise the net income figure," said Mr. Johnson, "than any other figure on the board." To get the per unit cost down, producers like Mr. Johnson have had to increase the size . . . and spread fixed costs over a larger operation. This new farmer-businessman is a bigger customer. "Skip" Johnson spent $3000 for fertilizer in a year, $700 for seed corn, $1200 for tractor gas. He replaced about 10 per cent of his machinery each year—that's $3000. He spends $1 a head to vaccinate his pigs. His insurance bill is sizable. He spends $200 a week, or $10,000 a year, for hog feed. To-day's farmer, exemplified by "Skip" Johnson, is a sharper businessman, tougher to sell. His decision-making depends less on tradition or habit, more on economic rationality.

The difference between Johnson and Henry Hamilton tells the story of the revolution in American farming. Hamilton was not a good customer for the goods and services of the outside world. The Johnson type, by contrast, buys a great deal. No time is wasted on the production of eggs and milk for the family, when the same hours and energy can be applied more profitably and the family's food obtained more conveniently at the local supermarket. By 1970 farmers like Skip Johnson will spend three-fourths of their annual gross income for feed, fertilizer, seed, machinery, stock, and household supplies purchased from outside.

This progression from the insular world of Hamilton to the more sophisticated one of Johnson has produced a new social order with a new system of doing business. Ezra Benson, former U.S. Secretary of Agriculture, commented on the efficiency of the new type of American farmer. ". . . these twenty million people, less than one per cent of the world's population, are producing between two-fifths and one-half of the world's eggs, red meat and milk. This is the major factor enabling the American consumer to have the best diet in the world and spend a smaller part of his income for food than in most other countries."

The transformation in American farming has changed the procedures of those who cater to agriculture. How the feed department of The Quaker Oats Company met the challenge of the new order is an example of management dealing with change. Commercial feeds were first manufactured to realize income from byproducts of cereal and flour milling. Close-fisted Ferdinand Schumacher refused to float his oat hulls, corn bran, and barley residues down the river or haul them off to be burned; he found a use for them in cattle feeds. The advent of specialization in agriculture, which Schumacher was quick to sense, created a profitable market for his wares. During Schumacher's career, the free open range of the prairie states gave way to fenced land. As pasturage became more restricted and the land more valuable, the dairy, poultry, and livestock producers augmented their supplies of home-grown feedstuffs with preparations bought off the farm, particularly during

times of war, drought, or pestilence. The need thus was
created for an industry which would manufacture feeds
for the farmer. Schumacher pioneered this with a mixture of corn, oats, and barley byproducts which he
named *COB*. The early feeds like *COB* were improvised
from the cereal materials available, and thus they varied
in formula with the season and with retail demand.

The following reminiscences of an early mill worker,
printed in a trade journal, reflect the casual standards of
nineteenth-century feed manufacturing:

> We had a little dab of cottonseed meal, a few sacks of
> bran, and a few sacks of corn chops, and a barrel of salt.
> We dumped it on a pile in the middle of the floor and Mr.
> Edgar, he gets a shovel on one side of the pile and I get a
> shovel on the other. Mr. Edgar shovels awhile, then stops
> and wipes his brow; then I shovel awhile. Then you know
> when we got that feed made up and shipped it down to
> Opelika, Alabama, those mules wouldn't eat it because it
> had too much salt.

Unknown to Edgar and his foreman, animal nutrition
was receiving scientific attention. Two Germans named
Wolff and Lehmann had been responsible for creating
the original standards for nutritive values in animal
feeds. The Connecticut Experiment Station and the University of Wisconsin were the first to teach the Wolff–
Lehmann standards in the United States. Later F. B.
Morrison adapted the German standards to American
feedstuffs, and the Morrison standards became the de-
finitives of nutrition in feed ingredients. These standards gave the state governments a basis for laws to
regulate the content and purity of commercial feeds.
Connecticut led the way, followed by Pennsylvania. National action caught up with the states when feed regulations were added to the existing federal Food and Drug

*Donold B. Lourie, chairman and chief executive officer,
(left) with Robert D. Stuart, Jr., president since 1964.
Hired as a statistician in 1922, Lourie became executive
vice president in 1945, president 1947, chairman 1962.
Stuart, grandson of the founder, served fifteen years on
the rugged firing line of sales and retail merchandising*

*Colin S. Gordon, vice chairman, for many years pro-
duction specialist, fact finder and trouble shooter; with
the two executive vice presidents, John D'Arcy, Jr.
(operations) and Augustin S. Hart, Jr. (International)
both of whom became vice presidents in 1954, members of Board of Directors 1960*

Quaker executives are noted for their public service. Chairman Lourie being sworn as Undersecretary of State for Administration by Secretary of State Dulles in 1953

John Stuart led Illinois committee pressuring Congress to adopt good government recommendations of the Hoover Commission. Here with former President Herbert Hoover

Robert D. Stuart, U.S. Ambassador to Canada 1953–1956, welcomes to his embassy the then British Prime Minister Anthony Eden and Canadian Gov. Gen. Louis St. Laurent

President Robert D. Stuart, Jr., active in many youth programs, here encourages Company-sponsored Junior Achievement group at 1965 Junior Trade Fair

Quaker expansion emphasizes ultra-modern operations. Cedar Rapids plant (top) largest of 32 production units in U.S., and (below) manufacturing-marketing complex serving east coast from Shiremanstown, Pa.

Foreign operations expand. Peterboro (top, above) is one of nine Canadian plants; Southall, England (above) one of three in Britain; Nakskov, Denmark (below) one of seven on European continent; Cali, Colombia (below, bottom) one of five in Latin America

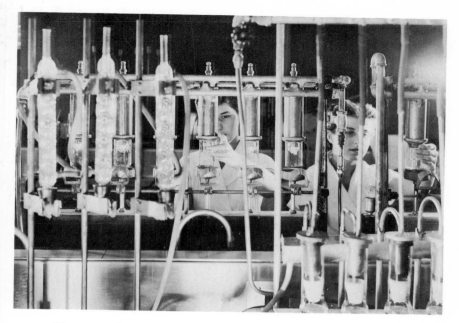

New product research, quality control, nutritional studies center in modern plant at Barrington, Ill.

Quaker's model farm, also at Barrington, tests better feeds for cattle, hogs, poultry, pet dogs and cats

Quaker's galaxy of 200 products includes chemicals,
commercial feeds, plus this line for grocery shelf

Act. Most states now require a feed registration generally showing the brand name, a guaranteed analysis, list of ingredients, net weight, and name of manufacturer. Meanwhile, to protect their own interests and to give them greater voice, millers formed The American Feed Manufacturers Association in 1909. This organization became a potent trade association but had no office in the nation's capital until 1964.

Quaker's management recognized the need for more exact feed formulation by establishing a separate division in 1905 with George A. Chapman in charge. Chapman had been a student of W. A. Henry at the University of Wisconsin and was thus a pioneer in the science of livestock nutrition. Quaker's feed division has continued to rely heavily on university agricultural schools such as Wisconsin and Iowa State College (now Iowa State University) for basic research, technological guidance, and executive manpower.

The first recruit from a university faculty was J. A. McLean, who in 1921 reached Quaker from the Massachusetts Agricultural College at the invitation of William Suits, then manager of Quaker's feed division. McLean brought the scientific approach to research and formulation of Quaker's livestock feeds. Later Quaker established a livestock experimental feeding farm at Madison, Wisconsin. There McLean conducted research into the feed value of mill-run oat hulls, middlings, and shorts under the observation of the College of Agriculture of the University of Wisconsin. As a result of this program, the combination of the three byproducts achieved an identity as mill feed of accepted nutritional value.

A scientist in the field of poultry husbandry made himself heard during the same years. Olney Brown Kent, the second man granted a Ph.D. in poultry husbandry, became a professor on the Cornell faculty. Doc Kent, as he was affectionately known, was a crusader. Possessed of great imagination and stubborn drive, he was an energetic advocate and a fluent speaker. In Kent's day the time lag between the scientific development of a new technique in farming and its general acceptance by farmers was estimated at seven years, an inertia that stimulated Kent to action. Certain that discoveries made in his years of research at Cornell would pay important dividends to poultry farmers, he joined the Quaker organization in 1922. Two years later he established the company's experimental poultry farm at Libertyville, Illinois. Here Kent engineered the first great scientific breakthrough in poultry feeding. General acceptance of it led to "taking the poultry industry indoors," as one expert put it, and made possible the production of poultry meat and eggs on a year-round basis.

Doc Kent had been watching closely the nutritional researches of Hart and Steenbock at the University of Wisconsin and of McCollom at Johns Hopkins. These pioneers in vitamin science discovered that the leg weakness and general debility which overcame poultry confined indoors and deprived of natural sunlight was a form of rickets. This malady could be eliminated, they found, by fortifying the poultry ration with cod-liver oil, a substance naturally enriched with Vitamin D.

The new knowledge inspired Doctor Kent to add cod-liver oil to Quaker's feed for baby chicks. Advertisements during the autumn of 1923 announced "sunshine in the bag," his term for the first vitamin fortification of a poultry feed. At first, disbelief and ridicule greeted the idea. Later, poultry farmers reported that baby chicks fed on the sunshine feed had negligible losses from leg weakness. Soon vitamin fortification of poultry feed became common. Kent's innovation had opened the way for modern meat and egg factories to house huge flocks indoors for the entire life cycle of the birds.

Sunshine in the bag was Doctor Kent's most dramatic and highly publicized contribution to poultry husbandry, but he was author of and advocate for many others. He theorized that when young pullets were forced to mature slowly by restricting their feed, instead of being rushed into egg production, the retarded birds would reward their owner with a considerably longer productive life. Gradually this idea took hold, and restricted feeding became standard procedure. Kent also amazed contemporaries by a proposal of "better teeth for hens." Since a hen uses her gizzard to grind up her expensive feed, why not give her a hard, insoluble granite grit to aid the digestive process, Kent asked, instead of the traditional grit of ground limestone which dissolved and lost its attrition value. Every tenth of a cent of feed cost was critically important, and Doc Kent's new way of improving feeding efficiency became common in the industry.

To O. B. Kent must also go credit for pioneering antibiotics in poultry feeds. The use of these medicines in fowl feeds is usually dated from the publication in 1950 of research done by Lederle Laboratories. A paper published by Stokstad and Jukes indicated that drugs of the antibiotic class promoted growth in chickens and at the same time combated the intestinal bacteria that interfered with the assimilation of protein. Before publication of this research, however, Kent had made one of his characteristically impatient forays. Hearing of the Lederle work, he secured the watery residue left from the manufacture of aureomycin for human treatment, reduced it to a concentrate, and inserted it experimentally in poultry feed.

Quaker made splendid use of Kent's unusual teaching abilities with a radio program, "The Man on the Farm," on a national network. Every Saturday noon for sixteen years—one of the longest consecutive runs in radio network history—Doc Kent dispensed advice on poultry management. Guest farmers discussed their problems and, under the coaxing of Master of Ceremonies Chuck Acree, shared their human experiences, which—stemming from real life—were often more hilarious than professional comedy scripts. Arno "Denny" Dennerlein, then manager of feed-dealer services, conducted the Blue Ribbon interviews in which poultrymen told of their successes with Quaker feeds. The climax of the program was Kent's editorial message for poultry raisers. Here was the forum for which he had always yearned, a place he could expand his ideas to a million-fold audience.

Kent will be remembered by Quaker feed salesmen for his evangelism at meetings and in private talks. He was the first scientist in the feed business to equip salesmen with an understanding of nutrition. On road trips with salesmen, Doc would stay up all night if he had an attentive pupil. To him the first precept of intelligent salesmanship was product knowledge.

"Doc has spent so much time watching chickens that he even thinks like a chicken," an associate observed. He even ate like a chicken, having observed that healthy birds gulped down their rations with great zest and no ceremony. "There's really no physiological justification for wasting a lot of time at meals," he explained to a companion as they visited the dining car during one of the doctor's missionary journeys. Then he deftly consumed his soup, a pair of rainbow trout, and the accompanying side dishes in five minutes flat, devoting his total attention to the matter.

After his death in 1956, his professional career was memorialized by his election to the Poultry Industry Hall of Fame, established by the American Poultry Historical Society, of which he had once been president. As the feed business grew in volume and complexity after World War II, a team of specialists in animal nutrition was recruited from the graduate schools of a number of leading agricultural colleges by Isaac S. Riggs, vice-president for Quaker's Feed Department. Riggs was an agricultural economist from Iowa State College and an early recruit of Doc Kent and was familiar with the broad areas of fundamental research going on in the nation's agricultural schools.

Soon after World War II, university laboratories achieved a milestone with a high-energy protein diet for producing poultry meat. The prevailing standard among commercial broiler raisers in buying feed had been price. H. M. Scott, then at the Connecticut Agricultural College at Storrs and later a professor at the University of Illinois, maintained that a higher-quality and therefore higher-priced feed was more efficient. The grain ration, he argued, should be fortified with a liberal amount of energy and protein supplement.

In 1945 [he wrote later] the decision was made to test the high energy ration in the field through a feed manufacturer operating in Connecticut. . . . The cost per ton of the ration was considerably more than the conventional rations being used. Several growers consented to run divided house tests when the feed company agreed to make up any difference in profit that might result from using the more costly feed. Relatively few of the original growers completed the experiment. They could see quite early in the test that they were going to increase their profits by using the more costly feed. By 1946 the word was out, and we were off to the races. I do not mind saying that we were astonished and somewhat perturbed at the speed with which the concept came into use, since we had not published our findings by so much as a single word in print.

Quaker formulated a new broiler ration based on the Connecticut standards, and extended credit for a term of ten weeks, the time then required to feed a meat bird to market size. The new policy soon developed a record feed business.

The effect of the new ration on poultry led Quaker's researchers to suspect that energy might also be the most important element in feed for livestock. W. R. Graham, director of nutrition research, commented on this reasoning: "The biological conversion of food intake into eggs and meat for human consumption imposes a heavy bodily strain on the chicken. Given sufficient energy intake in the form of carbohydrates and fats, the bird can acquire the strength to transform balanced increases in its protein intake into eggs and meat. The great significance of the Connecticut research was the recognition of this work load on the birds, and how the new high energy ration equipped them for it."

Pursuing this promising line of thought, Quaker made grants for research on the effect on livestock of the Connecticut type of ration for poultry. Such a study was begun at the University of Maryland, under the direction of Dr. Joseph C. Shaw. Ration tests based on the high-energy protein theory were carried out by putting a hose into a cow's stomach and withdrawing samples of her rumen at two-hour intervals. These were analyzed for clues to the amount of energy which the animal converted from each feed tested. A long series of experiments indicated that a threefold increase in energy-producing secretions had occurred in the stomach of one of the test cows. Some mysterious element in her feed had increased greatly the amount of energy she derived from it. Here was the first inkling that cattle could be equipped to manufacture more milk and beef by the proper use of some as-yet-unisolated nutrient.

Shaw finally discovered it to be an amino-acid protein energy factor called methionine, which acted as a sort of catalyst to step up the energy by changing the balance of the acids in the rumen to carry different carbon values. This gain in energy was accomplished without additional volumes of feed.

Eager to translate these research findings into practical form, Graham engaged William L. Ensor, a student of Dr. Shaw's at the University of Maryland. At Barrington, Ensor took charge of Quaker's experimental dairy herd. Later he was joined in the project by Ralph McCall, manager of beef cattle research, in comparable tests on steers that were being fattened in the Quaker feedlots. Within a short time, Ensor and McCall were getting increases of 10 per cent in milk and beef production.

The result, Quaker's researchers were confident, was "the first major breakthrough in dairy nutrition in fifty years." To the livestock producer, the discovery meant less feed per pound of gain, thus more meat at lower cost. Nor were dairy and beef cattle the only beneficiaries. A new Ful-O-Pep hog feed, Gro-Pork 280, cut from 3.5 to 2.75 pounds the amount of feed required to put one pound of weight on a fattening shoat.

When Quaker's feed department was formally organized in 1905, management's main purpose was to find a sale for the waste byproducts of the cereal mills. First improvement in feed formulas was the addition of molasses in 1908. William Suits, manager in 1917, is given credit for coining *Ful-O-Pep,* which has become a valuable trademark in industry. He applied it to Quaker's hog feeds in 1917, and the agreeable increase in business inspired Quaker in 1924 to establish its pioneering poultry-research farm at Libertyville.

World War I taxed agricultural production to the utmost. A seller's market in manufactured feeds resulted and Quaker's business flourished, particularly in the high-volume areas of hog and chicken feeds. "Our feed department," stockholders were told in 1919, "is constantly growing in size and importance." But the disastrous 1920 losses were centered principally in the feed department, and some wondered whether this end of the business could be continued profitably. A compromise left the organization intact, and it flourished until the economic depression of the 1930s, when almost every country store installed a feed grinder and manufactured-feed sales suffered drastically. To save money, Quaker's management merged feed sales with cereals, a move that proved unfortunate. Salesmen of cereal products were ill-equipped by temperament or knowledge to market agricultural supplies to the conservative farm trade. Feed sales languished and did not recover until the unusual demand of World War II created another seller's market.

By 1944, the civilian and military demand for eggs, meat, and poultry once again required Quaker's five big feed mills to operate at capacity. In this prosperous era, the feed department won back its autonomy. New postwar forces and technological improvements began to reshape agriculture. Small inefficient farms were absorbed by larger units. The new college-trained farmers traced to tenths of a cent the cost of feeding for a pound of meat, a gallon of milk, a dozen eggs. The feed manufacturer who could lower that cost won the business. Most traditional feed-merchandising practices became obsolete, and Quaker reorganized its feed operation.

When Isaac S. Riggs left the post of general cereal sales manager in 1948 to become manager of the feed department, Ful-O-Pep and other commercial feeds were sold almost exclusively in 50- and 100-pound bags—usually burlap, but sometimes of colorfully printed cotton material in an assortment of patterns. These florals, checks, and plaids were appealing to the farmer's wife as a source of tea towels, tablecloths, aprons, and housedresses. Many a feed dealer swore softly as he shifted several tons of feed in his warehouse to get at a single 50-pound sack of chick starter in the twining rose pattern "because Jane needs a couple more yards of that stuff to finish some sewing." The colorful bags, and much of the burlap as well, disappeared during the 1950s as new methods of distribution emerged. Bulk delivery was devised to meet the needs of poultry and livestock producers whose once-small operations had grown into enterprises involving the feeding of hundreds of cattle, thousands of pigs and chickens. Mass-production methods were called for; technicians devised the bulk truck, which could deliver in one load several tons of loose feed and unload it by means of an auger conveyor directly into on-the-farm storage bins. By 1965, some feed was still sold in sacks, mostly of kraft paper, for the convenience of smaller customers. But more than three-quarters of Ful-O-Pep's tonnage was in bulk, much of it custom-made for dealers and farmers who drove to the mill and watched their feed move straight from the blenders to their trucks.

Riggs and his staff of marketing-research people were convinced too of the need for more flexible formulas for Ful-O-Pep feeds. For years these formulas had been created by production planners at the Chicago headquarters and given management approval, thus rendering them unchangeable at the mill. With the development of a farm clientele of greater sophistication, this rigid system was no longer practical. Nor was it economical. John C. Huckabee, later general feed-sales manager, was articulate and persistent in advocating more elastic formulas. He pressed his viewpoint starting in the early 1950s, when he became manager of the southern feed division at Memphis. As a young salesman in Texas he had often seen good accounts get away from him simply because of price. He reasoned that Ful-O-Pep could be competitive only if the feed division had authority to take advantage of ups and downs in the cost of various feed ingredients. This the company's feed mills were unable to do, under a management policy which made them a sort of captive market for the byproducts of Quaker's own cereal mills. Feed sales at the Memphis mill had been dwindling steadily, with some speculation that the operation might be shut down entirely. Required to accept many of its ingredients at a price that advantaged Quaker's cereal milling, Quaker feeds could not compete in the market place.

Management was convinced and the feed division authorized to buy what it needed on the open market, using Quaker's cereal products when economy so dictated. A flexible new formulation policy permitted exchange of more economical ingredients for those high in price, so long as nutritive values of the finished feeds were strictly maintained. W. R. Graham recalls: "It was a change in thinking that several feed ingredients were considered to be equivalents, or roughly so. Thus we could substitute one ingredient for another within a given class. These formulas allowed us to move quickly as prices changed or as ingredients became more or less available. Over a course of ten years we went from almost a recipe system to formulation entirely by digestible nutrient values."

The new flexible procedure enabled Quaker to make feeds on the basis of an optimum formula, representing the most efficient nutrition at the lowest cost possible at any given time. Ingredient prices on the commodity exchanges fluctuate hour by hour and day by day. A sudden drop in the price of soybean meal is a signal to Quaker's feedmen to maximize the use of soybean meal so long as this source of protein costs less than equivalent sources. Most other feed grains and ingredients likewise have nutritional twins.

Computer technology was required to handle the astronomical number of calculations required each week to price Quaker's many manufactured feeds to reflect changing market quotations. Typical is Ful-O-Pep broiler ration, a combination of 11 different classes of ingredients. To compute the optimum formula for this feed alone requires thousands of intricate computations each week. Today, the task of flexing all of Ful-O-Pep's formulas is accomplished in half an hour of computer time; a team of mathematicians, working the clock around on hand computations, would need a week for the same task.

Having solved the problem of immutable formulas, Riggs and his associates proceeded to extend the principle of flexibility to manufacturing. Quaker had been a "big mill" company, producing feed at a few plants and shipping it great distances, sometimes hundreds of miles. The trend in the industry was toward decentralization, with smaller feed mills located closer to customers. Fifteen per cent of the farms were producing nearly 90 per cent of America's agricultural output. The cream of the market was about 400,000 customers, each a specialist in beef production, or pork, or turkeys, broilers, eggs, or milk. These specialist farmers tended to become concentrated in geographic areas where conditions favored them.

Quaker finally abandoned the concept of Ful-O-Pep as a national brand. The old-line mills continued to make feeds, with their market areas deliberately contracted to a hundred-mile radius. Modern Ful-O-Pep mills were constructed in centers of agricultural production and equipped for bulk handling, which saved customers four to five dollars per ton.

The concern of the Quaker feed salesman in the new order was "territory management," analysis of opportunity, and rendering service to his customers. He came to be expert in his customers' operations, an adviser and trouble-shooter. Selling feed was no longer a matter of driving down a dirt road, calling on every farmer and stockman. The modern salesman researched his prospects ahead of the call, and brought to the first interview a knowledge of the customer's financial condition, service requirements, and product needs. He understood in a broad sense subjects such as finance, credit management, accounting, manufacturing, farm management, agricultural marketing, and the general economic outlook.

The 1960s saw a pronounced trend toward integration of two or more links in the agricultural-industrial chain, through operating partnerships of farmers with packers or feed companies.

Integration had begun tentatively some thirty years earlier, in the middle of the classic depression. Jesse Jewell, a Gainesville, Georgia, feed dealer, began to finance local poultry raisers who were short on cash. Jewell extended loans enabling farmers to buy baby chicks, provided they agreed to use his feed, which he supplied on credit. In turn, likewise on credit, Quaker advanced the feed to Jewell. When the chicks reached market, all parties were paid. By the 1960s, Jewell had his own hatcheries to supply baby chicks, and he guaranteed to buy back the grown birds for processing in his own plant. His production was ten million birds a year, packaged, labeled, and delivered frozen to the grocery trade.

Ninety per cent of the nation's total poultry meat in 1965 was produced by similar mechanics, and the trend toward integration was evident in beef raising, dairy production, and (to a lesser extent) in pork.

There were infinite variations in the new working relationships developing among farmers, feed companies, processors, and distributors, and Quaker experimented with a number of combinations. The company's first experience with integration occurred in the broiler industry in 1953, when a large poultry processing plant in Decatur, Alabama, overextended itself and headed for bankruptcy. Its chief creditor was The Quaker Oats Company, from which it had bought feed on credit. Quaker's treasurer, William H. Ball, left for Decatur under instructions to make the best settlement he could manage. A few days later he telephoned Donold Lourie from Decatur. "You may not like the idea," he told the president, "but you're in the broiler business." He had accepted ownership of the plant in settlement of the feed bill. A dozen years later, Quaker was still operating its "involuntary acquisition" at Decatur and had substantially enlarged operations there.

Henry Crutchfield, who succeeded to the vice-presidency for feeds when Riggs retired in 1965, had been working out a variety of "alignments" whereby Quaker money was being used to back successful operations generated by local entrepreneurs. "We're inclined to think that we'd rather let successful local businessmen do the actual integrating," Crutchfield said, "but there are almost limitless ways in which we are willing to invest Quaker's money in support of well-managed operations." In some cases, Quaker actually became a minority stockholder in local feed distributorships, leaving the intricacies of integration to local businessmen. In other instances, the investment by Quaker took the form of a revolving line of credit, or even contracts in which broiler growers or turkey producers were guaranteed against loss at market time, with the provision that profits over a certain level were to be divided with Quaker. Innumerable variations on this share-the-risk, share-the-gains plan were possible and Quaker's management has moved with the times in a blend of daring and prudence.

Chapter 13 * *Quaker*
across the World

I N the autumn of 1897 Great Britain received a shocking foretaste of the advertising age.

Travelers returning from the Continent by the overnight boat from Calais to Dover saw, on approaching Britain, an enormous sign profaning the historic chalk cliffs. How it got there nobody knew. But there it was, in letters high enough, reports said, to be read three miles at sea:

QUAKER OATS

Inquiries were made at once by the proper authorities. The culprit was not hard to find. He had already made a nuisance of himself at Liverpool by converting a lorry into a huge replica of the Quaker Oats package and driving the contraption through the streets until the Watch Committee set him down with a two-guinea fine for operating a van of larger than prescribed dimensions. He had also made a preposterous proposal to the national ministry to be given permission to nail a tin sign heralding Quaker Oats on every telegraph line pole in the British Isles. He was sent packing for that one.

This brash fellow was Frederick A. Seymour, an enterprising young man from the home office of the American Cereal Company, which had a branch office in Liverpool and agents in London, Bristol, Newcastle, and Glasgow,

Scotland. Seymour's father had been Henry Parsons Crowell's salesman in the Quaker Mill at Ravenna, Ohio. Young Frederick had assimilated the promotional flair of Crowell himself with such zest that Robert Stuart sent him to England to conduct an advertising campaign on American lines, including sampling every doorstep in England with a two-ounce package of oatmeal.

Seymour refused to take down his sign from Dover's cliffs, determined to keep the controversy in the public print as long as possible. Every newspaper in Britain was talking about Oats, indignantly but effectively. The attention Seymour's offense against national propriety attracted was enormous and—from his point of view—a windfall. After several weeks of public bickering, the House of Commons directed the Company to remove its sign from the cliffs, and Frederick Seymour complied.

This was not the first time Britain had had cause to raise an eyebrow at Quaker Oats. The first shipments to England had been purchased in 1877 by the commission firm of Lathan & Company, London, one of whose executives had been intrigued during a visit to America by the choice taste of the cut oats from the Ravenna Mill. Henry Parsons Crowell, purchasing the property, was delighted—and flattered—that the Ohio product had found favor with the discriminating British palate, and moved at once to exploit the phenomenon. He named as his agent for the British Isles the highly reputed pioneer importer of American delicacies, Ebenezer Thompson of Liverpool, who had also represented Ferdinand Schumacher. Crowell urged the wholesaler to try an exceedingly questionable undertaking, that of selling Quaker Oats in Scotland, the home of oatmeal.

The British salesman told Crowell that cut oats would never do for Scotland. The Scots liked the dry, nutty flavor of stone-ground grain such as Robert Stuart had sent occasionally from his mill in Cedar Rapids, Iowa. These were the traditional Scottish oats, not flaky but more like granules. Such cereal required several hours of cooking to be edible as the classic Scottish porridge. The nutty product was also highly regarded in oatmeal cakes —biscuits made by mixing thoroughly kneaded oatmeal, butter, and shortening with salted water, shaping the resultant mass into half-inch thick scones and baking in an oven or, as some preferred, in a tight-lidded iron kettle swung from a trivet over the hearth. When baked, the scones were then toasted a crisp brown in front of the hot coals at the side of the stove and served with butter or cottage cheese. Travelers often carried the scones in their pockets and, at some inviting stream, dissolved a cake in fresh water and drank the broth, a nourishing, revitalizing, and thrifty lunch. For all three uses, the old-fashioned oats were thought to be mandatory.

Crowell, however, believed otherwise. To prove his point he cited the purchase of quantities of Quaker Oats by certain British and Scottish landed estates. If the nobility were eating Quaker Oats for breakfast, Crowell knew he had a worthy promotion. To his chagrin he discovered that his noble customers were buying Quaker Oats "not for consumption at their own tables at the morning meal, but to be cooked and fed to their hunting dogs."

"We were sobered and saddened by this experience," Crowell wrote years later in an employee publication, "for good as an English hound is, it was not the kind of consumer we were seeking. Our pride was touched and our ambition was aroused and our resolve was made that we would not be turned aside from our purpose but continue until we proved that we manufactured the finest cereal products and made them welcome articles of diet in every family high or low, rich or poor, throughout the length and breadth of Great Britain."

He had very little luck, however, until he began to make the flaky rolled oats he called *Quaker Oats Regular*. The old-style ground oats became known, for the benefit of Scotland's preference, as Scottish or Standard oats. Reinforced by a more attractive package design and a quicker-cooking cereal, Crowell began a round of vigorous promotion. "We were laughed at," he recalled, "by the Scottish and Irish millers who felt secure in their position which they had held through many centuries and which was deemed impregnable. We were told we were wasting our money, for no foreigner had ever succeeded in getting coals to Newcastle or oatmeal into the land of its origin. No one, not even our import agents, gave us more than faint-hearted encouragement."*

Crowell persevered, inviting comparison between the crisp, flaky, easy-to-cook, easy-to-digest Quaker Oats and the traditional product offered by Scottish millers. Local suppliers fought back. They put up their own oats in canisters that almost duplicated the Quaker Oats carton in appearance. A highly publicized court action was necessary to stop this invasion of trademark rights. Domestic millers cited that the importation of oatmeal endangered British agriculture and industry. An effective device of this campaign was a billboard which depicted a handsome Durham bull at the water's edge, goring and stamping a horde of little Quaker packages surging out of the sea on spidery legs.

* Not only did Quaker carry oatmeal to Scotland; in 1919 it also successfully invaded Italy, the home of *pasta*, with a macaroni and a spaghetti. In the 1920s Quaker introduced Puffed Rice into China and Thailand. In recent years ready-mixes of regional specialties have appeared in many nations under Quaker labels.

The concentrated attack was splendid publicity for Quaker. The public became curious enough to accept Crowell's invitation to compare Quaker's with British oatmeal. Many were converted to the rolled flakes and much pleased with the greater ease of preparation. "It was all that we asked," Crowell wrote in retrospect; "it proved to be the turning point, the beginning of success, the opening of the way to ultimate victory."

In 1894, Quaker sold in the British Isles 23,000 barrels (4,140,000 pounds) of bulk oatmeal and 31,000 cases (of two dozen 20-ounce tins each) of the packaged rolled oats. Six years later sales had expanded to 121,000 barrels (21,780,000 pounds) and 331,000 cases. Quaker organized a British subsidiary, Quaker Oats Limited, with Frederick Pleasants as its managing director. Quaker had also established itself on the Continent with an office in Rotterdam, from which base Ernest Noell had set up sales organizations covering most of Europe.

All three of the principals in the formation of the American Cereal Company had had earlier experience in foreign trade. Ferdinand Schumacher exported his Akron-made oatmeal to his native northern Germany. On the day that saw his milling empire consumed by fire, Schumacher told newspaper reporters, "I asked the boys last night about the orders and they said one carload left for Germany yesterday." Schumacher's British agent, as noted, was Ebenezer Thompson of Liverpool.

The promise of export trade by way of the ports of the Atlantic seaboard in part motivated Robert Stuart to persuade his father to move their milling operation from Canada to Cedar Rapids, Iowa. Later, their agents in Philadelphia and Boston supplied Stuart's oatmeal to ships' chandlers and foreign purchasers.

After the great 1899 proxy fight, Stuart and Crowell

were free to move fast toward world distribution. They would, said Henry Crowell later, "develop rapidly in all parts of the world, wherever oatmeal could be sold, an advertised brand . . . the Quaker brand." Organization of the British subsidiary was the first large result of this policy.

At the company's office in Saint George's House, Eastcheap, London, an agreement was effected whereby American Cereal transferred its assets in England to the new domestic corporation and pledged to sell in the United Kingdom only to Quaker Oats Limited. Having accomplished this business, Robert Stuart, who went to London for the negotiations, continued on to Hamburg for conferences with Noell, and shortly thereafter returned to Chicago.

The British company flourished. A year later Frederick Pleasants was rewarded for his seven years of achievement abroad with a position in Chicago as assistant to Henry Crowell, American Cereal Company president. An associate of Pleasants in the English company, Richard E. Bridge, was promoted to the post of managing director, a position he held for the succeeding twenty years. Finally he was succeeded by the ingenious motivator of the chalk-cliffs signboard, Frederick Seymour.

At first the new British subsidiary sold only Quaker products exported from the United States. Then tariffs on imports suggested either a manufacturing unit in England or a Canadian mill from which duty-free goods could be shipped throughout the British Commonwealth. The Canadian alternative appeared more attractive. The oat crop of eastern Canada was abundant, and even finer grain was beginning to flow from the western provinces. A Canadian plant could be supervised by U.S. technicians without great expense. And Canadian-born

Robert Stuart understood the natural resources and people of the country. He also felt some pride in returning to his motherland under such circumstances.

At Peterborough, Ontario, Stuart found what he wanted. A canal about to be built would connect Peterborough with the seaboard by way of the St. Lawrence, giving finished goods low-cost transportation to seaports. Two important railroad systems intersected at Peterborough, offering freight service to all points. Canadian railroads, to encourage the grain traffic from the West, offered "milling in transit" rates whereby western oats could be held at Peterborough for milling and then shipped as far east as Montreal at no extra transportation cost. To encourage Quaker, the farsighted Peterborough city council offered attractive concessions, including a maximum assessed value for tax purposes of $58,700 for forty-two years, during which time company personal property would be municipally tax-exempt. Under such favorable auspices, a plant was completed in 1902 with a capacity of 4200 barrels of milled products per day, at that time the largest capacity in the Quaker system.

The company did not promote domestic sales in Canada from its new mill at Peterborough, concentrating rather on supplying Quaker Oats to England. Sales in Canada itself were for some time restricted to flour supplied by mills in the United States.

Robert Stuart and Henry Crowell personally supervised the establishment of the company's first outposts in foreign trade. Both made regular European trips to counsel with foreign managers and agents and to establish subsidiaries across the world. The Rotterdam office was put in charge of a steamship executive from New York, G. H. Voorhoeve, who knew the export trade.

Later, as the European business throve, Ernest Noell was made chief of European operations. His first decision was to move headquarters from Rotterdam to Hamburg, where he set up a mill to escape oppressive German tariffs. Northern Germany had been a prize target in Quaker's planning. Schumacher's prestige should have made it easy, but the Germans had resisted the invasion with a retaliatory tariff wall. Domestic sales companies were formed in Sweden and France. The western Mediterranean was considered a franchise of the British subsidiary's office in Cairo.

By 1908, Quaker's export catalogue proclaimed that the Quaker trademark "is known by more people in more countries than any other brand on any kind of goods in the world."

One of the earliest export opportunities had developed in Central and South America. A Quaker sales agent had written: "This is Quaker Oats' land of promise. Other than lottery tickets, nothing in Latin America is more staple than Quaker Oats." The remark was hyperbole, but revealed the willingness of Quaker's salesmen to penetrate the hinterlands of every nation on earth. A traveler to Uruguay sent word: "We scoured the town of Montevideo and in a little grocery store we found a few packages of Quaker Oats." Members of the Stuart family, traveling abroad, made a game of inquiring at remote stores and trading posts in many lands for the Quaker product, and were rarely disappointed.

From London to Tokyo, company advertisements appeared in newspapers, on billboards, and in other media. To reach the illiterate masses, symbols and signs were employed, word-of-mouth campaigns spread. In China, a colorful billboard proclaimed "Old Man Brand Quaker Oats." Lantern slides, printed handbills, cooking demon-

strations, samplings spread the message of better nutrition. *"Kuacher Oatch"* was known, said a Quaker agent,
"in the Arabic language the length and breadth of
Egypt." In Calcutta, a brilliantly illuminated sign proclaimed *Quaker Oats* from the top of the Bristol Hotel.
From Canton, China, a correspondent wrote: "At the
Victoria Hotel yesterday a party of tourists were talking
at the table of what they had seen in their sedan chair
tour of the shops. We saw a lot of American goods . . .
especially Quaker Oats." From Manila came back the report of the popularity of oatmeal with coconut milk. A
Japanese wrote to Chicago that Quaker outsold other
brands two to one. An African agent, deep in the Congo,
then one of the more inaccessible jungles, returned this
word: "In this land of malaria, black water fever and
sleeping sickness, the sanitary watertight can of Quaker
Oats has great appeal to the planter, missionary, hunter
and pioneer." Many doctors prescribed Quaker Oats for
infants or invalids, which greatly spread the sales, often
providing the first breakthrough in a newly entered
country. Summing up, a Quaker export executive told
the company's stockholders, "We frequently hear that
the sun never sets on the British flag. This saying can be
applied even more literally to Quaker Oats."

The export tin, devised originally by Ferdinand Schumacher for his overseas trade and modified by Crowell,
was a durable and ingenious container. It had to protect
the cereal from rough handling, sea water, humidity,
pests and filth of all kinds, and at the same time ship
economically and advertise itself through an attractive
label. Twenty ounces of oatmeal were compressed into a
metal package half the size of the cardboard container
used in the United States. This economy of space led
famous pioneer arctic and antarctic explorers to carry

along Quaker's export tin on their expeditions. More than thirty years after one of these packages was shipped to the South Pole by British explorer Robert Scott, it was opened up and the oatmeal found perfectly sound and edible. The tin also traveled to both the North and South poles with Scott, Shackleton, Nansen, Amundsen, and Byrd.

The label was an important line of communication in foreign markets and was printed in dozens of languages and dialects. From the beginning Quaker adapted to foreign customs and practices in its labels, advertising and suggested uses for oatmeal. Rather than attempting persuasion of other nationals to adopt American breakfast habits, Quaker conformed to local customs. In much of Scandinavia—where consumption of oats was the highest per capita in the world—the product was offered, in the tradition of the area, to be eaten raw. In France, Italy, and Spain, where breakfast is negligible, oatmeal was advertised for general cooking. The old Scottish cold broth, which Robert Stuart introduced to his workers at Cedar Rapids, was adapted and sold as a *refresco* for the hot climate of Latin America and as *mingão* in Brazil and Portugal. A different-consistency oatmeal was suggested in recipes for countries using chopsticks.

Before World War I, Quaker claimed to be the most widely distributed product in the world, not excepting Singer Sewing Machine. When the war began, Quaker reported to its stockholders, there were "shipments moving to or contracts accepted in nearly every nation in the world." As a war measure, the German government turned the Hamburg plant into a flour mill, Ernest Noell remaining there in charge of the enterprise. The Canadian plant stepped up its operations substantially to supply British war needs until fire destroyed the Peterborough facility in 1916. A new complex was built immediately, with nearly double the old capacity, giving Quaker the largest cereal mill in the British Empire in 1919. As for the rest of the world, stockholders were advised, "War conditions have interfered somewhat with the distribution of our products throughout the world, but in the larger markets our volume has been increased and our position well maintained. Trainload after trainload of our products is being shipped to Europe."

In his reorganization of 1922, John Stuart gave the foreign operation corporate status for the first time with the appointment of Clifford C. Coldren as Company vice-president for export. The war had left the industrial nations of the world with surplus plant capacity. Many companies pushed for the first time into foreign markets to keep busy their overbuilt manufacturing facilities. Soon nations were erecting sharp tariff barriers against each other to protect home markets. At one critical point Coldren reported, "Since the passage of the last tariff bill by the United States, over forty countries have increased their tariffs."

Quaker, however, managed to expand. In the years between the world wars, the company purchased or built additional mills in England, Denmark, Holland, and Germany to produce Quaker Oats. In 1936 the management sent Earle Muzzy, manager of the export department under Coldren, to search for a manufacturing site in England where ready-to-eat cereals and livestock feeds might be made. Muzzy settled on Southall, a London suburb adjacent to three forms of transportation: canal, railroad, and paved highway. The new plant in England, with the four manufacturing subsidiaries on the Continent, gave Quaker the ability to compete on a broader front throughout Europe.

When Hitler attacked Poland in 1939, setting off World War II, Quaker's annual volume of foreign trade was more than $16 million—27 per cent of gross sales. Of this amount, 75 per cent was contributed by English and Canadian sales. Dutch and Danish subsidiaries yielded about 10 per cent of the gross foreign business, Germany 5 per cent, and the remaining 10 per cent was export trade from the United States to the West Indies, Central and South America, Africa, and the Orient.

All communication with the German, Danish, and Dutch companies ended when the United States entered World War II. A shortage of tin, placed under U.S. government priority, hampered overseas shipments. At one critical period, 50 carloads of Quaker goods destined for overseas were stranded in United States ports because the ships destined to transport the merchandise had been sunk. Often cargo space reserved for Quaker was preempted for strategic military materials.

As early as 1939 the familiar Quaker package had disappeared from the British Isles. An embargo was declared on all imports of packaged oatmeal, although the Canadian mill supplied to Britain huge quantities of bulk oatmeal and flour. To retain its label in British markets, the Quaker management sought to expand its production facilities at Southall, but shortages of building materials prevented the step.

Quaker's export staff was tested by bizarre events throughout the war. A sizable deal with the Finnish government called for the shipment of 20,000 sacks of oatmeal from New York. The Finnish sales agency had been financed by the United States government, and the transaction seemed troubleproof. On Saturday, June 14, 1941, 10,000 sacks of the oatmeal were loaded on a ship about to sail for Finland, and the remainder of the order was piled on the dock to await a later vessel. With the

banks closed on Saturday, Quaker did not secure payment for the first 10,000 sacks before sailing. The ship
anchored at the mouth of New York Harbor to make
ready for its voyage. On Monday, President Franklin D.
Roosevelt, advised over the weekend that Finland was
entering the war on Germany's side, froze all Finnish
funds in U.S. banks. Quaker could not collect on its bill
of lading. A potential loss of $58,000 was involved.
Quaker's Gaylord Whipple, then export manager, met
the emergency by persuading the U.S. State Department
to return the ship to dockside so that the cargo of oatmeal could be unloaded. Whipple then sold the shipment to the British Mission in Washington for $2.80 a
sack, just eight cents a sack short of the price the Finns
had contracted to pay. Even this amount of loss annoyed
Whipple. He persuaded the Finnish government agency
in New York to make up not only the eight-cent differential, but to pay all of the out-of-pocket expenses of the
resale.

Three of the four Quaker mills in Europe suffered surprisingly little damage during World War II. The English plant at Southall, only a mile and a half from
Heston airport, was almost untouched; its office doors
were blown in by a bomb blast during the 1940 blitz. For
four years there was no communication with the plants
in Holland, Denmark, and Germany. After V-E Day, May
7, 1945, Earle Muzzy assessed the damage. He found the
German mill in Grevenbroich, near Düsseldorf, gutted
by bombing raids. With typical German industry, the
Quaker employees reconstructed their mill, utilizing
storage buildings that had escaped damage, and with
their own hands fabricated new machinery from make-
shift materials. Within a year the plant was in operation
at double its prewar capacity.

At Rotterdam Muzzy discovered that the company's

grain elevator had been used in May 1940 as a German command post in the bombing of the city. But this war use of the facilities protected them from destruction, and the Quaker mill operated throughout the occupation under a Nazi trustee. The Germans pressed insistently for export of the Quaker production to Germany; the Quaker personnel saw to it that their supplies were distributed to the famished Dutch. One day the Nazi trustee suggested that the millers might be sent to German labor camps unless they complied, but the manager, Arrie van Noortwijk, Dutch and stubborn, refused at the risk of his life. He further defied the Germans by concealing quantities of Quaker Oats, parceling them out to Quaker personnel for food and something to barter for other necessities. The sole war damage to the Dutch plant occurred when the Germans blew up Rotterdam harbor in their retreat, causing minor wreckage. The mill, however, after five years of peak operations without replacement of worn parts, was in need of a thorough overhaul.

Domestic business in Denmark continued as usual during the German occupation. The mill at Nakskov was not bombed by either side. Gerhard Boesen, the Danish manager, kept the operation in repair and at peak capacity. But Quaker's business had vanished in France. As the Nazis invaded Paris, the Quaker bookkeeper disappeared with all the office cash. Whether he meant to hide the resources from the Germans, was killed in his flight, or absconded intentionally is unknown, since no trace of him was ever found.

The market for exports to the Far East was erased by the war with Japan. On V-J Day in 1945, a twenty-ounce tin of Quaker Oats sold in Shanghai for about $1.50 U.S., or $3000 in Chinese Nationalist currency.

The distributive network that had supplied Quaker's channels of trade in the Orient was demolished.

After the war, damaged properties were rehabilitated and a sales organization re-established in the free world. A separate corporation, Quaker Oats Company of Canada Limited, had been formed during the conflict, with Canadian management and staff, the stock wholly owned by Quaker in the United States. The first postwar concern of the Canadian company was to sell packaged oatmeal in Canada to absorb the production no longer sent to England. With continued refusal by the British government to permit imports of packaged oatmeal after the war, Quaker began to mill oats in England from a new unit at Southall. Late in 1946 the "figure of a man in Quaker garb" became available once again to British customers after a hiatus of eight years. The way back to a leading market position was long and expensive. Not until 1952 could the Quaker management report "The British company's earnings have reached a new high."

The establishment in postwar Europe first of the European Steel and Coal Community, then the Common Market in six nations, with another grouping of the "outer seven" stimulated freer circulation of manufactured goods from plants located within the member nations. Quaker was well prepared for this development, since it had manufacturing facilities both in Common Market countries and in Denmark and England. Latin American markets were bolstered with new milling subsidiaries in Buenos Aires, Cali (Colombia), Porto Alegre (Brazil), Valencia (Venezuela), and Mexico City.

Ten years after the end of World War II, Quaker had re-established itself in world trade excepting only the countries behind the Iron and Bamboo curtains. The report to stockholders for 1954 revealed that the foreign subsidiaries represented a book value of $7,500,000, with earnings around $1,500,000 a year, a high for the post-war period to that time. Less than 10 per cent of Quaker's overseas sales were by export from the United States, so solidly was manufacturing entrenched abroad. The domestic exports were principally to the Far East, with aggressive marketing in the Philippines, Hong Kong, Ceylon, Malaya, and Japan.

Profits to the parent company from foreign operations have been subject to many impacts. In the postwar period, currency devaluations and inability to repatriate earnings were reflected in the earnings statements of some of the foreign subsidiaries. In 1956–1957, on a consolidated foreign gross of $72 million and net of $2,800,-000, only $312,000 was recaptured by the parent company. The remainder was plowed back into growth or held locally in reserve because of the inability to transfer credits. In 1960, on $85 million of gross foreign sales, the profit contribution was only $1,064,000.

As the 1960s progressed, Quaker's increased foreign-capital investment induced a mushrooming of overseas sales. In 1960, a furfural alcohol unit was added to the mill at Southall, England. A pet-food factory was purchased in Holland. Creamoata, Ltd., a leading grocery processor in Australia, was acquired. Gross sales from foreign sources leaped, reaching $90 million for the first time in 1963 and advancing another $6 million in 1964. A big market for convenience foods was developing in Europe, the standard of living improving rapidly, its economy transfused with new life blood by the Marshall Plan. By the mid-1960s Quaker Oats had regained its world position fully, representing one-half to two-thirds of the total sales of oatmeal consumed in the various countries.

Canadian operations expanded in the postwar decades, with ten manufacturing plants located in that country by 1965. Quaker Oats of Canada had achieved the largest sales volume of any of the company's foreign establishments, with Quaker brands there in a commanding position.

Quaker's introduction in Colombia of a low-cost, high-protein food called Incaparina, emphasized that convenient, easy-to-prepare foods can be popularized even in less affluent societies.

In Italy, Brazil, and Argentina, a ready-mix *polenta* was successfully introduced, cutting by hours the traditional time of preparation which this staple corn-meal product required. FrescAvena, Fortavena, ChocAvena, and Areparina were new versions of oatmeal nutrition devised for Latin American markets. Quaker products for man and animals adorned the new Australian supermarkets, doubling in number every year. Livestock feeds and chemical products were increasingly evident in international trade.

By the mid-1960s, 22 foreign plants manufactured a diversified list of Quaker products for human and animal consumption at a rate approaching $100 million a year.

Robert Stuart's and Henry Crowell's vision of self-supporting subsidiary units world-wide appeared to have been substantially realized.

Chapter 14 * Service
in War and Peace

Early in January 1942, scarcely a month after the Japanese had bombed Pearl Harbor, John Stuart received a call from U.S. Army Ordnance in Washington. Colonel Joel G. Holmes had been assigned the job of recruiting help from American industry to meet the awesome goals set for the production of munitions.

One of these requirements was a bomb-loading complex near Grand Island, Nebraska. "This came to Mr. Stuart out of a clear sky, so to speak," said Holmes later. "As I remember, he was a bit shocked, since a bomb-loading plant was not exactly in Quaker's line of business."

Stuart summoned Quaker's vice-president for production, Robert S. Laird, to monitor the telephone conversation. The obvious question Stuart asked Colonel Holmes was "Why Quaker?" The colonel replied that Ordnance, because of peacetime budgets, had been unable to improve or develop substantially its production methods since World War I. "You have been picked because you are fine housekeepers, you are experts at mixing ingredients, and you have techniques for high-speed packing. We want to take advantage of that."

An obstacle occurred to Stuart. His company, he said, had no previous experience with high explosives.

Holmes replied that Ordnance was aware of Quaker's exceptional know-how in the prevention of dust explosions, a traditional hazard of the milling industry; this had influenced their decision. Later Colonel Holmes recalled, "The Quaker Oats Company had, we felt, a keen appreciation for and considerable experience in safety, as they were subjected to the possibility of dust explosions in their own plants."

As the conversation continued, Stuart realized that he had little choice. The Quaker Oats Company must accept the responsibility. He sent Laird to Washington. Meeting with General Wesson's staff, Laird reiterated the company's naïveté concerning explosives. But, as Laird reported later, "They maintained that Quaker knew how to mix ingredients, how to pack them, and how to do both at high speeds, and that was what they wanted. So I returned to Chicago with a government contract to present to our executive committee."

Under the agreement, the government would pay Quaker's ordnance subsidiary a fee of $200,000 a year for its supervisory services. All costs of construction of buildings, machinery, materials, and labor for manufacturing bombs and shells, maintenance, and policing of the properties were to be paid from a revolving fund supplied by Ordnance. Quaker's executive committee approved and sent its engineering chief, Myer Avedovech, and the general counsel, James M. Best, to Washington to confirm the details. Avedovech recalled later that during the meeting Best had said, "There are some things in this contract that I would like to discuss." The federal attorney replied, "We don't have time now, Mr. Best. Let's get the contracts signed and we'll talk about the details later." The Quaker Oats Company had gone to war.

A wholly owned subsidiary was created to perform the assignment, known as The Q.O. Ordnance Corporation. Its officers were John Stuart, president; Robert S. Laird, vice-president; Myer Avedovech, general manager. Said Laird, describing the unusual situation, "The moment we committed ourselves to the task, we surveyed our plant personnel, selecting men we felt would fit best into this situation. We listed sixteen experienced engineers, production men, shipping and packing experts, chemists, mechanics, and personnel directors." This cadre created on 20 square miles of flat Nebraska corn land a munitions plant that would exceed every production quota the Army set for it and produce, before war's end, millions of artillery shells and aerial bombs. Emil J. Petranek, production superintendent at Cedar Rapids, went to Grand Island to supervise construction and recruit personnel for the ammunition-loading lines. He saw the Nebraska farms disappear and the foundations of a munitions assembly appear. "When we arrived in March 1942 bulldozers were taking away the farm buildings. Road crews as big as a county highway department followed. Miles of railroad track were laid by the Burlington Railroad and Northern Pacific. Plants were operating on sites that had been farm lands six months earlier."

The Quaker task force set up its headquarters in the six-story Masonic Building in downtown Grand Island. The ranks were increased by 500 army and civilian engineers, draftsmen, and procurement functionaries. Another 16,000 were engaged in construction of what the Army named the Cornhusker Ordnance Plant. Production Superintendent Petranek's big problem was the hiring of people capable of becoming supervisors. "I went to every school superintendent and football coach in the state," he said. "They came to us from small towns all over Nebraska and made good supervisors. We also had several hundred persons in training all over the United States for jobs as inspectors and safety engineers."

Within six months Cornhusker was operational. The completed plant cost $30 million. Its more than 800 separate buildings were scattered over 20 miles, the entire area fenced by hurricane wire. Four ammunition-loading units, each a mile long, were also fenced off inside the rest of the plant, accessible only through security gates. Two of these lines loaded 105-millimeter artillery shells; the other two assembled various sizes of aerial bombs ranging from 100 up to 2000 pounds. Each loading line had its own bomb shelter, cafeteria, and first-aid room. At a remote corner of the site, as far removed from the loading lines as possible, was the "igloo area," consisting of several hundred buildings partially underground, in which were stored reserves of TNT and an even more powerful booster explosive known as tetryl.

Movement of production materials and the work force was facilitated by a fleet of diesel locomotives operating on 30 miles of standard-gauge railroad tracks, and several hundred trucks rolling on 90 miles of hard-surfaced roads. A central fire station and seven branches were manned constantly, and a force of 500 uniformed guards maintained security over the installation and its personnel. In all, nearly 8000 persons were employed, many of them women. Laird had high praise for the feminine work force: "They were splendid workers, and not as scary as a lot of the men who didn't like to work in an explosive area."

Once Operation Cornhusker was under way, Laird returned to Chicago. Avedovech ran the operation for the duration of the war. Metal shell and bomb casings poured by trainloads into Cornhusker from eight fabricating plants. Bomb casings rode an assembly line and were loaded with a basic charge of TNT, along with a booster of tetryl inserted at either end of the bomb to make sure it detonated on contact. The artillery shell cases were filled with gunpowder in bags, with a percussion cap inserted to explode the shell on contact with its target. Toward the end of the war, the efficiency of this munition was increased by the Army's development of the then-top-secret proximity fuse. This contrivance contained a tiny radio receiver rugged enough to survive the shock of being fired from a cannon. As the shell approached a mass of metal such as an airplane, the receiver was activated, exploding the shell.

The amount of destructive force represented by the output of the Cornhusker plant can be approximated by one statistic—it loaded 800,000 pounds of TNT every 24 hours, a volume four times the original estimate of the plant's capacity. The achievement was made possible by a machine designed and built by Quaker engineers in the machine shop at Grand Island. This mechanism filled 48 105-millimeter shells simultaneously by the pull of a lever. The same machine was adapted to the loading of bombs. In all, Grand Island produced 11,500,000 artillery shells and more than 3,000,000 aerial bombs. During the critical phase of the European campaign, Ordnance asked Operation Cornhusker to step up the ammunition production to 35 carloads in a specified period. The plant more than doubled this request—73 carloads in the allotted time.

In four years no mishap occurred from lack of experience in handling high explosives. The only accident was caused when lightning struck on May 26, 1944, with a loss of nine lives. The structure hit was the last that had been constructed at the base. Army engineers had taken a calculated risk and had not grounded each piece of machinery with copper conduit, because of the scarcity of the metal. The lightning rods proved inadequate. A stock of high explosive was touched off, and the building and its workers vanished.

WAR'S END BRINGS C.O.P. CLOSING was the front-page headline September 7, 1945, on the *Co-Planter*, the ordnance plant's newspaper. The edition also carried tributes to Cornhusker's men and women from ranking Ordnance Department officers. The corporation had received the Army and Navy *E* for excellence of operation. After the war, a further citation of merit was presented to the Company by Secretary of War Stimson.

The Quaker Oats Company, as noted earlier, also played an important part in the synthetic-rubber program. When Japanese invaders cut off the U.S. supply of natural rubber from the Far East, federal authorities turned to American industry to produce a substitute. A crash program pooled the resources of federal government and private industry through the Rubber Reserve Agency. Private industry was asked to erect a network of plants in natural-gas fields for the production of butadiene, the basic petrochemical used in the fabrication of synthetic rubber. Enormous quantities of furfural were needed as an intermediate in butadiene manufacture. The Quaker Oats Company was the only important supplier of furfural in the world, but its total manufacturing capacity for the chemical at the war's beginning was a fraction of the need. To meet the emergency, The Q.O. Chemical Company was formed to build and operate a new plant in Memphis, Tennessee, with sufficient capacity to supply furfural to all the butadiene plants in the synthetic-rubber program. Again, as at Grand Island, seemingly impossible target dates and production quotas were met to solve one of the more critical emergencies of World War II. (The story of Q.O. Chemical Company appears in Chapter 10.)

Shortly after World War II, a swell of opinion developed in the American business community for better control of federal-government expenditures. The Executive branch, which had grown increasingly complex through the 1930s, had been enlarged further by the urgencies of war. Waste and duplication of effort in scores of agencies drained tax dollars, ballooning the federal budget. The Executive branch had become a tangle of bureaus so complicated that effective administration was almost impossible. Communications between agencies—and even within agencies—were confused or nonexistent, despite a mountain of costly paperwork that had itself become part of the problem.

President Harry S. Truman sought to correct the disorder. To modernize the structure of government, he urged the 1947 Congress to pass the Lodge–Brown Act. This measure created a bipartisan commission for reorganization of the Executive branch of the federal government; the agency became known as the Hoover Commission when President Truman appointed Herbert Hoover its chairman. An early and ardent participant in Mr. Hoover's crusade for better government at a better price was John Stuart, then chairman of the board of The Quaker Oats Company.

During the war, John Stuart had experienced firsthand a memorable example of how duplication wastes money. Late in the conflict, Cornhusker Ordnance Plant produced more bombs and shells than the Army withdrew. Despite this, Stuart was astonished to learn that duplicate facilities would be built near Grand Island. "We got wind," he said, "of Navy plans to build a bombloading plant of its own. We were producing so far ahead of withdrawals that we had to store the surplus bombs in igloos. It seemed senseless for Navy to build another plant of the same kind just a few miles away. I telephoned to Frank Knox, then Secretary of Navy. I had been on his board of directors when he published the Chicago *Daily News*. I told him my view on the Navy wasting money duplicating our plant at Grand Island, and he agreed with me. He said he'd follow through on the matter and let me know. Later he returned the call to say that he could do nothing. Regulations did not permit Army and Navy to share facilities. Further, start of the Navy program at Grand Island would kite wage scales in the area. I called Knox on that, too, and again he agreed with me that it was bad management. When he looked into the matter he found that in the Navy scheme, Nebraska was within the Saint Louis area and was entitled to its metropolitan wage rates. Fortunately the war ended before the project was really under way."

After two years, the first Hoover Commission issued a report. This document presented 300 recommendations for changes in federal business methods, representing potential savings of $5 billion a year. The figures were too astronomical for public comprehension. Public apathy led to a national organization known as The Citizens' Committee for the Hoover Report. The group interpreted the Commission's findings, mustered public support, and brought pressure on Congress to translate the Hoover recommendations into law. John Stuart was chairman of the group for the state of Illinois. As a result of the volunteer committee's work, public opinion crystallized. Letters supporting the Report deluged senators and congressmen. The Eighty-First Congress adopted about half of the 300 recommendations.

Twenty additional laws and 51 reorganizations relevant to the Hoover plan were introduced into the Eighty-Second Congress, but only one minor recommendation became law. Again the call went out to the volunteers. In Illinois, John Stuart told his organization, "The big drive to push this legislation through must be made between now and the thirty-first of January, when Congress is expected to adjourn." Nearly 72 per cent of the Hoover recommendations eventually became law.

Shortly before the presidential conventions of 1952, the volunteer committee disbanded, to avoid any appearance of political activity. President Eisenhower appointed a second Hoover Commission after his election. John R. Staley, Quaker's vice-president in charge of traffic, served as vice-chairman of the Commission's task force on transportation. He learned, among other things, that The Quaker Oats Company's traffic department, with 75 employees, handled 60 per cent more carloads of freight than did the Navy Department, which had assigned nearly 2000 people to the task. After two years of further work, a new Hoover Report caused the volunteers to mobilize again. John Stuart this time was vice-chairman of the national committee and state chairman for Illinois. Within two years, Congress adopted about 40 per cent of the 314 recommendations. Significantly, 492 government-operated business enterprises competitive with private industry were closed as a result of the second Hoover Report. Its goals substantially achieved, the volunteer committee disbanded in 1959.

World War II caused rigid controls of the civilian

economy. The program involved national management of much of the production and use of goods and resources. A prominent agency in this emergency operation was the Office of Price Administration, which governed price controls and the rationing of consumer goods.

Quaker's vice-president for grain procurement, Colin S. Gordon, made a substantial contribution to O.P.A. The son of Robert Gordon, first secretary of the American Cereal Company, young Gordon grew up in the Quaker tradition. In 1927, fresh from the University of Chicago, he became a Quaker trainee in Akron, then transferred to the grain department in Chicago, where after twelve years he became vice-president. Early in 1943 he was called to Washington to cope with a developing black market in corn futures. He was tapped on recommendation of the regional O.P.A. office, which reported to Washington, "There are two men particularly on the Chicago market of high character and fairness, coupled with wide experience, whose counsel is especially valuable." One was Gordon. He recommended that the government set up an emergency grain corporation to administer the movement of cereal crops from farm to consumer and to designate the grain exchanges as war agencies. (The Canadian government had a somewhat similar system.) Circumstances made this severe action unnecessary. Rather than shortages, a huge surplus of grain accumulated due to shipping sunk by submarines. The grain surplus eventually eliminated the black market. Gordon remained in Washington for 27 months as a pricing executive of cereals for the O.P.A., dealing also in feeds and agricultural chemicals. During the closing months of the war, he was director of the O.P.A.'s food division.

A lifelong Chicagoan, Gordon resided in a north side apartment and was actively interested in Chicago's problems. For many years he was a member of the Chicago Crime Commission, serving that watchdog organization as president and, in 1953, as chairman. Chicago's business and civic leaders had founded the Commission in 1919, with Henry Parsons Crowell of Quaker as a charter member. The organization aimed to discover and expose corrupt conditions under which organized crime flourished. This was the Capone era. As a private body, the Crime Commission had no official powers of investigation or enforcement. It was nevertheless a useful adjunct to the law through continual probing of the Syndicate's octopuslike operations.

Quaker's Colin Gordon later headed a Committee of Nineteen, composed of civic leaders who studied the broad social and political structure of Chicago and environs, concerning themselves with such matters as reapportionment of voting districts, modernization of the criminal code, reformation of the antequated Illinois judicial structure, better law enforcement, redevelopment of blighted areas, and better housing. The Committee evolved into a permanent organization called Citizens of Greater Chicago.

Quaker Oats Company's personnel felt a special pride in the White House announcement of January 1953 that the President had appointed Donold B. Lourie, then president of the company, Undersecretary of State for Administration. For years Lourie had been a member of the Business Advisory Committee. This group of leaders from major industries acted in liaison with the Department of Commerce. The State Department needed an administrative overhaul, Secretary Dulles told Lourie in asking him to undertake the task.

"Mr. Secretary," Lourie replied, "I've never been in the State Department building." "That's fine," replied Dulles.

"Moreover," Lourie continued, "I don't know anyone in the State Department." The Secretary answered, "That's great."

As the office of the Undersecretary was then constituted, Lourie would be responsible for the reorganization and for other duties as well, including high-level policy-making in the Secretary's absence. Lourie thought such responsibilities should be reserved for someone familiar with American foreign policy since its earliest days and thoroughly schooled in international law. Pondering the matter at home, he told his wife, "Mary, I ought not to take the job—I can't even spell Afghanistan." To which she replied, "Spell it—you can't even pronounce it!" Her response confirmed his conviction, and he decided to decline the appointment.

But Dulles was persistent. He telephoned. Would Lourie consider going to Washington, he asked, for a year or two, provided his duties were limited to those of Undersecretary of State for Administration, a new post that might be created by a special act of Congress? Lourie accepted. The directors elected H. Earle Muzzy to serve as Company president in Lourie's absence.

Lourie's confirmation by the Senate Committee on Foreign Relations in 1953 had a light moment. When Lourie appeared before the committee, Senator Wiley, as chairman, opened the proceedings with the request, "Mr. Lourie, tell us where you are from, where you were born, your background and so on."

"I was born in Alabama," Lourie began, drawing a friendly nod from committee member Sparkman. "Shortly after that, my family moved to California," to which another committee member, Senator Knowland, smiled an acknowledgment. "From California my family moved to Racine, Wisconsin," which brought a salute from the chairman. "Then we moved to New Hampshire," and a grin came from Senator Tobey. At this point the chairman interrupted. "Mr. Lourie, are you trying to cover the entire Senate?" Senator Alexander Smith of New Jersey then spoke. "Go ahead, Don, tell them the rest." So Lourie continued, "Well, later I went to Princeton," which pleased the senator from New Jersey. "After Princeton I went to work for The Quaker Oats Company"; here Senator Hickenlooper of Iowa signaled his approval. Then Robert Taft, the senior senator from Ohio, spoke up. "Don't forget, you have a plant in Akron."

The Senate hearing made one of the more pleasant days of Lourie's Washington stay. The job was a grim assignment for him. The roster of State Department employees had grown to 42,154, seven times the prewar complement. To reorganize it into a compact policy-making body as envisioned by Secretary Dulles involved the relocation of thousands of employees and the dismissal of thousands more. Antagonistic pressures were severe.

At that time, the State Department was also suffering the public castigations of Senator Joseph McCarthy of Wisconsin. McCarthy had shortly before made a speech in West Virginia in which he maintained that the State Department was the haven for 138 security risks, whose purge he demanded. Lourie called on the senator at his office and said, "After all, Senator, you and I are working the same side of the street. We're going after these fellows you've been talking about, but we want to do the job ourselves." McCarthy agreed to cease his criticism, and he kept his word.

Within a year Undersecretary Lourie had accomplished substantially his plan of reorganization. In twelve months, 390 were separated for security reasons. Of a total of more than 42,000 employees, Lourie transferred 17,000 to other agencies. Nearly 26,000 still remained. In another year, 6000 additional jobs had been abolished, reducing the State Department force to 20,000, less than half its peak strength.

His objective completed, Lourie began to think of going home. "I'd better get back to rolling oats before the company finds out it can get along without me," he told newspaper reporters, announcing his resignation.

Dulles wrote: "Although I do so reluctantly, I feel I have no choice but to keep my part of our bargain, that you would serve for only about a year. . . . I am aware of the particularly complex problems which we have had in the administrative field, and I am heartened by the substantial progress which you have made in meeting and overcoming them."

On his return to Chicago, Lourie was reinstated in the presidency of the company and again became a member of the executive committee and the board of directors. "He has again assumed active supervision of the company's affairs," said Chairman John Stuart in a letter to the stockholders.

The White House announced on May 23, 1953, that President Eisenhower had appointed Robert Douglas Stuart, then vice-chairman of The Quaker Oats Company, U.S. Ambassador to Canada. Douglas Stuart had been equipped for this role by careers both as a civilian in government and as a businessman of prominence in Canada. During the 1930s, Stuart had been chairman of the Industrial Advisory Board of the National Recovery Administration. His ambassadorship in the Eisenhower

administration was a recognition of the Stuart family's
Canadian background as well as of Stuart's knowledge
of Canadian affairs and as a substantial investor in Canadian industry. He had been active in the Republican
party all his adult life and treasurer of the Republican
National Committee in 1948, a critical assignment
which mobilized the finances for the 1952 victory.

During his stay in Canada, Stuart reduced the personnel in the American Embassy by 20 per cent and
closed three substations—at Hamilton, Victoria, and
Regina. A primary objective of his tenure was to solicit
the good will of the Canadian people for American investments in Canadian industry. The Ottawa *Journal*
described him as "The busiest member of the diplomatic
corps in Ottawa. . . . His natural gift for friendship
and complete absence of side have made him a very
popular person." He traveled throughout the Canadian
provinces in the embassy's airplane; for trips to more
remote areas of Labrador, Nova Scotia, and the subpolar
regions he used a Canadian Army transport plane. "I
averaged about thirty thousand miles a year," he estimated later, "covering cattle shows, moose shows, fairs,
and other places where I could meet the rank and file of
Canadian citizens and spread some good will. I also
curled a lot.* A great way to meet people in Canada is at
their bonspiels." As a result of his travels, the Ottawa
Journal said, "Newspaper editorials across the country
have expressed Canada's satisfaction with him."

Stuart had planned to stay in Canada only two years.
He extended his service to three and a half years, after
which he returned to Chicago. Before leaving, he made
what came to be known as his best speech in behalf of a

---

* Curling is the prototype of lawn bowling, played on ice with
specially fashioned stones.

better understanding between Canadian people and American capital. This message suggested that the opposition Conservatives were playing politics with Canadian–American good will, and he expressed the conviction that American investors in Canada were completely aware of their responsibilities to the Commonwealth. Stuart had been bold beyond precedence in his reference to Canada's internal political strife, courting a charge by Conservatives that he was meddling in purely domestic matters. Secretary of State for External Affairs Lester B. Pearson formally declared the speech "of a character likely to provoke controversy." Public discussion of the subject was Stuart's purpose. The opinion generally expressed by the Canadian and American press was that the Ambassador had made an accurate and courageous statement of the facts.

Chapter 15 * *Toward the Future*

A BOOKLET published in 1964 to acquaint prospective employees with career opportunities in The Quaker Oats Company began with the sentence "Marketing is our business."

The statement was that of Robert D. Stuart, Jr., grandson of the founding Stuart, made Company president after fifteen years of rugged conditioning in the highly competitive fields of feeds, pet foods, and grocery products.

Robert Stuart thus put new emphasis on the truth that amid bewildering changes in food distribution and consumption patterns in an age of self-service stores and convenience products, a consumer-goods company succeeded in direct ratio to how big a share of the market it could command. Inventive manufacturers offered chain buyers hundreds of new products every year. Only the fastest sellers survived; about 85 per cent failed. The large supermarkets stocked 8000 items or more. Volume sales and rapid turnover necessary for the survival of low-margin operations reduced profits commonly to a cent on each dollar of sales; slow-moving items were dropped quickly. To strongly promoted, heavily advertised, attractively packaged products went the precious shelf space. The battleground was at the point of sale, an inescapable fact of life.

Young Stuart's attitude highlighted a good many things that had been happening at Quaker, some of them almost unnoticed, since the advent of Donold B. Lourie as chief executive officer. Lourie, a professional manager with no relation by blood or marriage to any of the founders, had been president through the Company's transition from a solid, well-to-do, family-flavored enterprise to a greatly expanded world organization. Donold Lourie's era saw automated manufacture and distribution of instant oatmeal and presweetened ready-to-eat cereals, gourmet cat foods, $43,000-a-minute television advertising, multimillion-dollar launching costs for a new product, nearly half a billion dollars worth of annual sales for Quaker generated by more than 200 products, advertised in 16 languages in 40 different countries.

John Stuart, elder son of founder Robert, headed the company from 1922 to 1942 as president, was chairman for another 14 years, a director until 1964; when he stepped down, he was designated director emeritus. His legacy was one of superlative production facilities in a broad sphere of manufacturing. Chief executive officer for 34 of his 64 active years in the business, he had led the company through a period of growth in which domestic sales rose to $277 million and overseas business to $72 million. He had brought Quaker past the midpoint of the twentieth century, preserving an atmosphere of personal management, at the same time guiding a diversification program which took the company into such disparate lines as chemicals, pancakes, baking mixes, and cat and dog foods. During the careers of

John and his brother, R. Douglas Stuart, as heads of the company, Quaker Oats stock became entrenched as a blue chip, desirable for trust-fund portfolios.

John Stuart introduced Donold B. Lourie into the management echelon as the first top "outsider." Lourie might well have been a Stuart from his upbringing and point of view. John Stuart was a trustee of Princeton, and naturally admired a young quarterback who led Old Nassau to an unbeaten football season and was tapped as All-American quarterback by Walter Camp in 1921, when Camp chose *the* All-American team. After graduation, Lourie further demonstrated his resourcefulness when sent to scout a Notre Dame–Army game in advance of Princeton's encounter with the Irish. Lourie sat on the sidelines bench with Walter Camp and, deep in conversation, completely missed a pass play on which Notre Dame scored. So he went to Knute Rockne for help. "Well, here's the play, young fellow," the Notre Dame coach said, and with the toe of his shoe obligingly scratched a diagram in the cinder track that circled the field. When Notre Dame played Princeton later, the Irish used the play twice. "And one time they made it work," Lourie recalled.

Lourie went to work as a statistician for Quaker Oats on July 5, 1922. He trained at Cedar Rapids, then moved up quickly through sales and advertising to the positions of sales manager in 1936, vice-president for sales in 1942, and executive vice-president in 1945. When Douglas Stuart became vice-chairman of the board in 1947, Lourie was chosen president.

Lourie was an innovator, although not a believer in change for its own sake. Neither employees nor outside observers sensed any break with tradition when he became president. Managing a corporation like Quaker required complex teamwork, he felt; yet he strove as far as possible to preserve an intimacy between the head man and the organization. He was proud of the record of growth but cautious about depicting Quaker as *big*, feeling that people did not like bigness, especially in business. "World's largest cereal mill," applied to the sprawling Cedar Rapids plant, made him wince. Despite these reservations, Quaker's promotion-minded marketing staff and the newly acquired public relations men found him generally receptive to their plans. Sometimes he said yes *and* no. In 1948 he authorized a motion picture about the company's history, but he was dubious when a script was submitted for his approval.

"Don, I'm sure this will be a fine, successful film," a public relations man declared. "If I'm wrong, I certainly won't expect to keep my job here."

Lourie grinned and replied, "Well, I suppose that might be fair enough—but how do we get back our fifty thousand dollars?" The movie was not made. Later, however, Lourie approved several product-promotional films, as well as other general publicity on Quaker products—even to the extent of presiding at occasional press conferences, innovations for traditionally publicity-shy Quaker.

As growth continued, inevitable changes occurred in the physical character of The Quaker Oats Company. More plants meant more people, and the personal touch in management became more difficult. In the Chicago offices, administrators, typists, accountants, and clerical workers proliferated. So did technical experts. With plant construction and modernization proceeding apace, the Company's engineering department expanded tenfold. Veterans in the home office found disconcerting the numbers of strangers in their ranks. Nameplates appeared on desk tops, a necessary evil. One Company officer, meeting a new public relations man, roared in dismay, "Public relations? Good God, when did we get that!"

There was even a new appearance about the Company's traditionally old-fangled offices, along with modification of some practices for improved efficiency. For many years, high-ranking executives had no private secretaries, a custom Lourie broke during World War II when he was vice-president in charge of sales. At that time and in the postwar years, private offices were few. Most employees, including many important functionaries, sat at desks in the open office. Some department heads were housed in small pens constructed of plasterboard. These waist-high partitions were known to the rank and file as ego fences. Executives answered their own telephones and used dictating machines or, if of sufficient rank, summoned a stenographer from the central pool. Office walls were a drab "Quaker green," presumably restful to the eyes. Carpeted offices and hallways were taboo.

Then a new research laboratory replaced an old converted automobile showroom on Chicago's south side. The architect, Frank Voorhies, was appalled at conservative suggestions from Quaker's executive committee. "Do you really want your research facilities to reflect the Victorian period," he asked, "or do you want to take a stance in the contemporary world?" To the delight of research vice-president Fredus Peters, John Stuart backed the architect, the committee took a modern stance, and Voorhies designed at Barrington a superbly functional yet strikingly attractive edifice. There were bluestone terraces, marble sills, modish offices—one with a balcony—and contemporary furnishings. Even a thick-carpeted conference room emerged with grass-cloth walls and yards of rich drapery. At the dedication in 1956, the executives from Chicago paled at the grandeur, then returned home to undertake a gradual restyling which by the 1960s had transformed Quaker's headquarters in the Merchandise Mart into a model of attractive efficiency.

Lourie kept his leadership flexible. He shunned tables of organization and avoided rigid channels of authority. But he laid the groundwork for scientific definitions of responsibility by retaining outside consultants to study the Company's management structure. He also instituted planning conferences, spiriting his department heads away from their offices for annual sessions of group introspection at resorts in northern Illinois and Wisconsin. Day by day and year by year, the tempo of planning and reshaping accelerated, and a Quaker Oats Company fitted to the new competitive challenges began to emerge. For the first time in Company history, Quaker began to look outside its own echelons for mature, specialized skills in marketing, manufacturing, and administration. *Grow your own executives* had always been the motto. But the company burgeoned at such a rate, and in so many directions, that the intracompany incubator could not supply the demand. In a number of departments, boxes on the new organization charts were filled by talented "outsiders," professionals with special experience and proved records.

The influx of new talent and the sharp emphasis on marketing as the Company's prime motivation were powerful stimulants. Result, an emergence of new products in profusion. Daring entries were made in such already crowded but lucrative fields as ready-to-eat cereals. Unavoidably, these outlays curbed profits. By mid-1960s, however, the investment was beginning to pay off. The earnings curve slanted sharply upward in what marketing-minded Robert Stuart, Jr., publicly described as the beginning of a long-term rise. Shareholders were gratified to find sales in 1965 at another record high with earnings up 15 per cent over the previous three-year average. A company-wide survey made in 1956 indicated that people generally regarded Quaker as "a great place to work." Friendly. Secure. Warm. Wonderful people. The survey also turned up some dissatisfaction with salaries. The more open-handed executives had distributed more liberal pay increases than were given by their more tight-fisted counterparts in other departments. A more centrally administered program ended the inequities.

Manpower planning became a full-time activity within the employee relations department. Specialists took a searching look at management and supervisory personnel needs for the years ahead, systematically appraising the probable availability of rising young people within the Company. Training programs were strengthened. Recruiters combed colleges and universities for potential leaders. Excellence was the criterion in screening candidates. In its search for ability, the Company hired without regard to creed or color. In earlier days, the Company tended to regard Scotch Presbyterians, Episcopalians, and Princetonians as particularly well qualified for a Quaker career. This notion has long since been dissipated.

In help-wanted ads, Quaker long has billed itself an equal-opportunity employer. This position was affirmed in 1963 when Quaker joined President Johnson's Plan for Progress and published a program for hiring on the basis of ability and promoting for merit. This became the working policy throughout the Company. The organic process of any successful corporation, including Quaker, demands a constant recruiting of fresh, young manpower. Particularly, as Robert Stuart put it, there must be a steady flow of bright people "with the drive and dedication really to *manage* in an increasingly sophisticated market place."

Throughout the period of midcentury growth and change, Donold Lourie sought to preserve the atmosphere of personal management. His friendly personality served to cement the organization during the stresses of rapid expansion. He made decisions but appeared not to give orders. "Maybe we'd better not do that," he would say, and everybody got the message. Or "Why wouldn't it be better to try this?" In manner and method he seemed a hundred management generations removed from Henry Parsons Crowell, "the godly autocrat" whose commands to the staff had carried the weight of Biblical injunctions.

With his top lieutenants, Lourie called the signals like the quarterback he was, tagging some with nicknames which stuck throughout their careers. Told to "clear it with the Judge," the petitioner in Lourie's office understood he was to check with Merrill E. Olsen, vice-president and general counsel. H. Earle Muzzy, onetime vice-chairman of the board, was "Unk" to Lourie, and George Whitfield, the company's outsize controller, was called "Big Foot" after his size-13 shoe. Colin S. Gordon, a genius at trouble-shooting and fact-finding, who prided himself on knowing what was afoot throughout the world organization, was "Chi," a nickname that for obscure reasons was pronounced *Ky*, although it dated back to his student days at the University of Chicago.

Gordon saw all, knew all, and remembered everything; the trophies in his office as vice-chairman of the board included two presented by Lourie: a double-visored deer-stalker cap and an underslung pipe—both reminiscent of Sherlock Holmes.

Characteristic of the new men singled out by Lourie was John D'Arcy, Jr., elevated in 1964 to the role of executive vice-president in charge of operations. A University of Michigan graduate, Jack D'Arcy was an anomaly at Quaker, a liberal arts production chief rather than an engineer. D'Arcy was both technically competent in production methods and well educated in the liberal arts. Sandy-haired and slight, he looked young for his responsibilities. More precise, serious, and thrifty with words was D'Arcy, one associate said, than anyone in Quaker's management since the first Robert Stuart, who years before had advised sons John and R. Douglas to talk as little as possible. One of D'Arcy's accomplishments was Quaker's new eastern manufacturing plant and distribution center at Shiremanstown, Pennsylvania, a vast computer-coordinated facility for servicing the big eastern markets. Among other economies, this multipurpose complex introduced palletized shipping to speed service and accomplish a saving of about $25 per freight car in loading costs, a system gradually extended on a nationwide basis. Entire orders were stacked automatically on wooden skids or pallets that accompanied the goods to their destination; then the pallets, like empty milk bottles, were returned through a cooperative arrangement with other shippers and the railroads.

Under D'Arcy's direction, improvements in distribution and customer service also received close attention. A computerized car-control system was inaugurated to keep track of shipments and guarantee definite delivery

dates. Substantial savings in damage claims and a reduction in grocers' complaints were achieved through
the railroads' development of "damage-free" cars, minimizing losses in transit. Damage at the retail level was
reduced as well. Since inexperienced store personnel
sometimes put gouged or crushed cartons on the shelves,
to the annoyance of retail customers, Quaker also introduced a zipper-top shipping case. Instead of ripping
open the cardboard case with a utility knife, occasionally
damaging the inner cartons in the process, stockroom
boys merely unzip the outer case, saving time, money,
and ultimately the tempers of store managers and har-
ried housewives.

In modern supermarket operations, a penny saved is
often the difference between profit and loss. Helping the
big markets save those pennies through better merchandising was the job during the modern era of Vice-President William G. Mason and his sales organization. Such
help extended even to developing a packaged training
course for supermarket employees. The training materials, based on the new technique of "programmed
learning," were prepared by a psychologist in the sales-
development section of Mason's department.

In earlier days, new acquisitions had been largely the
results of judgment by the shrewd Stuarts that certain
modestly established companies could be built into bigger properties as part of The Quaker Oats Company. In
those days, national prominence could be achieved for
Aunt Jemima for a promotional outlay of $100,000. By
the mid-1960s, the introductory costs of Cap'n Crunch
cereal were $5 million in a single year, and new ventures
were the result of prolonged and many-faceted research.
Looking to a future in which already appalling costs
seemed likely to increase, Lourie again sought scientific

counsel, and as a result a corporate planning department was created and made responsible to him. This sort of thinking was new for Quaker. The new department would provide an integrated pattern for progress and lay out a total, constantly updated plan for company action, short-range and long.

The first head of this department was Frank C. Schell, Jr., another of Lourie's "new look" executives, who in 1951 had entered the company, fittingly enough for the job at hand, in finance after training as a banker. Under Lourie's flexible system of crossing department lines to recruit talent, Schell was called on to exercise his aptitude for product development, becoming vice-president in charge of that area in 1957. He moved to Barrington in 1959 as vice-president in charge of research and development, and in 1964 became vice-president for corporate planning, a member of the executive committee, and a director of the company.

Quaker's new willingness to spend money to secure its place in the market was nowhere more evident than in recent appropriations for advertising. *Advertising Age* estimated in 1965 that the company's advertising budget for the preceding year was $21,500,000, of which $6,500,-000 was national television network billing and another $5,434,000 was for "spot" commercials on local television stations. From the beginning, Quaker had been reticent to discuss publicly its present or its future. For decades, the annual report to stockholders was a model of minimum information: accurate, brief, dignified, and somberly packaged. The company's relations with the press were minimal.

In 1947, Quaker inaugurated formal public relations activities. The company had traditionally been shy of corporate publicity, personality interviews with members of management, and news addressed to the financial community. In 1958, for the first time, a Quaker executive addressed the influential New York Society of Security Analysts. In May of that year, Donold Lourie presented to the analysts a statement containing the type of information of interest to financial specialists. Several years later, Robert D. Stuart, Jr., addressed the same organization, using charts, samples of new products, television commercials, and inviting questions about the company's future.

Robert D. Stuart, Jr., said a close associate, "looks like a god, talks like a lawyer, acts like a Stuart, and thinks like a huckster." He was tapped as successor to Lourie in 1962 and designated president, though Lourie retained the authority of chief executive officer. Much like his father, R. Douglas Stuart, in manner, Robert was an equally hard worker—poised, urbane, articulate, thorough, always in motion. In his school years at Princeton, he had held summer jobs with the Company. His liberal arts training was followed by a law degree from Yale. During his apprenticeship in feed sales in California, the younger Stuart made copious notes of his ideas and observations which, on his return to the home office, he translated into suggestions and actions.

As president he continued the custom, and manifold change accompanied the jottings. In the division of administrative responsibilities among top corporate officers, sales and marketing fell naturally to him. When profit-sharing bonuses were distributed after the prosperous 1965 year, department heads were directed to meet with employees to discuss the Company's marketing goals and their importance to individual men and women on the production line. Copies of the annual report and other publications were mailed to employees' homes, accompanied by messages from the president. Marketing, Stuart stressed, was the ultimate goal, which could be accomplished only as the end effort in a complex process of production and distribution. Costs were to be controlled. Quality was to be maintained without fail. Every job was important as a step forward to that payoff in the market place.

In 1965, personnel totaled 6500 people in the Company's U.S. plants and offices, and the world-wide complement was a bit over 10,000. A profit-sharing plan reached every domestic employee, except relatively few in operations not integrated directly with the Quaker organization. Since 1936, the bonus plan had paid out almost $35 million to employees below the level of eligibility for management incentive plans, and the payout had been amounting to an extra three and a half or four weeks' extra pay every year.

As the Company grew larger, the world grew smaller, and overseas plants seemed closer to home. The Company's foreign operations once had been as remote as a celestial galaxy. Top management knew what went on in the subsidiaries, of course. The closest in touch was Earle Muzzy, who ran the Foreign Department in Chicago. A production man by training, he had supervised the building of the Quaker Oats Limited plant at Southall, England, in 1936. He and other topmost executives made trips abroad from time to time to inspect the "foreign subs."

As intercontinental air travel became practical after World War II, Muzzy began to bring his European managers to the States for frequent brief visits. By the time Augustin S. Hart, Jr., succeeded Muzzy as the Company's international executive, Quaker's foreign facilities were no longer just faraway places with strange-sounding names. Late in 1964 he had been named executive vice-president for international operations. He was a director and member of the executive committee, and one of the five senior officers of the company.

Cross-pollinization was the term employed as Quaker's domestic managers were brought into contact with operators of satellite companies abroad. An engineer from the Marion, Ohio, plant went to Australia on permanent assignment. One Englishman found himself settled for a two-year term as plant superintendent in the Pony Express town of St. Joseph; another was in Chicago as an executive on lend-lease in pet-food marketing; two U.S. marketing men and a financial executive were on the staff in England, injecting the British company with some American marketing know-how, along with the sharp-penciled discipline of Stateside budgeting and cost control.

Managers of the subsidiaries employed increasingly sophisticated U.S.–style advertising and merchandising programs. As in the United States, new products were introduced at a fast clip, especially in the well-to-do areas of Western Europe. Gus Hart, executive vice-president for international operations, saw that the fruits of Quaker's research and product development work at home were made available quickly to his companies in Canada and abroad. He pushed for introduction of convenience-style products wherever local living standards and dietary habits warranted, urging his managers to boost their budgets for introductory marketing costs. The ready-to-eat cereal, Cap'n Crunch, quickly went international—as *Capitaine Crouche* in French-speaking areas of Canada and *Kaptajn Knas* in Scandinavia. Pet foods made in the Netherlands were sold in France. Instant Quaker Oatmeal, still in limited distribution at home, was made and sold in England as Instant Porridge.

Hart absorbed himself in the task of welding a loosely coordinated group of semiautonomous foreign companies into a modern, market-oriented machine. He insisted that the subsidiaries retain their local character. They continued to be manned, for the most part, by nationals of the countries in which they were located, and individual managers had operating authority and responsibility for profits.

Hart had risen to the top through a succession of promotions from a trainee's berth in 1937 to a position as one of the "big five" in Quaker's management 27 years later. A native New Yorker with Princeton University background, he was the only member of the top management echelon to be reared outside the Midwest. As a novice, he had spent some time at Cedar Rapids and was assigned to the old St. Joseph flour mill for a few weeks. In 1938 he was transferred to the export department in Chicago, then spent most of the next 22 years abroad or in New York. He was on assignment in Holland when German troops blitzed the Low Countries in 1940. As a citizen of the still technically neutral United States, he observed Nazism's frightful military efficiency firsthand. Later, as a U.S. Army officer, he revisited the Rotterdam plant after the city's liberation. Very late in the war, he also managed to look in on Quaker's *Nahrmittel Gesellschaft* in devastated Hamburg, finding to his astonishment that the business-minded German manager was speedily rebuilding the plant with machinery and spare parts he had concealed beneath the floors early in the war.

Hart's designation in 1964 as one of Quaker's two executive vice-presidents reflected management's awareness of the growing importance of international markets. In 1965, for the first time, an annual report was published consolidating the operating results of all subsidiaries around the world with those of the parent company. The completely consolidated report showed investors that more than a quarter of the sales dollars were garnered outside the United States. Quaker's gross sales that year were $461 million, of which $102 million came from business outside the United States. The aggressive management philosophy of sowing now for a later harvest was absorbing money; earnings growth slowed between 1960 and 1965 as sales rose 20 per cent and profits only 10 per cent.

Then, in 1965, new momentum produced new trends in the earnings picture. Every cereal in the Quaker line showed higher profits; even feed sales improved their contribution; the Chemicals Division hit a new peak in sales and earnings. Net income leaped 15 per cent, to $16,300,000.

Quaker's greatest expansion, Robert Stuart reported, was in the grocery industry's fastest-growing lines: pet foods, convenience products, and ready-to-eat cereals, selected by industry forecasters for even greater gains in years to come. Population projections anticipated nearly a third more food consumers in the U.S. alone by 1975, and a 20 per cent higher income per family. Much of the world was undergoing a revolutionary thrust toward better living standards, which promised larger markets for Quaker and its affiliated companies. In America, both prosperity and children were in abundance; household pets increased in number at a much faster rate than humans, and all had to be fed. Happily, Quaker products representing more than half its total sales catered to these two categories, and 90 per cent of its new products were tuned to the new social trends. By 1964 Quaker had captured 10 per cent of the ready-to-eat cereal business, advancing from sixth place in the industry that year to fourth place in 1965. Almost 6 per cent of the booming presweetened market belonged to Quaker. Five years earlier, the company had no presweets whatever.

Quaker continued during this time to hold its position as the world's largest seller of corn meal, hominy grits, and other dry-milled corn products. Meanwhile, the bellwether of the Quaker grocery products line, rolled oats, continued to produce more sales volume, although its growth was less spectacular than that of the ready-to-eats. Despite the dry cereals' progressively greater popularity, an average of 8 million Americans ate a bowl of Quaker or Mother's Oats each day in 1965. In a number of markets, Instant Quaker Oats gained new customers for hot cereals, generating in eat-and-run breakfasters a renewed interest in a hot breakfast. Moving with the trend, Quaker offered hurried housewives frozen Aunt Jemima waffles and other toaster-ready products. As a related item, the company launched Aunt Jemima bottled syrup 76 years after the world's first ready-mix had been introduced.

In 1966 Quaker tested new products in 25 different domestic markets. One of which the general public was unaware was a Danish-pastry mix for restaurants, hotels, and institutions which, without the addition of yeast or shortening, could be prepared in 90 minutes, compared to the previous kitchen time of nearly 12 hours. "The convenience food market," said Robert Stuart, "is the big one, and the ultimate in convenience is eating out. Therefore, we're developing products for restaurants which will save them time and work."

The Quaker Oats Company's future, as it exists on the

drawing boards or in the creative imaginations of its corporate planners, might bewilder the most sophisticated. Accustomed as the modern homemaker is to miracles of food processing and packaging, she may be surprised by some of the innovations already well within the reach of modern technology.

The literature of the food industry contains intriguing clues to the sort of future that may be in store for American families. Possible are foods cooked in attractive, edible baking dishes that can be put on the table hot and—like an ice-cream cone—eaten along with the contents, thus eliminating a great deal of dishwashing. The trend toward more packaging of foods in individual portions seemed certain to continue. The prospect was for more complete meals, increasingly elaborate, packaged in their own disposable serving dishes and perhaps with disposable cutlery. Prognosis: less fuss and bother in meal preparation; no expensive leftovers in the refrigerator; and maybe—through new preservation techniques of freezer drying and irradiation—no refrigerator.

How far would the world move toward push-button meals? At the Barrington laboratories, Research Vice-President Hartley C. Laycock, Jr., and his staff were prepared to anticipate the trend. The housewife had demonstrated that she was willing to pay for products with built-in maid service, saving her hours of drudgery in preparing meals from scratch. However work-free the products might be made, Quaker's planners did not envision that the woman of 1975, or of the year 2000, would willingly surrender entirely her creative role in feeding her family and her guests. Dr. Fredus N. Peters, who as vice-president for research had persuaded management to build the new Barrington laboratories, talked with reporters at dedication ceremonies in 1956. "We'll see a lot of fascinating developments in consumer convenience in the next few years," he predicted with accuracy. "But there won't be many drastic changes in the sort of foods we eat. It's no technical problem to condense nutrients into pills, but they'll never take the place of steak and apple pie."

Viewing the situation from retirement, Fredus Peters saw no reason in 1966 to alter his opinions of a decade earlier. A great deal of what he had forecast already had come to pass; yet, as he had said, steak and apple pie were still high on the hit parade and likely to stay there. The per capita intake of calories had diminished as the requirement of physical exertion in earning a living declined. There was more emphasis on quality and variety in family fare. An affluent society had upgraded its eating habits. For American housewives of the 1960s, food was a bargain of bargains—infinite in variety, easy to prepare, costing a smaller and smaller share of the family budget—18½ cents of the income dollar in 1965, compared to 26 cents a dozen years earlier. The typical housewife of the 1960s was a smart shopper, far wiser about nutrition than her mother had been. She insisted on, and she got, value in convenience as well as value in nutrition. According to a comprehensive survey by Opinion Research Corporation, she was well pleased with her grocer, with the wealth of new products offered by food processors, and well satisfied that she was getting her money's worth.

In the employee relations department, recruiters observed by the mid-1960s that many outstanding college graduates were attracted as job applicants by Quaker's reputation for integrity and the honest verities espoused by the first Robert Stuart and Henry Crowell. These students preferred a career with a company that offered them a sense of moral stability as well as a good income and other collateral benefits. Perhaps this stemmed, the staff psychologists thought, from the younger generation's anxiety over newly developing attitudes in large parts of the world toward established moral values. Quaker offered a durable platform on which to stand in this changing world, as well as an opportunity for a satisfying career in a basic industry. The Quaker Oats Company's history revealed a continuity of values that seemed likely to endure through decades to come.

Donold Lourie had been impressed with these values early in his management career. Years ago, in a luncheon conversation concerning the assets of The Quaker Oats Company, John Stuart told him:

"If this business were to be split up, I would be glad to take the brands, trademarks, and good will, and you could have all the bricks and mortar—and I would fare better than you."

That is the core of The Quaker Oats Company's management philosophy.

Index